C000226423

ALAIN PROST

Also by Christopher Hilton

NIGEL MANSELL
CONQUEST OF FORMULA 1
AYRTON SENNA: HARD EDGE OF GENIUS

ALAIN PROST

CHRISTOPHER HILTON

PHOTOGRAPHS BY KEITH SUTTON

PARTRIDGE PRESS

LONDON · NEW YORK · TORONTO · SYDNEY · AUCKLAND

TRANSWORLD PUBLISHERS LTD
61-63 Uxbridge Road, London W5 5SA

TRANSWORLD PUBLISHERS (AUSTRALIA) PTY LTD
15-23 Helles Avenue, Moorebank, NSW 2170

TRANSWORLD PUBLISHERS (NZ) LTD
Cnr Moselle and Waipareira Aves,
Henderson, Auckland

Published 1992 by Partridge Press
a division of Transworld Publishers Ltd

A catalogue record for this book is available from the British Library

ISBN 185225 1506

Typeset in 11/13 Sabon by Chippendale Type Ltd, Otley, West Yorkshire

Printed in Great Britain by
Mackays of Chatham, PLC, Chatham, Kent.

To Alain Prost himself
for so many magnificent memories

CONTENTS

1
FUTURE TENSE

> The guy is so intense he wakes up and wanders around sleep-walking. I remember once in Austria where he was out on the balcony of the hotel in the middle of the night and for him it was like he was on the rostrum.
>
> PATRICK TAMBAY

Heavy folds of cloud hung over the bay. Down the morning, calculating eyes glanced up at them noting their height, monitoring how quickly they were being pushed on the wind, gauging whether darker cloud was coming over the ragged ring of hills which encircled the bay. Drizzle would be difficult, never mind heavy rain or, worse, a thunderstorm playing out its violent echoing melodies. The hills compressed the weather into great extremes and did it quickly. Everybody knew that. It was why they kept glancing up.

Towards midday the cloud began to lift and shafts of sunlight tumbled through. By early afternoon that beautiful purified sky described as azure spread and consolidated itself. Beneath it sixteen cars were arranged on a grid for the Monaco Grand Prix. Jackie Stewart, a crisp and concise man, had put a March in pole position; a New Zealander, Chris Amon, also in a March, was on the front row alongside him. Denny Hulme, a taciturn compatriot of Amon, and Jack Brabham, an extremely taciturn Australian, filled the second row in cars which both bore Brabham's own name. He made them. Jacky Ickx, a neat and thoughtful Belgian, had a Ferrari on the third row alongside Jean-Pierre Beltoise of France in a Matra;

Jochen Rindt, an Austrian wreathed in all manner of charisma, was directly behind Beltoise in a sleek, low, red-and-gold Lotus.

10 May 1970, moving towards the start of it.

The crowd which ticked off the minutes was largely in temporary stands, skeletons of scaffolding covered with plain seating in regular, descending tiers. The stands ran full down to the rim of the racing circuit, hemming and almost overhanging it so that each spectator had an intimate view, was close enough to taste the acrid exhalations from the exhaust pipes, could see gloved hands pumping and churning steering wheels.

There was already a resonance of noise. The Italians had come in a flood tide from across the border just over the hills, bearing their battle insignias: flags which would billow, banners on poles, red hats to be flung in the air. Their voices were lubricated to bellow but now, ticking off the minutes, they chattered and gesticulated and fidgeted. Their restless dreams rested not upon Ickx but his Ferrari. They loved the car, merely respected the man and if the Ferrari was in the lead they would rise in a subliminal unison and make the stand vibrate.

Among them – your seat was dictated by your ticket – a quiet furniture maker from an obscure town in central France sat next to his fifteen-year-old son. They had come to savour the spectacle as part of the holiday they were on. It is what dads do and where teenagers go if dad gives them the chance by buying the ticket. To see an exciting spectacle. This teenager, small, muscular, wiry and with his face encased by long hair nearly à la mode – it was fractionally too long and would remain so into adulthood except for an interruption when a military barber got at it – was certainly going to enjoy the race, just as he was enjoying the antics of the Italians. Their behaviour was remote from him; he came from a solid, dependable family in a solid, dependable part of the country where men said what they meant and held to that and did not necessarily feel the need to say it loudly. A man's word was enough.

A good day out, this, nothing more. Father and son were emotionally indifferent to motor racing beyond these dimensions and the teenager intended to be a great footballer. More likely in the real world he would work with his father making furniture, respecting the wood, savouring the craftsmanship, learning how to read the movement of the grain, where it was weak and where it was strong. Within eighteen months he would be doing exactly that. He would have smiled his wry, tight, semi-defensive semi-offensive smile if he had had a vision of the day when these same Italians – they and their descendants but all of exactly the same tribe and impulse – would throw stones at him and cast straw in front of the racing car he was driving to make him crash and in doing so risk killing him; when this tribe would hate him so much he would need the President of France's own bodyguard to protect him from them; or, more fantastic still, a handful of years further down the road when they would come to venerate him as the Chosen Son to make their yearnings come true and would have rent asunder anybody who plucked so much as a single hair of his shaggy mane. The story of a life, no more, no less, but a big life, never a meagre one.

There were no lights this May 1970 to call the cars to heel after the parade lap and hold them obedient, unmoving, breathless until the red blinked to green and they were all unleashed in a single instant. No. The moment was controlled and enacted by a venerable old man clutching a real flag which he hoisted with a great and laboured sense of theatre, every driver's eyes upon it, monitoring how quickly it was being raised, gauging its fall. When it fell Stewart's March hiccuped, fired and he pressed it into the lead clean and swift, the way he had done so many times before here and in plenty of other places scattered across the globe. Amon clung to him, Brabham clung to Amon, then Ickx, Beltoise, Hulme, Rindt, rat-a-tat nose-to-tail all the way round the thread of a circuit a couple of miles long and past the stands to complete lap 1 of eighty. A long way to go. The story of other people's lives, no more, no less, and none of them meagre, either.

Stewart, friend of the Rainier family who watched at this moment so intently from their own box, siphoned out a lead of 7 seconds by lap 10, Brabham attacking Amon for second place. A couple of laps later Ickx came to a complete halt, the Ferrari crippled: driveshaft.

The teenager in the stand would have smiled his defensive smile very hard if he had had a vision of exactly this place fourteen years down the road when there would be a thunderstorm playing out its violence and he would be in the lead of the Monaco Grand Prix, gesticulating to stop the damn thing: it is too wet to go on, stop it this instant; or that behind him a black-and-gold Lotus utterly dissimilar to the one Rindt now had in seventh place would be coming, coming, coming through the spray, the driver of which, this May day 1970, was experimenting very seriously in a kart around the Parque Anhembri on the outskirts of Sao Paulo, and was only ten years old. The stopping of the race on 3 June 1984 would provoke a storm of its own because in another lap or two the black-and-gold Lotus would have won it. The man who decided to stop the race would have by then – 1984 – a very great deal of experience.

His name: Jacky Ickx.

On lap 19, Bruce McLaren, the third New Zealander, rammed a safety barrier, limped another lap and was out. Like Brabham he made the cars which bore his name. He had been racing a long time and within three weeks would be killed doing private testing.

The teenager in the stand would have smiled all right if he had had a vision of 1980 when he would drive for the team which still bore the name McLaren, would come to feel unsafe in the car, betray an ethic and break a contract to be free of it, return to McLaren in 1984 and win three World Championships and damn nearly five. An absurd notion. It must be repeated: he intended to be a footballer but would become a furniture maker, a sensitive hand feeling the texture of a piece of wood and what it could be made to do, what it could stand under the pressure he would apply to it. Otherwise, everything breaks.

On lap 24, Stewart, most rational of creatures, was safely siphoning the lead further out and continued to do so through 25 and 26, but on 27 when it had become a lovely, lovely 17 seconds, his engine began to misfire slightly and quickly worsened. He angled the March into the pits and the mechanics seized it to see what they could do. Thus far in his career Stewart had won twelve races and this would not be number thirteen; but before he retired he would win twenty-seven, an absolute record which some thought unassailable. It remained so for a generation, remained so until a dry and dusty afternoon at Estoril in 1984, when the teenager in the stand in 1970 crossed the finishing line 20.493 seconds ahead of Gerhard Berger, who like Rindt was an Austrian and via Niki Lauda in direct succession to Rindt. A Very Important Person made sure he was in Estoril to witness his own diminution and would say from the heart: 'I'm glad it's him because he deserves it. There is no doubt in my mind that he is the best driver of his generation.'

His name: Jackie Stewart.

An absurd notion, crazy, crazy, crazy. Soon enough the teenager would obtain his Junior Licence from the French football federation enabling him to play for the Saint-Chamonais in the Lyons Regional League, which might remotely lead to a trial with St Etienne, a big-time club known as Les Verts with a vocal and vociferous following all their own. *Allez les Verts* stickers were plastered everywhere, stirring the fervour, pressuring their own importance. More remotely still, he would be playing for his country, which is where the visions of teenagers lie – although uneasily because they are already aware that it almost certainly will not come true. He has said himself where those dreams lay: Colombes, which was then the national stadium in Paris, Wembley, Maracana. Or make furniture.

Along the promenade by the stands, Brabham had outbraked Amon and 'scratched' through. There wasn't much room. With Stewart gone Brabham led the race, Amon still clinging, Rindt fifth but coming, coming, coming. Rindt was a man of impulse and the impulse held him hard. No race was safe from him when the mercurial and mysterious mood touched the skill. On lap 36, he passed Henri Pescarolo (Matra) at the hairpin called Gasworks and now was fourth. On lap 41, he passed Hulme and now was third but Brabham was too far away, Amon was too far away, surely? On lap 61, Amon's suspension went and now Rindt was second but still too far away, surely? Rindt squeezed the Lotus and nibbled a bit here and sliced a bit there and cumulatively it brought him to within 9 seconds of Brabham but there were only four laps left. He remained too far away.

Surely?

Flowing up the hill to a place called Casino Square, Brabham came fast upon the March of Jo Siffert which occupied the middle of the track and, no more petrol in the engine, was weaving to and fro trying, literally, to slop the dregs from the tank. Brabham remembers that with some clarity. He nearly ran full into the rear of Siffert because their relative speeds were so different and Siffert was so preoccupied he didn't see Brabham at all. The flag marshals, aware that this could decide the whole race, were waving at Siffert to get out of the way, *faster, car behind you! faster, car behind you!* Brabham, impelled by an impetus of his own, mounted the pavement to get through, hustled on but it cost him 4 seconds.

As Brabham passed the pits with the crowd ticking the laps down he could not miss Colin Chapman 'hopping up and down' to urge Rindt on. Chapman, creator of Lotus and arch-psychologist of the battlefield, was doing it long before Rindt actually appeared, was doing it to prey on Brabham's mind that Rindt was coming, closing, coming, closing. See that, Jack?

On the last lap Rindt drew up to within two cars' length but there was no space to overtake: not as they emerged from the tunnel into the sky so azure, not as they descended to the chicane which flung them into the left twist called Bureau de Tabac, not as they flowed along the promenade where the skeletal stands loomed and pressed, not as they reached out for the tight, tight horseshoe of Gasworks corner which was only a gasp and a lunge from the finishing line itself.

Another backmarker limped forward in the middle of the road, Piers Courage in a de Tomaso, engine seemingly dead. Should Brabham take him on the outside or the inside? He hesitated and missed his braking point and when he did brake his car skittered over a thin film of sand which happened to lie on the surface. The car struck some straw bales stacked there to stop anyone hitting something harder, like the tall stone wall behind. As Brabham extricated the car and tried to hold off two marshals who wanted to give him a push – that would have disqualified him – Rindt went through and won the Monaco Grand Prix.

This was the first time Rindt had won it and only the second victory of his career. If the teenager in the stand had had a vision it would not have been that he would win here three successive years and four years out of five; nor that only one other human being had a real chance of beating him: the ten year old moving around the Parque Anhembri, Sao Paulo, 5,000 miles away.

His name: Ayrton Senna.

One of the marshals had fallen across the bonnet of Brabham's car as it reversed from the bales. Brabham tapped the brakes to deposit the marshal on to the circuit – nothing personal you understand, you have just made yourself into an obstruction, cobber, and cheerio – and crossed the line 23.1 seconds after Rindt. Brabham had been in Grand Prix racing for fifteen years and had won fourteen times. The teenager would have seven wins in a single season twice. In the visions he would not have heard himself saying, as he would: 'To drive a car is my passion. It is not just the speed, it is a whole life: to travel, to meet all sorts of people, earn money, live as most people don't live.' Nor that in time his relationship with the kid in the Parque Anhembri would become so intense that he felt the need to savage him verbally and, just for a moment, physically too. Nor that threats to his life would drive him from France altogether, moving his family to the safety of Yens, Switzerland. Nor that here in Monaco he would have an interesting encounter with the police and the police would happily conclude that boys will be boys, nor that encased in a small, sleek car he would seize a race for apprentices here because in his mind he was so strong and he wanted the race so much and in winning would find another life altogether, namely Formula One, nor that . . .

It had been a good day, a great day as teenage days go, what he calls a 'fabulous memory of my first Grand Prix'. He had seen six drivers who had been or would be World Champions, Stewart, Hulme, Brabham, Rindt, John Surtees and Graham Hill. Leaving Stewart aside the other five would total forty-eight wins between them. No sane vision on 10 May 1970 could have shown the teenager that he would have forty-four of his own by 1991 with plenty of running still left in him, nor that people who knew would make a profound judgement: he is probably the greatest tactician of all time – and even if he wasn't, he is certainly better than Hulme, Brabham, Rindt, Surtees and Hill. A lot better.

But now Rindt is holding the winner's silver bowl so slackly that it nestles limp against his waist. A vast garland encircles his neck and trails down so far that its fronds partially camouflage the bowl. Prince Rainier, a man of considerable and studious dignity, is positioned next to Rindt having just presented him with the bowl. Rainier's right hand clasps the tiny paw of a sweet five-year-old girl wearing a navy blue jacket all buttoned up and a pleated white skirt; her left hand is clasped by her mother, Princess Grace, who has simultaneously arranged herself to face the cameras. Always there would be cameras, particularly at moments like this. She had spent a lifetime knowing it and knowing how to arrange herself for them. The temporal smile remains immortally beautiful. And bless the little girl, she yawned. She would grow inevitably into a celebrity in her own right, a singer of pop songs, a model of fashions, a leggy creature of the Euro-culture of the born-rich trying to find themselves – members of the ancient House of Grimaldi would never do that, sing pop songs.

Surely?

She would come to know well the teenager just over there among the Italians.

Her name: Stephanie.

A sheet of cloud hung over the Enzo and Dino Ferrari circuit and from it, driven hard on the wind, snow poured in broad, moist flakes. In time, on a subsequent day, there would be the violence of a thunderstorm announcing itself across the paddock with a shriek of reverberating, wretching, unloading thunder so low and so sudden that people actually screamed fearing the Day of Judgement was at hand and, as it happened, no one was ready for it. Then the rain came, pounding and stabbing the surface of the paddock so virulently that it bounced back up a foot, two feet, three feet, something like that.

Imola, April 1991.

It was also bitter cold inside the Ferrari team, spiritually cold, while far away over the border posters were being placed at just about every strategic vantage point in France. They advertised a new magazine, *Course Auto*, to be launched three days after the end of this official test session at Imola, if the session ever did end. The snow fell on the Wednesday and they extended it, the thunderstorm was on the Thursday and they extended it again.

The posters were an enlarged reproduction of the cover of the magazine. A single face was depicted, dominated by a large oft-broken nose and pursed lips. The shaggy long hair had become shaggy bushy hair with unfurling curls down the forehead and positive thickets over the ears just like, well, like fronds. The eyes seemed entirely locked on to the present. Across the red Marlboro driving overall that he wore a headline was overprinted in large yellow capital letters. It said in French: THE 'I ACCUSE' OF ALAIN PROST. It was a hell of a headline, almost a scream, almost another unloading of thunder.

No Frenchman could mistake the undercurrent it distilled. Just before the turn of the century Alfred Dreyfus, a captain in the French army and a Jew, was convicted of spying and shipped to Devil's Island. The novelist Emile Zola became so convinced Dreyfus had been framed that he wrote an open letter to the President of the Republic where again and again he hammered out the fateful phrase *J'ACCUSE* as he castigated the people involved name by name. It was so devastating and so profound that even ninety-six years later *J'ACCUSE* was not a phrase to be wielded lightly and no Frenchman could mistake its implication. Prost, true to the region of France which nurtured and shaped him, had always said what he meant and held to it when he had said it. The article promised his judicious and judicial sentence on Ferrari, a team in great turmoil and for whom Prost was now The Chosen Son. Many, many people during that Imola test waited with anticipation or trepidation for the first issue of *Course Auto* to hit the streets hard on 23 April. Would he accuse the whole team, name by name?

Perhaps 2,000, perhaps 3,000 people were at Imola, most camped in the long grandstand directly opposite the pits. They had brought their battle pennants: flags, banners and red hats, they had brought the open, untrammelled emotions of a football crowd; they had come to hiss and hoot and jeer Ayrton Senna whenever he brought the red-and-white Marlboro McLaren Honda from the pits or returned to them; to rise whenever young Jean Alesi – Prost's partner at Ferrari – completed a lap and the flat nasal voice from the loudspeaker announced a fast time. The crowd could see deep into the bowels of the Ferrari pits and could sense even across the width of the track the tension there. Politics are endemic at Ferrari, you could always sense that – they had been for thirty, forty years, while Enzo Ferrari himself was alive and now in his hereafter. These April days, Prost would judge that the atmosphere had 'calmed down'. It is what people say. The mental hills surrounding Ferrari still compressed the atmosphere into great extremes and did it quickly. Whenever the crowd glimpsed Cesare Fiorio, the team's Sporting Director, they hissed and hooted and jeered him, told him to get back on the beach to touch up his tan.

So, there was the snow on the Wednesday, the deluge on the Thursday, an uninterrupted day on the Friday and the extension to Saturday. This was important; a last chance to run before the San Marino Grand Prix at Imola on 28 April which, as it happened, was five days after the appearance of *J'ACCUSE.*

On that Saturday, Prost pressed the Ferrari out of the pit lane with qualifying tyres on it, warmed them nicely and threaded through the geometrical left-right corners which brought him to the start–finish straight and the line itself. As he crossed it the timing device began counting to one hundredth of a second. He knew the 3.13 miles of the circuit very intimately by now, yard after yard. One minute 22.412 seconds later he re-crossed the line and the crowd were on their feet making the stand vibrate. No man had ever gone round Imola quicker, none of them.

Monaco 1970 and Imola 1991, two poles – if I may use the word in its other sense – of a life and a lot had happened in between.

To understand Alain Prost's professional career you must (ironically) listen to the words of Senna, who learnt that if you spend years driving cars of this power in open competition with other drivers of a similar disposition, in front of a television audience spanning the globe and numbered in hundreds of millions, adding all the stresses of stressed machines and ploughing in enough dollars to rescue a Third World country, extreme things will happen. You have to accept that, make some space in your mind to accommodate it.

Across a career, Alain Prost tamed the beast which is Formula One motor racing, bent it to his will, rode it like a jockey, all taut, economical movement. He mastered the mechanisms in the most profound way. Beyond it he presented himself as a normal, chirpy chappie who liked a joke and had everything in focus in what scientists are pleased to call real time. Vanity was remote from him as were many other social vices. Because of that he was genuinely respected and popular, a star as people want stars to be; but we must never forget the extremes. They come with the territory. There are darker sides, as there surely have to be.

The life was enacted on a stage of great extremes. Some fragments: 'You're drawn two ways about Alain Prost', Tyler Alexander will say. Alexander, laid back in the classic American way and bearing a waspish turn of phrase, was part of Marlboro McLaren's management in 1980 when Prost first penetrated Formula One. 'The guy's brilliant, a fantastic guy in a race, one of the best guys to understand how to win motor races. He's very good at trying to get the best for himself – which they all are, they all want the best for themselves. That is the very nature of the good guys and the good teams, too. It's a huge ego trip to have everything that they want and when it does go wrong not many of them say, "Sorry, but I guess it was my mistake." Once in a while Prost has said that.' He is not damning Prost with faint praise, only moving among the verities he has observed and experienced the best way he can.

John Watson spent that year of 1980 as, ostensibly, Prost's senior partner at McLaren and lost his place in 1984 to Prost when Prost returned. This in no sense diminishes his respect. 'The thing that Alain has understood, and it's something you learn with age and maturity, is that you do not have to be on the front row to win the races. It's not about being in pole position. Of course to be there is very fulfilling but not a sure way to winning the races.

'Alain's ability to read situations is something he has evolved and when you are in the quickest car, significantly the quickest car, it's not difficult. What is difficult is to win when you aren't. We've seen drivers in the past achieve this – Stewart in the Tyrrell for example because he was the smartest driver then and Prost is very, very smart now in situations. He is very prudent in the way he drives. In overtaking he won't go for gaps which are not there.

'I remember watching him in 1984 and I'd think, "Bloody hell, what is he doing?" He was leading the race by an Irish mile and the way he'd pass people he'd be exposing himself to their mistakes and errors – and that's what happens. It is not necessarily that you make a mistake but that you trust the judgement of somebody else too much. You cannot always anticipate what the person you are passing is going to do. The irrationality of those situations is on such a scale that you cannot anticipate. Because of his level of intelligence – and he is very intelligent – he has worked this out in his mind and he is able to keep himself out of trouble.

'Race-craft is to recognize your potential and your car's potential and know how to use them effectively: where you need to apply pressure; how to sustain that pressure. It is to know the characters of the other competitors, know their weaknesses and strengths and those of the cars they are in. It is Kasparov versus Karpov, it is a game of chess and you have to put all the pieces together on the board and then know how to play them.'

This is a legitimate art-form, delicate, transient, very complex, maddening, all-enveloping, full of strange subtleties and it is extreme because it must be exercised at very high speeds on narrow strips of tarmacadam shaped to snake and snap amidst the jostle of other drivers travelling at approximately these same high speeds, some of whom will be young, red-blooded, Italian and myopic, to name but a few.

You ride the beast by consciously arresting the pace of your thought-processes so that the corner coming at you in a great flicking, fleeting surge in real time will click frame by frame in slo-mo; or as Prost puts it: 'When I look fast I'm not, I'm ragged. When I look slow I'm fast because I'm smooth.' You can't do it and few other human beings can, either.

Nor can you do this: 'Alain was brilliant on tyres,' designer John Barnard will say, 'brilliant on looking after them, brilliant in telling you when a tyre was going off – in telling you after a ten-lap test that this tyre is going to be too strong for the race or too soft or whatever. The race might be sixty, seventy laps and as a team you've got to know: will these tyres last the whole race? Will they keep going off? Have they stabilized? Will they stay like that? All these sort of questions. His ability to separate the tyre data and feel from what the chassis was doing was unbelievable. I had never met anyone who could separate it that well.'

From the very beginning he was sure of himself to an absolute degree and we shall have many witnesses to testify to that. Most found it genuinely astonishing and at least one so improbable that he needed a decade and a half to begin to believe it. He believes it now. Few doubt Prost was born with it, whatever it is.

Sometimes the public persona fitted uncomfortably with the events which surrounded it, a matter for legitimate discussion. Marlboro McLaren were glad of the bounty he brought them in 1980, Renault glad of it next, McLaren joyous after that and yet he left each embattled. Someone intimately connected with a lot of these years (and still intimately connected) whispered to me in early 1991: 'Makes you think and makes you wonder, the leaving, doesn't it?'

Another fragment: in 1984 Prost joined Lauda at McLaren. 'I never had a problem with him, maybe because he wanted to learn, maybe because he arrived in a situation where I was an established World Champion and he was the upcoming star, if you want to put it that way', Lauda will say. 'So we had a situation which was different. But I think he's a difficult character, to be honest. He's a moaner, he is not a good politician – this will be a problem for him with Ferrari – he has a lot of problems in his private life which I don't want to talk about.'

His riding of the beast itself was beyond question. Brian Hart, engine maker and shrewd observer, rationalizes it as well as any. 'He developed the talent he had. It's what very few drivers have, this all-round ability, this belief in themselves, this natural talent. He understands racing and the fact that the race lasts sixty-four laps or seventy-two laps or whatever. Over the years we have seen many who have not registered that fact at the start of a race. Drivers like Prost think the race through on the Saturday night, think through the various permutations, where they'll be and when they'll be there and it's all locked in their brains: by about lap 15, they'll think, *he'll* drop out, *he'll* be too hard on his tyres, *he'll* . . . and it's just amazing. They'll probably never tell you but I believe that's how far ahead they think.'

The man himself is a curious mixture of contradictions (although I suspect we all are) and a biographer cannot separate the private person from the public property. Each feeds the other and each depends on the other and you can examine neither in isolation.

Here for example is Prost discussing his profession from a human point of view.

'You have apprehension, stage fright, but fear is not the same thing. Fear paralyses the reflexes. Why so often does a driver have the air of being closed in on himself, a little sad perhaps? I am persuaded that it's because every day continually – when he wakes up in the morning, when he goes to bed at night – he has to think a bit about the risks he is running.

'I don't see how I can explain the desire to drive itself. It is something impalpable. Eventually, one day in a hundred you might ask yourself what you're doing there behind the steering wheel. I imagine that this lassitude will keep evolving, it will become one day in fifty, one day in ten, one in two and the day will arrive when the boredom is constant and that will be the day to stop. Now in 1991 I'm perhaps at the level of one day in 365, perhaps not even that. On the other hand, more than the driving itself, what's hard to take is the pressure which comes from outside. That affects me more than I thought it would. When you are serene you have the impression that nothing can happen to you.'

The biographer faces uncomfortable moments judging how far he goes into the private person. Does Prost's Catholicism have any relevance to his career? Almost certainly, and inevitably too because it shapes childhood and the child is the father of the man. Do you pursue him into his bedroom? Does it matter that he likes women and golf in that order? When I was exploring this delicate territory with a friend of Prost – who wished, and will be granted, anonymity – he said that at moments it has been extremely relevant and added: 'It's so much part of the whole thing. He calls them up in the middle of the night, whispers, and is very romantic and he is very erotic and very sexy and you can imagine the type of things he is telling them. He turns such a big show on that somewhere they are so aroused they have to give in – and he sends flowers, he spends a lot of time at it.' Prost himself once replied that if reincarnation existed he would like to come back as a eunuch to keep out of trouble. He also said that because he was so 'little and ugly' he regarded women as a challenge although, as the friend attests, 'his success is that he had to become very successful in order to change the way people look at him. Now everybody thinks he is handsome and is after him – but really you'd have to ask a psychiatrist about all that.'

There are those who postulate that the act of driving a racing car is so macho, such a raw, primitive exercise of power that it can become sexual in (perhaps) much the same way as horse riding is supposed to arouse women. Maybe. Certainly Nelson Piquet, who down these years has shown exquisite taste in beautiful women, confesses that when Nigel Mansell broke down on the last lap of the Canadian Grand Prix in 1991 and Piquet passed him to win 'I almost came'.

Piquet was joking. He always jokes. Doesn't he?

To chronicle the sexual history of Grand Prix racing would be legally dangerous, extremely exhausting and require – if it was to be definitive – a tome to eclipse the *Karma Sutra*. The driver is in the prime of life, invariably good looking, extremely well paid, a celebrity, he glides among The Beautiful People on each continent and he has the fascination of facing mortal danger most weeks of his life which gives him an aura different to all other men, and rightly so.

There is a vein of sincerity which runs very deep in Alain Prost. How many men at the age of thirty-four would say this: 'Am I a believer? I have never prayed or asked anything of anybody before a race. I am very believing, however, and say my prayers every evening before I go to sleep, as I have done ever since childhood. Everything I have I owe to myself. God has other things to do than give victories to Alain Prost'? And on meeting the Pope: 'He's the person who's made the most impression on me. To a Catholic the Pope represents something very special but it is difficult to assess the sensations you feel. On meeting Pope Wojtyla I immediately appreciated his greatness. We talked of many things although I felt a bit confused. He even told me he occasionally watches the Grands Prix on television.'

The conjunction between the private Prost and the public Prost is there in that sentence, as it is always there.

He expresses the vein of sincerity with other words, too. The French newspaper *Le Figaro* asked him if he thought this is a decadent era. He replied: 'In full decadence from the human point of view and that's incontestable. Relationships between individuals are claustrophobic. And believe me Formula One is no exception; it is simply a reflection of life, a reflection of how the world is evolving. But what I find odious is not being able to speak to people any more, not put confidence in people any more. As soon as you live in a closed universe you become a prisoner, you become hermetically sealed.' There you have it, the conjunction again.

Usually he was very calm. Once in the mid 1980s he came to Silverstone on a promotional trip which drivers normally dread. Those invited to lunch numbered two or three racing journalists while the rest were production car people or from women's magazines, few of whom had the remotest idea about Prost or his world beyond the obvious. He sat at a large circular table and he was asked childlike questions (are the cars very fast?) and this went on for an hour. At no stage did he betray boredom or irritation. On the contrary he sensed that these were precisely the questions people who didn't know would ask, he was grateful for their curiosity, he was in sympathy with these people and he made the answers interesting. In short he charmed the whole lot of them, shook a forest of hands afterwards, smiled a lot but not in any wooden way and then, wonder of wonders, appeared reluctant to leave. Perhaps he was.

This is the man who when he felt codes of conduct betrayed could use words like bits of broken glass. Of Senna after their crash at Suzuka in 1990 Prost even went so far as to say publicly, 'It fills me with disgust . . . I thought he was one of the human race . . .'

This is the man who, in the words of fellow driver Derek Warwick, 'has been a great leader in the last decade, a really great leader because he has the respect of the important people around us, the people in authority. He is the only person they respect. If Joe Bloggs goes up and says, "We want a barrier removed and a chicane put in", so what? But with Alain they know he has thought it out, spoken to his colleagues and he knows what is best – no, not what's best but what is possible. Without him there would have been a lot of situations where we wouldn't have had marshals, safety crews, helicopters. That rests on his shoulders not just because he is safety conscious but because he devotes a lot of time to it. Plenty of drivers are safety conscious too but they can't be bothered.'

Prost himself expands on this and we are at another conjunction. 'Road safety is something we have to face up to. Deaths caused by road accidents are something which affect me deeply. In France for example there are double the number of deaths that there are in England and, I believe, one and a half times as many as in Italy. The problem is that people are not valued. They are treated like children. It's an insult to people's intelligence when we see flimsy, tinny cars on the road and we know that technology is sophisticated enough to produce something much stronger. On the one hand cars are allowed to be built that are unsafe, on the other hand cars that are safer and built to the highest standard must not exceed certain speed limits. This is real hypocrisy. Take Formula One. You see the most awful accidents happen but cars hardly ever burst into flames whereas on motorways you only need an accident between two old bangers and the people inside are burned to death. If our safer petrol tanks were fitted to mass-produced cars hundreds of thousands of lives could be saved.'

There are many facets to the man: non-political ('I read the big headlines in the newspapers but it doesn't go any deeper than that'); resigned to being a much-discussed public figure ('there is nothing you can do about it'); a man who when he had been a Formula One driver for seven years would say of the death of his brother Daniel, who succumbed to cancer: 'It taught me that life is short and fragile' and 'I'm afraid of sickness and old age. After a full sporting life lived in good health old age is very difficult to come to terms with. Since the death of my brother I am petrified by illness. I never take medicine, I'm scared to go to the doctor. I do however have two complete check-ups a year.' Another conjunction.

And: 'Premonitions? I had an incredible one when I was a child. I dreamed my grandmother was dead. I woke up in an awful state and rushed to her bedroom which was next to mine. She was fine of course but the night after she died. Since then I have believed in certain dreams.'

That summer of 1970 long after the noise of the engines had melted into silence at the Monaco Grand Prix, long after the teams had decamped and the teenager and his father had descended the plain steps of the stand and made their way back to the bosom of the family the footballer-dreamer was to be given another treat.

One afternoon André Prost took Alain along Route Nationale 89, a road which runs snaking and snapping all along the ragged coastline of the South of France, to a place of various pleasures roughly midway between Antibes and Cannes. Like the Grand Prix this was another way of enriching a holiday by taking what was on offer and tasting it.

The Siesta looked appropriately Spanish, a cluster of smooth stucco-white buildings with a wall and tall shrubs all round. It was a disco and casino but that was of no immediate relevance to a fifteen year old.

The long car-park directly in front of the Siesta, flanked on one side by the N89 with its traffic ebbing endlessly by and on the other by a stony beach dipping down to the sea, welcomed visitors by a truly vast anchor set into a truly vast block of stone. It was the kind of artefact which looks inexplicably chic in places like this.

The car-park was broad and long and fringed alternately by parched palm trees and cactus plants with, superimposed on its surface, the contour of a miniature track, a kart track. Hire one, drive on, have fun, go home, just like that. André Prost hired one despite the fact that Alain had an arm in plaster, the result no doubt of some adolescent mishap. He was after all *active*. Alain clambered in (or rather on) and drove it put-put-putter, then the engine noise rose into a buzz and away he went into the corners, along a little straight, tight into another corner. He covered a few laps and didn't hit anything, started no doubt to go faster . . .

Many years later he described the impact these precious moments had on him as the equivalent of a thunderclap. He had discovered, he sensed, the life-process itself, had by a complete fluke uncovered the passion which would rule the last years of his teens and all his adult life. It happens.

A large and varied group of people have dug into their memories to help tell this story. All have struggled to be honest, many speaking – as they say – for the first time. I fear that not all of them will enjoy the book but that cannot be helped. What was, was. But I thank them all. They are in no special order: François Goldstein, Lionel Chamoulaud, Sylvie Shannon, Tony Jardine, Brian Lord, Mark Burgess, Dick Bennetts, Donald Davidson, Terry Fullerton, Nigel Clegg, Teddy Mayer, John Watson, Fred Opert, Peter Stayner, Simon de Lautour, Michel Hugon, Tyler Alexander, Kevin Cogan, Ken Tyrrell, Jeanette Chabot, Antoine Rafaelli, Bernard Droulon, Jean-Louis Bousquet, Jean Sage, Jacky Ickx, Stefan Johansson, Gerard Crombac, Elj Elgh, Kenny Acheson, Teo Fabi, Anders Olofsson, Michael Korten, Slim Borgudd, Martyn Pass, Brian Hart, Ron Dennis, René Arnoux, Keke Rosberg, Derek Warwick, Patrick Tambay, Pino Allevi, Ginetta Guarneri, Frederic Watelet, John Barnard, Alan Henry, Niki Lauda, Renaud de Laborderie.

Nigel Roebuck, Grand Prix editor of the British magazine *Autosport*, has fully and unashamedly savoured Prost's career. For his counsel, his active assistance and reading the manuscript I offer my gratitude, although I must apply the usual caveat that the mistakes are entirely mine not his.

I have used *Autosport* itself as a pillar and a comfort. I have taken quotations from it with the kind permission of Simon Taylor, the Deputy Chairman. *Autosport* misses nothing and knows exactly what it is about. *L'Equipe*, and particularly the reportage of its noted correspondent Johnny Rives, was another pillar. *AUTOhebdo* was of enormous value in the chapter entitled 'All Time High'. *Antenne Deux*, the French television channel, produced a programme called *Dossiers de l'Ecran* which was almost an hour-long confessional with Prost and for those insights I am grateful. I have delved deep into *Autocourse* and kept *Marlboro's Grand Prix Guide* constantly at my elbow. I pay due tribute to both publications, each superb in their different way. Pino Allevi was kind enough to provide a fascinating interview he did with Prost for *Gazzetta dello Sport*. Karting Magazine is a mine of amazing information, and for permission to quote from it, sincere thanks. The Olivetti Longines timing service has been a laboratory of precise information and for that thanks, too.

Prost has written his own book, *Life in the Fast Lane*, with Jean-Louis Moncet (Editions Michel Lafon in France, Stanley Paul in the English language) and I have ambivalent feelings about it. He naturally gives his side of the story but there are many, many other sides. I hope all of them are here.

The introductory chapter to my biography, *Ayrton Senna – The Hard Edge of Genius* (Patrick Stephens and Corgi), ended with a quotation from the German philosopher Hermann Hesse, which was going a bit in a motor-racing book. Never mind. Alain Prost deserves no less. 'Each individual, who is himself an experimental throw from the depths, strives towards his own goal. We can understand each other but each person is able to interpret himself to himself alone.'

Tyler Alexander will certainly be amazed (and amused) to find himself in the company of Hesse but in discussing Prost he used a quotation which in its way is equally profound and equally daunting: 'Someone once said there are two reasons why a man does something. One is the good reason and the other is the real reason.'

By journey's end I trust we will understand Alain Prost and both reasons.

2
IT'S A KNOCK OUT

> I was standing with my camera to get the head-on shot . . . I hadn't actually taken a picture and suddenly I saw a kart coming through the lens.
>
> BRIAN LORD

The sign on the padlocked double-gate has faded now, soaked by the rains of winter, burnished by the suns of summer. It says: *Piste Antoine Vernay, Property of the Association Sportiv de Karting. Reserved exclusively for licence holders.* The hours of opening are carefully set out below day by day. *Authorized sessions: Wednesday 13 hours–19 hours, Saturday 9 hours–12 hours, 13 hours–19 hours . . .*

There is another sign and this too is fixed to the gate but it is more recent and hand-written in large letters. *Track reserved for licence holders. All transgressions will be severely punished.*

That is all.

Rive de Gier lies a handful of kilometres from Saint Chamond and shares the same essential character although it is significantly smaller, going on 20,000 inhabitants instead of 40,000. It is strung out along what used to be the main road and it bears the appearance of a place having closed in on itself. In the evening the occasional person wanders the pavement, the occasional car drifts by, the buildings are of solid stone, shutters are drawn across windows. If you stop to ask the way to the kart track you are likely to be met by a shrug. Not everyone, as it would seem, knows there is a kart track never mind the enormous, thunderous thing which began there – and you had anticipated triumphal hoardings and big direction signs. After all not much else seems to have happened at Rive de Gier and for a naughty moment, surveying the long, dead street you wonder if *anything* else has happened at Rive de Gier.

There is a good reason why some shrug and others forage in their memories to tell you where it is. You have to leave the town altogether and ascend a narrow, twisting by-road into open fields where green hills roll gently away towards Lyons; some of the fields have crops, some are pasture for grazing and from the middle distance as you approach there is nothing to distinguish the one field you want from the others except the wire fence which surrounds it and the double-gate.

Peer through and you see a very small, humble, tight outline of a track uncoiling and folding back on itself. It is flanked by heaps of worn, ancient tyres and sturdy grass grows through them in profusion. There is no semblance of a building, not even a hut.

The teenager journeyed here in the late summer of 1970, asked how you joined, and joined. No banners were unfurled, no flags waved. As with so many adolescent episodes in a life it was done modestly, with a certain trepidation, the consequences completely unknown. 'He was about fifteen when he first came,' Bernard Droulon, now the club's president, will say. 'He'd done a bit for amusement on the Cote d'Azur and he came to look at the races at our circuit. That made him want to do it and he came back with a kart, an ordinary one, very simple.' It cost 700 francs, exactly the sort of sum adolescents pay to own something precious.

'To get a licence it was enough to write, there was nothing particular to it: a letter, a photograph, a cheque [Droulon chuckles at the latter]. In reality the money was a fee for insurance in case you had an accident. A little part of the cheque went to the club. Nowadays you need a medical to get a licence but in those days it was enough to show up with a kart. The licence cost 150 francs.

'At every meeting we had around a hundred drivers who took part in races which we called *Les Amicales* (friendlies). There were three kinds of engines so we divided the drivers into three categories, thirty drivers per category. The thirty didn't all race together. The rules said we could only run fourteen at a time so they went in a series a bit like a championship.

'His first few races he did nothing, he didn't get results. He'd come with his parents. His father is outwardly a very reserved man. He and his mother followed him everywhere, his mother was there all the time. With us they laughed and joked a lot, as a family they did every mischief possible, every mischief you can imagine. They were enjoying themselves. That first year I didn't get the impression Alain was deadly serious about it. He'd come to amuse himself.' The mischief revolved, no doubt, around Prost junior's sense of humour and he would never lose it.

'At the beginning', Michel Hugon, another karter, will say, 'he ran in his region, St Etienne. He did a few friendly races and that's how I got to know him because in those days I was in the French team and for him I was a good karter. As a bloke he was very *sympa* [all right], calm, he'd had a few knocks with other drivers. He began to drive and drive and drive, and then he joined the French Junior team which wasn't doing much – but it was a proper team.'

'In his second year', Droulon will say, 'he started to achieve what he wanted. Yes, he had become serious but at the same time he was still amusing himself enormously. That's normal, but when he got into the kart he had to win and his opponents began to understand that. On circuits which he didn't know at all and against the drivers of the region who were of a very high level he'd attack them in places where you thought it was impossible to overtake – his opponents were sure he couldn't but he did and that's how he got past them. It's almost something unimaginable, isn't it? All his results were like that.'

This is the first evidence, the very first, of something which subsequently people would call 'the balance in Prost's mind'. It means that instinctively he felt what a machine could be made to do and where its limit lay and could explore that limit in complete safety; others would reach for the limit and not find it because they lacked the innate ability: the mind balancing the body balancing the machine. Like the sense of humour Prost would never lose it.

There is moreover something deeply potent about competition itself, something intrinsically hard which draws a fierce spirit out of young people and karting, with the great advantage of being cheap and cheerful, is the perfect medium. This is why if you scan the grid of a Grand Prix almost the whole lot began exactly here. There is, too, a single word which captures the competition: aggression. It is a word which returns and returns, insistent as a hammer-drill.

'When I began', Prost will say, 'I was simply empassioned. I didn't think about glory or about money, I didn't think about anything except winning races. At first I knew absolutely nothing about the mechanical side of it but a year after my début I was preparing my own engines because I had become hyper-interested in the mechanics of it.' We can now add technical fascination to the balance and the sense of humour.

The passion grew in direct proportion to his exploration of it and this too is a familiar story. In 1973 he borrowed 1,300 francs (a lot for a teenager) and bought a Vacquand chassis. 'The difference was clear to see. First he started to get good results immediately and second he bought material from a very good kart preparer. The chassis was Vacquand. They were chassis constructors near Paris who don't exist any more. They only made chassis for karts and if they were not the best they were certainly among the best', Droulon says.

Karting is good for discipline, something which would be needed later on. 'When you did a European or World Championship you had to work all day', Hugon says. 'It was six in the morning until nine at night fixing the karts mechanically, it was hard even though the machinery was not as sophisticated as it is now.'

This year of 1973 Prost won the French and European Junior Championships but he was beaten into second place in the French seniors by a driver called Jean-Louis Bousquet, whose career would run parallel for a while. 'I started karting through curiosity, that's all. We began at approximately the same time although oddly perhaps I have no precise recollection of when I first met him. He was not someone who was hard during a race. He was correct, he didn't take excessive risks, he wasn't someone who would overtake at all costs but on the other hand he took defeat very badly. He was manifestly gifted because from his début he was competitive and you could see that clearly. He was someone who went fast naturally. That means he had the feeling of speed as well as being able to use an engine to its maximum. His results show he was gifted. I don't believe in gifted people who don't get results.

'In those days there were two permanent members of the French team (first and second in the Championship) and that was him and me. For a year and a half we did all the races together, sometimes abroad. Our relationship was never bad and never good – not good because, bearing in mind his character, he was someone who couldn't enter into friendship with a man who was his rival on the track. We did not however waste time fighting between ourselves.' This is the classic tension in motor-sport, an uneasy co-existence of egos and ambitions between direct competitors and the further up you go the more the tension increases. We shall see this, too.

Deep into the autumn of 1973 Prost travelled to Oldenzaal in the north of Holland for the World Junior Championships. However impeccable his behaviour would eventually become this was not the moment for that and to understand why we have to move back to the Worlds of the year before, held in Denmark.

Brian Lord, a schoolteacher, was acting as chaperone/adviser to a young Brit, Graham Roscoe, in Denmark. 'He demolished three of the French team in one go. He went into a corner fourth and came out first. He'd come up the grid like a dose of salts and as he came out of that corner first I thought "bloody hell". The French team manager decided he would have a little counselling with Roscoe when he returned to the pits, he dived on him and tried to rip him out of the kart. I was on the other side and dragged this Frenchman over the top of Roscoe. We had harsh words, then some people got between us. The Frenchman was only a little fellow and [deep chuckle] I was about to kill him at the time. After that the French karters all came out with *Ne Touchez Pas* (don't touch) written on the back of their karts . . . '

The French did not forget.

'In 1973 I took a young lad called Nigel Clegg, who was very good and one of the best in the British team. I had an old Ford Anglia van and we trudged all the way across Holland to Oldenzaal. The track was so tiny it was unbelievable. It was set in a sports park and it really was so little you could have put it down within a football pitch. We were accustomed to big long straights, wide tracks, and this thing twisted in and out and round itself but it was quite nicely laid out and well appointed. The French manager said they weren't afraid of the British this year, they could make "bumps" themselves . . .

'Alain Prost actually looked very, very old. He had a moustache and people were saying, "This guy's never a bloody junior." The thing was that British juniors went up to the age of sixteen but the Continental juniors went up to eighteen. Mentally there is a gap between those two age groups, that is to say there is a considerable difference between the attitude of a fifteen year old and an eighteen year old. There were even rumours that Prost was married and had a child!

'At night they had a barbecue on the side of the track, right on the grass down the main straight. His entire family which seemed to be about sixty strong were there, they set up this huge barbecue and they had a piece of meat the size of which I had never clapped eyes on before – enormous – and they cooked this damned thing. They were drinking wine and they were quite happy for everyone to come and join them. We said, "blimey, what a rum bunch" – this was a world championship, everybody else was cleaning their tackle and making sure it all worked and there they were knocking back gallons of wine. They were handing out beakers of wine, not glasses. I was threatening our lads not to drink it because they'd never get their heads clear. I remember the meat, too, rock hard on the outside, but blood coming out of the middle which does nothing for me, I'm afraid.

'The Germans turned up in white leathers with their national colours of red, black and orange stripes round them looking smart, looking like an army, the French looked rough and ready. I wouldn't say they looked a team as such and the Prosts seemed to be a law unto themselves, they were at the front of everything.' Yes, enjoying themselves.

Time trials were run in the morning and Clegg emerged from them with pole position for the first heat.

'Everybody was an official and everybody had a badge on,' Lord says, 'but it was total chaos. To begin with they'd never handled a meeting of that sort in their lives before. They appeared to be incredibly efficient, everyone with their badges, they had a proper clubhouse, a thing for this, a thing for that but when the racing actually started it was turmoil. They didn't seem to know what was going on.

'The competitors run in twin lines and go around in grid order on what's called the rolling lap, because if a kart comes to a halt it stalls and you've got to get someone to push you. I have a feeling that Prost jumped quite a few places but then everybody was doing that.'

Imagine it: the rolling lap threading through the ins and outs of the circuit and some very strong illegal jostling for positions by an awful lot of the karters. Clegg ('perhaps I was a bit too timid') didn't come round leading them as pole man should, no, he came round twelfth.

'Every driver had his eye on getting on to the front row,' Lord says, 'and given that people had spent all morning in the time trials to get that position it was just not on.'

They were all stopped, harsh words were exchanged, the proper grid was constituted and they set off on a second rolling lap to come round to start in grid order. During that rolling lap Clegg went fast and Prost went fast ('when the adrenalin starts flowing, it's very hard to get people round in a nice sensible way', Lord says, almost in a *cri de cœur*). As the starter raised his flag he saw what all those officials with the badges were seeing, too: Clegg and Prost were half a lap ahead of the rest of the field and still travelling fast . . .

The officials flooded on to the track to abort the start again and 'about fifty of them were dancing up and down on it', but Clegg, Prost and then the rest – all strung back – were still travelling fast. 'The drivers weaved between the officials', Lord says, 'and people were running here, there and everywhere.'

After the third rolling lap, and a stern warning to Clegg and Prost, the race actually began but 'with everything that had gone on before I began to lose oil', Clegg says. Prost seized the lead and led a pack of four all the way to victory. He was on his way to the title.

Neither Prost nor Clegg were in the second heat, which was just as well. Only five minutes were allowed between each, the temperature was in the nineties and one of the British team wandering round without even a T-shirt was blistered so badly they had to throw a bucket of cold water over him.

Prost and Clegg lined up for the third heat, Clegg on the front row and Prost somewhere behind. 'Clegg was not a particularly aggressive driver,' Lord says, 'but he was fast, clean and if he got a clear run he was excellent. If somebody was elbowing him he was less good. Being on pole he'd come up the inside towards the first bend and he whipped out to swing through it the way you do, and you're not expecting somebody to come through. [Echoes of Droulon and tales of the unexpected.] I hadn't noticed where Prost started from but I think it was the third or fourth row. He came whistling up the inside and hit Clegg absolutely amidships as Clegg swung into the bend, T-boned him good and proper. Clegg went flying.

'I was standing with my camera to get the head-on shot as they came into the bend, I was looking through the lens. I hadn't taken a picture and suddenly I saw a kart coming through the lens and I had to jump and Clegg missed me by inches.'

'No, I wasn't expecting anybody to come through,' Clegg says, 'but Prost had fire and aggression.'

'Clegg hit the edge of the track, came completely over the top of the tyre barrier and landed underneath a seat. I turned the kart the right way up for him and lifted it over the tyres again, put him in it and said, "get going", because there was no point in him sitting there licking his wounds. But that finished him for the meeting. It was a pity because we could have won it but the steam was knocked out of him and he drove terribly, he let so many people through, he was frightened of it happening again, he wouldn't shut the door. Clegg wasn't even sixteen.' All Clegg can remember is 'Brian lifting the kart back over'.

He restarted in twenty-fourth place and meanwhile the race had another Brit leading it, Shaun Walker. Prost was past him on the fifth lap – Walker was exhausted after winning the second heat and had had only the five minutes in between – and held that to the end. The title was a lot closer, two out of two.

The lack of a time-gap now affected Prost and Clegg for the next heat. They were on the front row again and, 'He got the drop on me and that was that', Clegg says. 'Had the crash knocked the stuffing out of me? At that age you should be able to bounce back. I'd already had a broken shoulder in my karting career so I knew what it was all about and when you're sixteen you don't really feel fear, you're full of youthful exuberance – or you should be . . . '

And that was three out of three.

The final was over two legs and Prost won both decisively. He had driven five times and finished first in all of them. He stood on the podium dwarfed by an enormous laurel wreath clutching the trophy and he was smiling wistfully. It finished 1 Prost (France), 2 Masseu (Germany), 3 Bernel (Germany), 4 Walker (GB), 5 Koene (Holland).

'After what had happened in Denmark in 1972,' Lord says, 'now it was Prost who was doing the same thing to us. He was battering the British lads all over the place. It was in our minds we could deal with them but with him we got a bit of a shock. It was a different breed of Frenchman. Prost didn't need *Ne touchez pas* on the back. We'd stuck it across them the year before and by and large they were pretty timid then. Prost certainly wasn't. He could hand it out with the best.'

'At that stage in karting', Clegg says, 'it really is about fire and aggression. I didn't speak to him. I've never spoken to him. I didn't remember him at all until he started to make it in Formula One and I thought "that name is familiar" – well, I thought "that nose is familiar . . ."'

'He began', Droulon says, 'to win races everywhere, including the World Junior Championship but with us he didn't change, he never changed – there was no difference.' Absolute self-control during and after races would come later but that aside the main facets of the man were already in place.

The World Senior Championships were at Nivelles, Belgium and twenty countries took part. This would be much more difficult, although he was second in the time trials for non-seeded drivers before they moved to the heats.

Karting Magazine: 'It looked as if Mark Steeds [a Brit] was teasing the new World Junior Champion, Prost of France, at the start of the fourth heat by hanging back on the rolling lap but if so it didn't succeed because he found himself third after a first lap mêlée. In fourth position the German Korten appeared to be waving drivers through and then shutting the door on them at the last minute going through corners. Showing a fine aggressive spirit Steeds finally managed to get past Prost, although he was later to drop back when other chargers squeezed through.' Among the chargers was inevitably Prost who finished third, a certain Eddie Cheever fourth. Prost was fifth in heat five, Cheever fourth and that made Prost seventh among the top non-seeded qualifiers, Cheever sixth.

Karting Magazine described the latter in a crisp and cutting sentence. 'This sulky-faced boy is actually an American.' Cheever himself, who would come to have the highest respect for Prost and partner him, had begun racing when he was ten 'and it was very competitive. I didn't do it for fun and in fact I didn't have any puberty as such. If I lost a race my father would jump up and down and scream so I got the lesson early on that losing was not what it was all about.' He also found Prost a difficult young man to beat and remembers the frustration all these years later.

The seeded drivers had not yet driven and among them were two proper combatants, Belgian François Goldstein and Briton Terry Fullerton. Of Goldstein, Fullerton makes this judgement: 'He was a very fired-up character, a real winner, loads of determination and aggression, he was very analytical about the way he went karting long before people were getting technical over their equipment. He was an excellent kart driver but he was quite an emotional, reasonably fiery sort of fellow.'

This had nothing immediately to do with Prost but it certainly would in time, and there is something else we must explore because it captures that epoch in senior karting. 'No, it wasn't violent, not all violent,' Michel Hugon says, 'but they weren't the same kind of people who do it now. Then it was older people who karted, very few young ones. If you want an example, in France there were ten cadets, that means only ten drivers who were fourteen and under, and the rest – three or four hundred – were adults. Parents didn't want their kids to start because the parents hadn't enough money. You got people like me who worked to earn a living and karted for their leisure and it stopped there. Now it's adults who lead their little ones to karting. That didn't exist before.

'Typically there were a lot of garage owners and it was very difficult for kids because kids did compete against adults and they didn't have their parents behind them. And the rules on the way you drove were not so strict. The right to push people, that doesn't exist now. Before it was the strongest who won, not always the quickest, and the people who run it these days are more professional. That's how the world has changed.'

Prost finished fourteenth at Nivelles and before we leave it we need to look at an incident and then at a man, François Goldstein. The incident is recounted by Anders Olofsson, a Swede and competitor. 'Prost was a junior but he was so quick that the French decided to take him on their senior team. For me he looked like a boxer because his nose was like that, rather bent.

'He was very full of energy. He and a German were both fired up and – it was an early round, a heat, I think – one for sure held the other one up. They were not satisfied with each other's driving and how to drive fair. They were young people, sixteen or seventeen, so young and aggressive and afterwards they had some body language. I watched this. It happened where you came in, slowed down and got out of your kart. They were very close to each other, they were saying some dirty words to each other. They didn't take their helmets off. They tried to kick each other and one was trying to kick the other between the legs although I can't remember which one. Then the marshals or mechanics arrived to stop it. I know that if you have a problem it's better to discuss it by mouth rather than by the body but you can expect young, fired-up drivers to do it like that.'

The key word is fair. It was, and is, something Prost holds precious and if down the years others transgressed he found it extremely difficult to accept. It violated a basic creed and was not something he ever felt was negotiable. You just did not behave like this on any racing circuit.

Someone of a suspicious nature might point a finger at Michael Korten who, remember, had been waving and blocking. 'It was not me', he says very firmly. 'My problem was that we seemed to be in every heat together, we were fighting each other but on the track when we were overtaking because we were equally fast. He was completely fair although he pushed hard and was aggressive.

He wasn't as good as he would become in a racing car, though I remember his kart wasn't well set up. I spoke to him a few times, in English I suppose, but a fight off the track? It must have been someone else.' And we'll never know who.

Now, Goldstein. What follows here will help to explain what happened when we meet him again, as we will.

Karting Magazine: 'In the race leading up to the final everyone who could get a vantage point crowded to watch the confrontation between Goldstein and Fullerton, both being on the front row. With excitement running to a high pitch a red flag was suddenly used to stop them all on the rolling lap at the furthest point of the circuit from the paddock. As mystified drivers got off their karts and mechanics sprinted to go and see what had happened, so a ring of officials formed keeping the drivers segregated like animals at a market. Prominent among the marshals was an agitated Mr Goldstein Snr., who strutted up and down and prevented Fullerton from taking a cigarette from a spectator. A short, sharp sentence deflated Mr Goldstein like a balloon and after ten minutes the drivers were suddenly told to restart. Later the organizers admitted that the purpose of the stop had been to allow any illegal alcohol in the fuel to evaporate from the open petrol tanks.'

During the race 'with a masterful out-bluffing movement Fullerton got past Goldstein into the hairpin, touching wheels on the way. This all seemed too much for Goldstein and going into a very fast right-hander in front of the grandstand he drove straight into the side of Fullerton's kart and both plunged into the banking. Winded and with injuries to his chest where Goldstein's kart had driven over his own, Fullerton managed to restart.' Both were disqualified.

The final was two legs, Goldstein had a puncture in the first but beat Fullerton in the second. Many in the crowd thought Goldstein had taken the title although it was decided on aggregate positions.

'The organizers did nothing to dispel the feeling that Goldstein had won [Goldstein a Belgian remember, Nivelles in Belgium remember] and the scrutineering after the race took on a funereal atmosphere with Goldstein running for shelter to his personal tent. Much argument centred around the taking of fuel samples from Fullerton in non-sterile soft-drink bottles, apparently as a result of a protest lodged by Goldstein. Eventually in pitch darkness a garland was put around Fullerton's neck on a podium and rumour – there was no written announcement – revealed the fact that the presentation would take place at the nearby Town Hall. With much difficulty this was located but the main doors were locked and barred . . .'

Yes, we shall meet Goldstein again.

In 1974 Prost became French Senior Karting Champion and competed in the European Championships which were reconstituted as a team event and held over four rounds, at Wohlen near Zurich, Nivelles in Belgium, Thiverval near Paris and Fano on the Italian Adriatic. There were two finals to each round and at Wohlen, Prost was fourth (behind Fullerton and Goldstein) in the first, fourth again (behind Fullerton) in the second.

Fullerton, an experienced judge of these matters and not one to gaze back with misty eyes, puts Prost into his true perspective. 'He was always quite a sensible driver but not really quick. That was the ultimate feeling I had about him: not a threat, not one of those I considered to be a racer. I remember passing him on a few occasions and it was easy to do so. In my mind that's the way I remember the guy – not a formidable force.

'He was a nice fellow, he was doing his karting on a bit of a shoe-string. I talked to him quite a few times. Once at Venice airport we were both waiting for our mechanics to turn up and we were chatting away and he had a transit van outside. That's the way he went karting. He didn't have anything very special in the way of a transporter, it was just sort of very ordinary. I didn't have much money either but there were teams about who had better facilities than I had and Prost had.

'In Europe he'd tend to finish fourth, fifth, maybe third – that sort of stuff – or not finish at all. He never really showed any world-class flair, he was never going to be a world star you could say. As soon as Ayrton Senna came along into karting [later in the 1970s] it was all happening. That was not the case with Prost whatsoever. In fact if you look at his career you'd have to say he didn't do anything particularly stunning except win the World Junior Championships. Those were quite early days for the Junior Championship and the category wasn't phenomenally competitive.'

This demands a little amplifying and is interesting because it provides a paradox. Karting is an entirely separate world from any form of single-seater car racing, karting demands distinctly separate skills and while youngsters destined for Formula One are invariably quick in a kart (or anything else) they tend not, as Fullerton attests about Prost, to dominate. The following list does not pretend to be comprehensive but it does tell you something.

On the left are the winners of the World Championship between 1970 and 1984, on the right the performances of drivers who would subsequently reach Formula One.

1970	Goldstein	No F1 driver.
1971	Goldstein	No F1 driver.
1972	Goldstein	Riccardo Patrese 4.
1973	Fullerton	Patrese 9, Prost 14, Cheever even further back.
1974	Patrese	Cheever 2, Prost not in top 10.
1975	Goldstein	Elio De Angelis 2, Prost and Cheever not in top 10.
1976	Larson	Andrea De Cesaris 6, De Angelis 10, Stefan Bellof 13.
1977	Rovelli	Corrado Fabi 4, De Cesaris 5, Bellof 7.
1978	Speed	Ayrton Senna 6, Fabi and Bellof not in top 10.
1979	Koene	Senna 2.
1980	De Bruyn	Senna 2, Stefano Modena 8.
1981	Wilson	Senna 4, Henri Raphanel 6, Ivan Capelli 9, Modena not in top 10.
1982	Wilson	Johnny Herbert 18.
1983	Wilson	Herbert 24.
1984	Haase	No F1 driver.

Of those who went on to Formula One, only Patrese actually won it although at this time (summer 1991) he, Prost, Senna and the late Elio De Angelis have won more than eighty Grands Prix.

'You need to be very, very good at top-level international karting and there are differences from single-seaters', Fullerton says. 'My experience is mostly in karts but I've spoken to a lot of people when they've moved on about the problems that crop up. What you need to be good at for karting is a certain aggression and determination on the track which in its raw form serves no purpose whatsoever in a single-seater. That demands a technique where you are smoother. In cars the whole approach mentally is a smooth approach as it is with the driving style itself. When you go from karts to Formula Ford (or Formula Renault) you can't believe how little grip there is, for example. Karts have a tremendous amount of grip. I've known drivers who were carried along well in karts because of that aggression and determination then they moved to cars and had an awful lot of trouble. In single-seater racing it's about channelling the aggression, about controlling it.'

Bousquet handled both disciplines. 'For me a kart is one of the most difficult activities in motorized sport. In cars you brake fifty metres before a corner, in a kart you brake at ten metres and, comparing one to the other, everything is divided like that. When you get out of karts and into cars it's easier because it's longer and slower.'

This is not the diversion it might appear. Kart racing is a tumultuous experience and they dart round a track like a shoal of nervous fish; a car is longer and higher from the ground, which inevitably makes it more cumbersome; a car has a gearbox, a car has many refinements and, at the risk of raising the wrath of the karters, it demands several kinds of finesse. To a man like Prost there could only be one satisfactory medium and that was the car, although as Bousquet adds, 'It's the contrary of what people think: we didn't have the idea that karting would lead to Formula One. I don't believe he had that idea either. Cars are something else, another world. I do believe the idea of Formula One may have come little by little after a string of subsequent events – it's certain that when he started in racing cars it began to germinate but not too much before that.'

The 1974 World Championships were at Estoril where he was ninth after the heats and nowhere at all in the final. In the spring of 1975 he went to contest the Alazar Trophy near Paris, a well-known event. The favourite was Goldstein and by way of introduction we must hear the echo of Michel Hugon's words: 'It was very difficult for kids against adults. For example the story of Goldstein and Alain. Alain was just twenty, Goldstein was twenty-six or twenty-seven.'

Obeying the dictates of natural justice the witnesses must be allowed to speak for themselves. First, Prost, here reminiscing about it during a television programme on Antenne Deux called *Dossiers de l'Ecran*, transmitted in February 1991, a full sixteen years later.

'I have never accepted injustice. Yes, truly. I had won three heats, I had won the first final and the second final would be decisive and I was leading the race. Two laps before the end a Belgian team-mate of Goldstein made me go off. I spun, I set off again just in front of Goldstein and at the last corner he pushed me from behind and won. I finished second. What annoyed me most was that after the finish he held out his hand for me to shake and understandably I was very, very angry. I put my kart behind his and I pushed him in a straight line to the far end of the track, we arrived there and it ended in a fight. I knew that for me it wasn't perhaps a very good thing to do, but . . . '

The second witness is Goldstein, who watched the television programme with mounting anger these sixteen years later. 'I can't remember where I first met him, although it was a kart meeting. He was just like a lot of people who compete in karting – you can never tell at the start. He was normal. I spoke to him a bit but I didn't hang around with him. In the World Championships he never did anything and I never bothered about people who came fourteenth or fifteenth. I was concerned with the first three.

'He says I made him come a cropper, that I drove against him to make him lose the race. He said on television that I blocked him, did silly things and I don't understand that. I think he's wrong, I think his memory has let him down. I didn't "organize" anything [with a team-mate]. We did the race, he was in the lead, the last corner I passed him and I jostled him a bit while I was overtaking him – but another driver wasn't involved. After we crossed the line there was the argument. The mystery to me is that we did the race and when I overtook I jostled, that's possible but normal in karting.'

They got out of their karts and Alain Prost walked smartly over to François Goldstein and punched him. As Prost himself estimates, Goldstein was at least a foot taller.

'There was no other person involved', Goldstein says. 'I don't even know if it was French temperament. I understood it was because I'd jostled him but I don't understand when he says it was someone else who'd made him lose. You understand what I am saying? It was just me. I attacked Prost at the last corner, I overtook him, I jostled him a bit, that's all. He hit me once. I was out! I was on the ground . . . '

The third witness is Michel Hugon. 'I wasn't driving but I was there that day. Alain led the race – it was twenty laps – and he was in the lead for eighteen and on the nineteenth Goldstein bumped into him, Goldstein took the lead because of that and won. At the end Alain was unnerved, which is normal. He told Goldstein off, gave him a punch in the helmet. In those days the helmets were not integral [covering the whole face; the cranium and ears were protected, the face exposed]. He hit him on the – how do you call it? – the jugular. No, it wasn't hard, it was a *sympa* way of doing it . . . in spite of everything.' *Sympa* is a very difficult word to translate because it involves a precise nuance which has no direct equivalent in English and the nearest you can get in this context is that it's what a normal guy would have done. 'The incident assumed a big importance with Goldstein's entourage because Alain hadn't been competing long and he had just dethroned someone who'd been karting for ten years and who won all the time.'

Goldstein, continuing his evidence: 'These are old stories. Now he's a good driver but I don't understand why he still recounts stories like this in 1991. [The sense of injustice still hadn't gone away, of course, and never would.] I can't say why he didn't do great things in karting. I think that maybe he wasn't interested enough at the start. If you ask him about the Alazar Trophy I'd been interested to know, too. After the television programme went out I telephoned him in Switzerland but I got a secretary. I left a message that I wanted to speak to him but I haven't heard any news. Tell him I'd like him to telephone me . . . '

The sentence was duly pronounced. Prost's licence was suspended although in a sharp little footnote to all this he says that they gave it back when they needed him for the European and World Championships.

The first round of the Europeans was at Wohlen and *Karting Magazine* produced this paragraph. 'As Fullerton gave a brief feint to one side then went to pass on the other it was all too much for Goldstein and he deliberately locked his kart into the Briton so they both ground to a halt. It looked like an action replay of the recent meeting in France when Goldstein had his face punched by the angry French champion Prost.

'Fullerton's arms came up so the crowd licked its lips [anticipating another knock out?]. The Belgian has few friends. Getting his priorities right Fullerton turned to his kart, push-started it and got away to reach the chequered flag in front of Goldstein and as soon as they reached the weighing-in enclosure they were kept apart by team-mates.'

In a faded and miniscule photograph you can see the incident, Goldstein and Fullerton on the grass scrabbling to get their machines back, stooping to do it, not yet facing each other as they rose.

The Worlds in the autumn were at the Paul Ricard circuit. The course had been fashioned along the Grand Prix pit-lane straight by laying bales covered by clear plastic in a zig-zag of artificial chicanes the way kart people like courses to be. Fullerton remembers that. 'In one of the heats I wasn't going particularly well. He was about twenty yards behind me. I hit a straw bale on one of the corners, did a 360-degree spin and kept going. I was doing about 80 miles an hour at the time and it was a fairly remarkable thing to happen. I just touched the plastic and it kind of grabbed the front wheel and flung me round incredibly quickly. Alain saw this happening and out of "sympathy" – thinking there was going to be a really big accident

– he drove off and had a big one himself! Just as I was emerging from the spin I saw Alain trying to get out of the way and he went into the bales, too. I don't remember speaking to him afterwards but I probably wouldn't have done . . . '

To the strongest, the race.

Karting Magazine said cryptically: 'In the time trials controversial French driver Prost, who is continually in trouble for one reason or another, had a spectacular engine seize yet somehow was attributed with a reasonable time.' (This was at Paul Ricard remember, Prost was French remember.) And of the sixth heat before the final: 'Gabbiani was so upset by his misfortunes that he refused to compete in the second chance final and went home and this event started with Prost and Buzzi of Sweden in the lead and somehow they managed to have a shunt in the chicane, so leaving Dismore and Heuvel to fight out the first two places.' It happens. In the final Prost was again nowhere at all.

'He was a member of the full French karting team and when he did the World Championships in 1975 we were together', Hugon says. 'I helped him because it was Paul Ricard [a circuit Hugon knew intimately] and in a sense we were behind the steering wheel together. I watched him closely because I knew he already had cars in his head. He drove the kart but karting was finished for him. He'd already let it go a little bit. The same day as the final he did some stages at Simon's . . . '

I have deliberately broken chronological order about this year of 1975. The natural flow of a career is easier to digest that way. We shall encounter Simon in just a moment, Simon who had his being in the other world altogether although within clear sight of these plastic-coated bales and these zig-zags along the straight, Simon and his friend Antoine who explained how dangerous it was.

But for now we are still in the karts, Goldstein is winning the World Championship again and a very young, very handsome Italian called Elio De Angelis is behind him – this same De Angelis who would charm all women and impress all men, who played the piano with a most delicate touch, who was born rich and never flaunted it, who is mourned and will remain mourned; this same Elio De Angelis who would meet his death on another day in another time when a Formula One car somersaulted and smashed, somersaulted and smashed at precisely the end of this straight. By then the innocent, artificial zig-zags had long been removed into memory.

A complete phase in the life of Alain Prost was closing. It had been many things but only an exploration, a beginning, a way of finding the way you would go and played out among large groups of strangers. 'I have a vague memory – but I'm not absolutely sure – I raced against him in karts. That would have been in 1974 but it's like that with karting, so many people around.' The speaker: Stefan Johansson, who would become a team-mate and Prost disciple, no less. But so many people around? I wonder how many of those forgotten racers who came in their humble vans never did know the names of their opponents or care about them and would today delight in proclaiming, 'I raced Prost . . . I was wheel to wheel with him . . . I overtook him', but actually have no recollection of it at all?

Terry Fullerton does remember. 'If you're talking about world-class people in karting, Goldstein was the best in the world for quite a while. Comparing Alain Prost to others is a bit unfair. He was considered in the top ten and he was capable of that so he was a good karter. He just never became the top one or two, never became the guy who was capable of winning the World Championship. He never put himself in that position.

'In those days you had to be your own motivating person to make sure you had the right equipment. You couldn't just go to a good team and get it all sorted out, you had to say: well, there are good motors in Italy, I'll drive down there and buy them or hire them. You had to organize all your own stuff. I know people who have been fairly average drivers who get into Formula Ford 1600 or Formula Renault or whatever and win the Championship because they're with the best team. In karting you couldn't do that, it's more level and people have access to good equipment much more readily. You can get hold of better stuff if you're motivated. In cars you can be as motivated as you like but if you're not in the right place at the right time you don't win.'

There was a right time, as there always is, and the right time was now, as it so often is. The right place was just over there.

Bernard Droulon phrases this in the dry language of an administrator: 'When you won the French Karting Championship as Alain did you automatically got a grant and it continues in the same way to this day. The champion gets a grant for motor racing. That's his prize.'

The prize would prove priceless.

3
THE OTHER SIDE OF THE TRACK

Knowing him these fifteen years later . . . I can believe what he says but it's taken me a long time to believe it.

SIMON DE LAUTOUR

You took the second turn as you circled the scenic pond whose rim was decorated by chunks of bleached yellow-white Provençal rock. There was a sudden temptation to take the first turn, a sharp right under a bridge which led to the broad, level paddock where the transporters went. Five or six years hence you might be able to take that first turn, the control marshals recognizing you and waving you through, enter that paddock where a piece of beautiful cargo would await your pleasure; but certainly not yet and most likely never.

They were mainly young men who circled the pond towards the second turn, an opening among trees, and their emotions were inevitably heightened. They were about to discover that they might be good; not as good as they thought; no good at all; or, worse, they might make complete fools of themselves.

As they moved slowly down the pathway towards the functional two-storey building they were taking a risk with the person they imagined themselves to be. They might come back along this same pathway diminished; they might spend a lifetime wondering about this one chance missed; they might, just might, come back fêted, famous for a moment and with the promise of more of that to come, but the odds were always long and always constant: 200-1 against.

The building is nicely placed: butting on to it from the left the big door of a workshop is opened like a mouth and deft hands tinker with single-seater racing cars. Over to the right past the little gravel car-park there is a high wire-mesh fence with a segment of track running along beyond it and beyond that, looming in an almost tantalizing way, the sequence of pit entrances set into the sweep of the main concourse; and this is a high, modern edifice, all hospitality suites and administration offices and rooms for the Press, booths for the television commentators behind a vista of wide windows which seem to shimmer endlessly in the sunlight. It was to the rear of this concourse that the transporters lumbered bearing the cars for the French Grand Prix. It was to the front of it that the kart track had been arranged.

The Paul Ricard circuit, lost somewhere in arid mountains to the north of Toulon, was custom-built. It had not evolved from humble beginnings as many tracks do. This spring day in 1975 there were no cars going round but that did not diminish the presence of the circuit. Twice the Grand Prix had been held here, won in 1971 by Jackie Stewart on his way to the World Championship and in 1973 by the gifted, subsequently lamented Swede, Ronnie Peterson. Clearly Paul Ricard would become the regular home of the race. That was why so much money had been lavished upon it.

Such notions had little or no meaning to a young man who had just pulled up beside the two-storey building over on the other side of the track. He might have glanced across through the wire mesh and reflected how close he was to it and yet how far away; but much better to simply enter the two-storey building.

You push the door open, you tell the pretty and friendly receptionist who you are and your eyes wander to a montage spread across the wall which flanks a narrow staircase. This montage, set out with more thought to impact than artistry, is of racing drivers in and out of their cars, of drivers brandishing the trophies they have won, of titles gathered, of signed photographs offered as dedications and it all produces one of two gut reactions inside the young man: I'll be up there, too; or, My God, what am I doing here?

The Winfield Driving School is small enough to be intimate, homely, nearly home-spun but large enough to suggest that it is a very serious going concern. A nice balance. The montage is a curriculum vitae for it. Many have passed this way and the merest handful have made it up there on to the wall, have been able to take the first turn at the pond.

He had come from Trier in the Rhineland where he was doing his National Service and that was evident by merely glancing at him. He had a severe version of the military haircut, not quite pudding-basin but cropped tight and close so that it followed the contours of the head; it bestowed, as it was intended to do, anonymity. You could hardly miss the nose, accentuated by the haircut, but there was nothing the Army could do about that.

He had come in an elderly Renault 16, which is what twenty year olds tend to have whether they intend to be a racing driver or not. His fingernails were heavily, obsessively bitten back up past the quick. That was misleading. He wasn't the nervous type at all, quite the contrary, but the nail-biting would stay with him down the years.

Soon enough he would ascend the narrow staircase and find seated behind a solid desk an agreeable and rather suave Englishman with the gloriously un-English name of Simon de Lautour and a Frenchman with a name somewhat closer to home, Antoine Rafaelli, which is Corsican or to be precise north Corsican. De Lautour and Rafaelli might sound like a tremendous double-act and in a sense they were. At Winfield they were instructors.

'He seemed to know exactly what he wanted but he was – how can I put it? – discreet. I have no recollection of him being noisy or difficult or moody or anything like that. I do remember him doing the right things and (up to a crucial point) never doing more than he had to', de Lautour will say, drifting gently among his memories.

'He was discreet', Rafaelli will say and it is interesting that unprompted they both employ the same word although my interviews were conducted separately; and since we are talking about the French word *discret*, it is perhaps better translated as reserved. 'He was modest, timid, very timid, he spoke very little and he spoke softly.' To illustrate this Rafaelli lowers his voice to almost a whisper.

Winfield had begun its life at the Magny-Cours circuit in central France and opened this branch in 1971. De Lautour arrived in 1973. Logically Prost ought to have gone to Magny-Cours for lessons because it was much, much closer to Saint Chamond but Paul Ricard – still comparatively new, of course – was being widely lauded and, although there would be a measure of irony in this, Prost judged that there was a better chance of fine weather. You certainly could not guarantee that at Magny-Cours.

First he had to actually get to the South of France. 'I was in the Army in Germany, I was competing in the European and World Karting Championships and I did the driving school, too. I was able to enter a very few kart races but I still needed permission to do them. I was secretary to the captain or the colonel, I can't remember exactly now, but above all I was the one who handled the passes.' At a later, strategic moment this would become invaluable and without having to stretch the imagination it is easy to foresee how.

'He came here with what the French call a *bourse*, like a grant, from the Karting Association which is affiliated to the Fédération Français de l'Automobile. We get that every year, boys coming from the karting world. Anyway he came here with his grant – which paid for most of the course – and he just did the course normally like any other pupil. The whole thing is about eight or nine days going from day one to selections for the final so it's quite spread out', de Lautour says in his interesting accent which has now become very faintly tinged at the edges by French.

A final? Oh, yes. A couple of hundred hopefuls moved through the course during the year and the best were graded until twenty remained. They were pitched into semi-finals and graded until five remained. They were pitched into the final itself and the winner became the holder of the title *Pilote Elf*. Of itself it did not assure the winner a future but it did guarantee a real tilt at a future, namely a car with which to contest the Formula Renault Championship the following season; and this could lead to Formula Renault Europe leading to Formula Three leading to European Formula Three leading to the first turn round the pond on Grand Prix day . . .

If you became *Pilote Elf* you had perfect entrée to a career. The rest was strictly up to you. Nor was this the only final. There was another running concurrently at Magny-Cours and the winner there would also hold the title *Pilote Elf*.

But it is still spring, he has parked the old Renault 16, pushed the door, said who he is but he still had to get into a racing car for the first time in his life.

'The early part of the course is not that selective. Guys don't really have a chance to stand out be they Alain Prost or anybody else when they go through what we call our first three stages – unless they do something really stupid or something fantastic', de Lautour says. 'The first stage is a straight-line exercise where they learn how to brake, downshift, heel-and-toe and so on, the second stage they learn the right line for each of the turns, different ways of tackling hairpins or fast corners or whatever, the third stage is the early lapping sessions at relatively low rpms, like 4,000 to 5,000.'

This is explained to the drivers in a room just past the reception. It is a classroom and carries the precise ambience of one. Blackboards have been arranged all along a wall. Chalk diagrams lead the pupil through the most elementary aspects of propulsion, arrows to chart the path through a corner, marks to indicate braking points. Many, many who have never experienced a single-seater imagine that you slip in, get your foot on the accelerator and vanish over the horizon. You don't. You are better advised to slip quietly into the classroom while a de Lautour or a Rafaelli explains the confines and constrictions of making the single-seater work; not that Prost accepted those confines and constrictions in their entirety and nor did a fellow pupil, Michel Hugon, also come from karting. Between them they would make the instructors very angry and in doing so launch what Hugon still believes was a 'little revolution'.

'Simon and I alternated in giving lessons and as it happened I took the first one that time. I made a little speech, which I always did, in the classroom saying that this might lead to a place on podiums, to glory and to joy but, "it is dangerous and never forget that". I said that only once at the beginning of the course but I said it in case they thought it was easy.

'There were five or six pupils at that lesson and when we came out I asked: "Who wants to go first?" The significance was that they'd just heard my speech on the danger. Over the years I'd learned to watch the feet not the faces when I asked the question. Some would instinctively move a foot forward revealing that they were keen to get into the car, some would instinctively move a foot back revealing that they were a little bit apprehensive and of course I noted that. You don't push people who are apprehensive.

'Prost did not move.

'I saw then that he had absolute control over himself and his reflexes.' Antoine Rafaelli is still nursing that memory.

There was an instant attraction to the Winfield School. It used a 2.2 kilometre segment of the Grand Prix circuit itself, the 'bottom half' as de Lautour puts it, so that whatever their fate pupils could always say they had been on at least part of the real thing. 'This was one of our selling points.' The karting had not been the same, it had of course been specifically and artificially created for the World Championship and consequently had no flavour of the proper circuit.

The segment began at the Verrerie curve, a fast and fearsome sweeper and favoured vantage point for spectators wishing to know quite how big a driver's balls were in the matter of stark courage, went through the chicane, the twisty Sainte-Baume corner, up half the extraordinary Mistral Straight – in its full form so long that it permitted and demanded the ultimate speed of which a Grand Prix car was capable – to a link road which fed the young men back to Verrerie and another lap. In effect it was a mini-circuit fashioned out of the full-blown 5.801 kilometres which Paul Ricard then measured and it was a good testing ground, just the right mixture – straight, chicane, corner, straight, corner on to the link road, corner off the link road.

Once he was in the car – Winfield were using Martinis – Prost made a swift and profound discovery. 'It was at this moment that I understood there is no such thing as an ideal rule (meaning the lessons on the blackboard are your guide, not your master). There is a way of driving which is a feeling. You feel how to drive.'

Rafaelli was to receive a practical example of this, another memory he still nurses. 'Talking about the Mistral Straight, I told him which was the best line and said it could save fractions of a second' – always precious commodities. 'He replied that he'd already tried various permutations on the track himself to find the best line. Himself . . . '

Prost drifts gently into memory now. 'I'd come from karting where you have an engine which doesn't have a gearbox, I'd obviously driven road cars – I'd had my licence for a year or two – and I just changed gear like any normal driver. I didn't even know what double-declutching was and in a single-seater you are practically obliged to do that.'

There is no mystery about the technique and in olden days you had to do it on road-going vehicles, too. You depress the clutch and move the gearstick to neutral, release the clutch, stoke the accelerator with your right foot until the revs have risen, depress the clutch, move the gearstick into the gear you want, release the clutch again.

'In the first couple of stages Alain wasn't super quick', Hugon says, a naughty smile dancing over his swarthy face. 'We took the karting styles with us and that didn't please the instructors, not Simon, not Antoine. They weren't hot for it because traffic cones had been placed to show you where the turning point for a corner was but instead of going as far as the cones Alain and I cut directly across into the corner. It really didn't please them but when they looked at the times we were a second quicker than everybody else – which was hard for them to believe.

'We used the link section and you needed second gear there. What he and I did was go from fifth straight to second instead of following the fifth-fourth-third-second sequence double-declutching each time. We didn't double-declutch at all! Alain didn't say anything about this but me, I had some problems because I talked a bit too much and again the instructors weren't happy. But I said: "That's OK, I'm going quicker, we're paying to go quickly." We kept on doing it our way but at the same time giving the impression that we were going down through all the gears by tapping the accelerator so what they heard was vroom – pause – vroom (fifth to fourth), vroom – pause – vroom (fourth to third), vroom – pause – vroom (third to second).

'Simon started to get annoyed because two gearboxes had been broken on the school's cars. "It's not normal for this to happen", he said. "You don't know how to double-declutch, one by one you get into this Renault van and I'll give you a double-declutch test." That was quite something, that was. It happened that Richard Dallest, a driver who was in Formula Two at the time and champion of Europe, was present and Simon said to him, "How do you double-declutch?" and Dallest replied, "I never do. With the Hewland gearbox you don't need to!" So perhaps that day we had a little revolution in the system of driving.'

The story gets better and better. 'In fact Dallest was in Formula Renault Europe', de Lautour says. 'Dallest said, "I can do that", he got into the van, an old workshorse Renault Estafette, but he didn't know how to do it either! He and they thought it was blipping the throttle as you changed down, not the distinct movements it really is.'

'They called me a damned nuisance,' Prost will say of the karting style, 'because firstly there is a line, a trajectory which is called and always called ideal. I did not take this. I braked very late and entered the corner very early. Understandably the instructors were not pleased but the stopwatch showed that I was consistently quick.'

All this is revealing enough about Prost, who was already doing things his own way and justifying them to himself at the same time; and now there was a much more revealing moment.

'We were getting into the course', de Lautour says. 'We don't drive in the wet because this is a very dry part of the world and the circuit just doesn't lend itself to rain that much either – meaning it gets very slippery – but in those days we did.'

'It was', Rafaelli says, 'the third initial stage. During the first two he hadn't done anything to draw our attention to him. They were limited to 5,000 revs and they were going slowly round. It rained and some of the drivers lost it; found themselves back to front. I was standing at the link from the Mistral – which is the fastest part of the course – and Alain was braking just where he'd done in the dry. Because he hadn't done anything to draw our attention, as I've said, I wasn't expecting him to do anything like that. Simon was monitoring things at the other side of the track, he came back in the Renault van and we both said together: "Did you see that?" It's very, very difficult in the wet.'

This particular memory remains so vivid that they are both still talking about it a decade and a half later. They are still talking about something else, too, something which it has taken de Lautour the decade and a half to believe. The key is the phrase of Hugon, 'In the first couple of stages Alain wasn't super quick.'

When autumn came the 200 were twenty, divided into groups for the semi-finals, ten to go on a Saturday, ten to go on the Sunday and the five fastest for the final which would be held later, in October. This was becoming serious now.

Jeanette Chabot worked in the Elf Press Office in Paris and journeyed to Ricard. 'I didn't know the pupils at the school, there were so many of them. Because the title was so important there would be a lot of journalists at the final and to help them with background for their stories I compiled dossiers on the twenty semi-finalists.' These young men would almost certainly be completely unknown to the journalists except perhaps Prost and Hugon and even they would only be names from karting where single-seater racing journalists rarely strayed.

'I asked them all what they would do if they didn't win. Some envisaged finding a small budget to get into Formula Renault if they could, some said unfortunately they would have to abandon their careers because they hadn't got any money – which could have been the case with Alain. He wasn't relatively well off. I think that, tenacious as he is, if he hadn't won he might not have been able to go on. When I asked him the question he said that he didn't contemplate losing. I was a little nervous about putting that in his dossier, I really didn't know whether to put it in or not but he'd said it so finally I decided to put it in.'

'The semi-finals were over the two days', Rafaelli says, 'and Prost was in the batch on the first day. The drivers had to be there at eight o'clock in the morning and when eight o'clock came he hadn't arrived. Simon said: "I don't care, we'll start without him and when he does come he can drive tomorrow." Eventually he did come and said he'd had a puncture. I was doing the time for the semi-finals to be sure they were accurate. Prost stood beside me, watching everything.

'The next morning he was on time and Simon said to him: "OK, you go first", and he selected car number 4, which was the best. Later Prost told me how he'd invented the story of the puncture so that he could see all the other cars and know which was the best. He was already calculating these things in his mind.'

De Lautour, making a general judgement, says: 'Prost knew what he was doing and subsequently we've found out how typical that is of him, isn't it? Suss it out, work it out, that's where his real strength lies – in his analytical ability.' *Yes.*

We must dwell briefly on this matter of the cars. 'In those days', de Lautour says, 'we had seven or eight but we only ran five in the selections. That way we got a very minor difference between the fastest and slowest and anyway one instructor drove all the cars until we had a time for each so that we knew the difference between them and we bore that in mind but to the driver the choice of the car is important psychologically.'

'In the semi-finals I was fastest and he did the third fastest time. A driver called Geynand [who is he and where is he now?] did the second fastest time,' Hugon says. Let us be absolutely clear: whatever he had revealed in the wet, overall he had done just enough in the dry to ensure his continued progress and precisely nothing more.

Once the five finalists had emerged de Lautour telephoned Madame Chabot with the names and she picked them out from the twenty she had interviewed, to make proper Press Kits.

Prost, back in Trier, had a much more pressing problem. He had used up all his passes, was not entitled to any more. It was he who, as a secretary, had jurisdiction over this matter. He did what a determined young man would inevitably do. He issued one to himself. He remains convinced that his superiors knew what was afoot because later one of them got in touch with him. 'Colonel Le Saint, if my memory serves me, wrote kind letters afterwards when my career in motor racing had begun but at the time I was near the end of military service and I was at Paul Ricard with a forged pass.'

De Lautour did not know this, of course. 'Obviously we thought he had permission.'

The final was no one-lap shoot-out, tough if you blow it. Winfield were far, far too wise for that. 'We had a training session which was all done for free,' de Lautour says, 'because naturally we wanted to put on a good show at the final. We had the five finalists and they trained for three days before the actual final. Towards the end of this we had a mock final. There is a certain amount of importance in that because the guy who has the best performance can choose his starting position on the day of the final – a lot of guys don't want to go first, a lot of guys don't want to go last. Choosing your position is therefore often important psychologically and all the time during the training Alain had only just managed to keep fractionally ahead of the other drivers. He wasn't dominating the situation at all.

'The mock and the final worked like this: each driver did a ten-lap session. Normally the first four laps were untimed (so the driver could get himself good and ready), the next five were timed, then an untimed slowing-down lap. Actually it's usually all very quick, over in a jiffy.

'The driver's placing is calculated by the total he has from the five timed laps although sometimes the best lap is taken into consideration – and it is very interesting because in the mock Alain did a fantastic one lap, suddenly he was a lot quicker than everybody else. It was an extremely demoralizing thing to do: the mock's over, the driving's finished for the day, it's the last time for the drivers before the final in two days.'

The others could do nothing but wonder.

'Funny. All the other finalists suddenly realized that he was very good, they were almost defeated before the final. Again in subsequent years we all discovered that this was a typical Alain Prost gesture.'

It was and, as it happens, is the very first recorded example of the genre.

Saturday, 25 October 1975.

'He was very calm, very timid and of course he was in the Army. He came alone, no parents, his parents never came, no, no.' Michel Hugon remembers that.

'He wasn't very happy on the day of the final in case he didn't win.' Madame Chabot remembers that, remembers the conversation they had.

Prost: 'I said I didn't contemplate losing but I didn't want you to put it in my dossier.'

Chabot: 'But you did say it.'

Prost: 'Yes, yes, but I just said it, it wasn't necessary for you to write it down.'

The final was a gathering. Elf had flown Ken Tyrrell, a seigneur of Formula One who ran his own team and was a large, benevolent man, from England to present the trophy, which he did annually. Jean-Marie Balestre, President of the Fédération Internationale du Sport Automobile (FISA) – the world governing body – was there. Didier Pironi was there and fittingly too, since he had been *Pilote Elf* in 1972, had moved on to the ladder in Formula Renault in 1973 and won that, spreading a whole career in front of himself. Patrick Tambay was there, a driver close to Formula One. Many journalists were there, among them Jabby Crombac puffing placidly on his pipe and keeping knowing eyes open. You never can tell what you might see, you know, a future World Champion but it wouldn't be 200-1 against that, it would be a million. Never mind.

'Prost had forgotten his driving overalls,' Rafaelli says, 'so I lent him an old pair which had been given to me by one of my first pupils, Tambay. They were Alpine blue.'

Suitably attired (or unsuitably? *Mon Dieu*, Alpine blue), Prost now applied his psychology again and it was more of the devastating kind. During the warm-up he broke the lap record for the school circuit.

'As I've said, for the final he had the choice of where he wanted to start because he'd won the mock. Most don't want to go early, first or second, most in fact choose third or fourth because they're not sure they've got the nerve to hang on until everyone's been. Knowing Alain as we do now, it comes as no surprise that he chose to go fifth.' Simon de Lautour remembers that and he adds: 'I should point out that Alain's year was a bloody good one and we had a very high standard of finalists.' Mr Lautour is not giving this final a particular cachet in order to make Prost seem better than he was by saying he beat a tremendous field; Mr Lautour, whose knowing eye has seen them come and go in their thousands, is merely reporting the facts.

The final was utterly, absolutely straightforward. 'I was', Tyrrell says, 'chairman of the judging panel as I had been for several years.

My Formula One team was sponsored by Elf at the time.' Tyrrell, nicknamed Uncle Ken by the French, knew talent when his knowing eyes alighted upon it. Pironi would make his Formula One début in a Tyrrell in 1978, to select just one – but in this context extremely relevant – example. 'Prost was outstanding, as I suppose you'd expect with the benefit of what we know now, but on that day it was a walk-over, he looked absolutely a natural.'

Hugon speaks from deep within himself when he says: 'I did a lap of 59.10, Alain did 58.8 and the other three finalists were all over 60 seconds.'

And there it was, all over in a jiffy.

'Hugon finished second and I think he thought for a long time that we wanted Alain to win and we were pushing Alain to win but when you get to know the school and the way the actual final works you understand that we can't lean towards anyone. The final is run by Fédération time-keepers and the Elf panel and we don't form part of that for obvious reasons. We might be slightly biased.' This did not prevent Hugon from being 'very, very disappointed', de Lautour says, 'although he's mellowed over the years and we have a good working relationship now.'

58.8? Oh yes, and the best total time of the five laps, too.

'We find in the finals', de Lautour says, 'that some guys perform better than expected, others pack up, but Prost . . .'

. . . was Prost.

'Afterwards he was happy about the dossier. He had a great confidence in himself and you could see even then that he had great possibilities, he was very advanced in what he did and he was also a very reflective person.' Madame Chabot remembers that.

Whatever bitterness Hugon felt then he speaks now from the heart – you can tell by the timbre of his voice – when he says: 'Alain didn't win because he'd got money behind him, he won because he was a good driver. He was gifted. There are a lot of drivers who know how to turn a steering wheel but are not necessarily very intelligent. He was. That was evident by his reactions, evident in what he was doing on the track. He felt immediately by reflex what he must do to make the car go quicker than other people. In karts it had been the same.'

Tambay himself was a member of the jury. 'Alain was exceptional, so exceptional that there was no doubt in our minds. We didn't have to think about it twice. I guess his kart experience had done all the schooling for him but he had the physical frame to make a great racing driver. It's a lot easier for a small compact body to fit in a kart and a car.'

The presentation was captured by a photograph which today is up there but on the other wall from the montage on the staircase to de Lautour's office; there in splendid isolation, there with a place of its own. Tyrrell, looking a pristine prisoner of a jacket, collar and tie, is smiling benignly as he shakes hands with this small, elfin Frenchman who clutches the tall, fluted trophy in the other hand, the position of his grip on it revealing those bitten fingernails. Balestre looms in the immediate background, judicious, wearing his solemn face as if the honour of France had been redeemed, or the future of France possibly secured. Pironi's boyish face peers from the semi-circle of well-wishers, Crombac peeks from somewhere under the tartan flatcap he habitually wore (and still wears) and yes, is puffing placidly on that pipe and looking rather cheerful.

'Of course,' Tyrrell says, 'Prost didn't speak any English so I really didn't talk to him. [Tyrrell does not speak French.] I just gave him the trophy and then got to the airport to get home as quickly as I could.' The honour of England had been discharged by Uncle Ken, Formula One people are busy people and what was there to hang around for, anyway? He followed the Formula One creed which, one fine day, the little chap shaking his hand would learn too. If in doubt, go for the nearest airport.

'My wife came to the final with me', Hugon says, 'and the three of us went out afterwards because we were staying in the same hotel. I still remember where we went: the casino at Bandol. But we couldn't get in because we didn't have enough money, we didn't have a sou to spare on gambling, we only had enough for a meal. And anyway you needed to be wearing a suit to be admitted.'

It is an amusing vision, the three of them being turned away from the casino, just kids really and there was as much chance of young racing drivers wearing suits as of old racing drivers wearing suits, which is to say about the same chance as them wearing suits of armour. 'Finally we ate at a restaurant and then we went back to the hotel.'

Of this final Crombac would write in the magazine *Sport Auto*: 'Five candidates confronted each other at the wheels of Martini-Renault MK 11s of which the power was held at around 120 horsepower to permit the jury to select the best driver. In these conditions Alain Prost imposed himself without meeting opposition. Prost is only 20 but he has already been French and European karting champion, a discipline which certainly allowed him to harden himself in the best way. He comes from Saint Chamond and his profession is furniture salesman in the family firm. Michel Hugon, also a karter, put in the second best performance in a flowing style but there was no doubt: Prost was the best.'

We have not yet explored the matter of credulity and the exploration must be conducted in some detail because it presages so much, opens up so much. 'Later,' de Lautour says, 'he claimed that he hid his hand slightly in the early stages and I always thought: can a young driver at pupil level have the confidence and the ability to do that; to take the chance he wouldn't make the final? I always doubted that but he stuck to it, he maintains he played his hand very cool and just went for it on the day of the final.

'The whole point about a kid in a racing car is to make it go as fast as he can, that's what he dreams about, that's right. Knowing Prost now these fifteen years later, knowing what he's done I can believe what he says but it's taken me a long time to believe it . . . that a young man, knowing full well how important it was, would not squeeze to the maximum because he felt he didn't need to.'

That was the point. Young, intoxicated men translating their dreams on to a racing car have the most vivid sensation of being alive, let's make the thing accelerate till it shrieks, it's what it was made to do. Alain Prost, aged twenty and who ought at this moment to be in a barracks at Trier continuing his national service, was on no carousel of mindless acceleration. He was calculating every moment and every movement. He saw with almost mathematical precision how to reach the future.

De Lautour is talking quickly now, urgently, repeating himself in a swell and a tumble of words because the thing still seems to be so extraordinary. 'I really have found that hard to believe although obviously he did because why would he keep saying it when he's won forty odd Grands Prix? I've never known *anyone* else hold back like that, no . . .'

This is what Prost says: 'I was also the "damned nuisance" because I didn't want to show that I was fast until the semi-finals and there of course I was obliged to go fast [but not too fast, only third remember], something which surprised a person or two.' Yes, and still does.

He dwells still on that Renault van which he had been made to sit in 'just to learn how to brake, to change down using the double-declutch, and I never did get it. I won the title in spite of everything and afterwards I learnt how to double-declutch, that I guarantee you.'

Staying his hand? You see that for what it is and it is threefold. First you have the actual confidence to do it, second you guard the element of surprise so they will never know what hit them, especially since they didn't see it coming. You didn't let them. Third you have already learnt the most significant lesson in all motor racing: you extract the maximum without stretching your machine or yourself a single fraction beyond what you need to. Not one in a thousand can. Ask Simon de Lautour. He has seen the thousands try.

In that sense Private Prost awaiting his discharge from the Army was the same Prost who would grow into the famed and fabled Professor Prost who made Grand Prix circuits his lecture rooms, not least this same Paul Ricard to which he would come many, many times, taking the first turn round the scenic pond, being waved through by the marshals.

'He was modest, timid, very timid', Rafaelli says and now I'll complete the quotation because I only used the first part of it earlier. 'He's not really like that, he's a lion. He must have made the decision to be timid to make it easier to integrate himself, to absorb all the information. He is called The Calculator and I believe he had that when he arrived at the school. He was out of the ordinary as a driver and what you had to do was bring that out.'

Or simply allow Prost to bring it out of himself.

But on Sunday, 26 October 1975, as he prepared to book out of the hotel at Bandol and make the long drive back to Trier in the Renault 16, he had not yet been in a race. He had done Winfield's time trials no problem, he was much better than the seasoned and experienced instructors knew and he had something else to build on: tenacity, that lovely word wielded by Madame Chabot. Self-doubt was a stranger to him, as it frequently is to people with natural gifts. On the way back to the Rhineland he had something to savour endlessly, courtesy of Renault and Elf.

He had his own racing car.

4

WHO IS THAT LITTLE GUY?

> Elf wanted a French World Champion, which there hadn't been before . . . Well, [Elf] paid us in petrol coupons but so what? They got their World Champion.
>
> FRED OPERT

On 4 April 1976 Alain Prost spent twenty-six minutes and 44.2 seconds covering fifteen laps of the Bugatti circuit at Le Mans to win his first race in a car. He was driving a Martini-Renault and it was the opening round of the Formula Renault Championship, a domestic French competition and the lowest rung on the ladder. He found it easy. Potentially great drivers often do.

The Martini was not, as you might imagine, sponsored by the Italian company famous for making a certain drink. Martini was a car manufacturer who had the same name. As *Pilote Elf* the oil giant presented him with a Martini MK17 and sufficient money for the 1976 season. He formed a compact and intimate little team of his own at Magny-Cours with a mechanic, Jean-Pierre Nicolas, and a man to look after the engines, Bernard Mangé.

Two weeks after Le Mans he won the second round at Nogaro. Simon de Lautour happened to be there because the Winfield School was in its infancy and not swallowing all his time. He watched Prost with understandable interest and 'he had the whole situation completely in hand, completely under control. I thought – this is fantastic.'

He won the third round, at Magny-Cours, where by a great stroke of irony the other *Pilote Elf* decided to retire. There were two *Pilote Elfs* (or Elves), one emerging from Ricard, one from this same Magny-Cours. Frederic Watelet had taken the title by a mere 43.1000 of a second at the latter and like Prost was given his own car to compete in Formula Renault. 'For me,' he says, 'Prost was completely unknown. I already had a business – I was running a pub in Paris – and that's why I left. I couldn't afford the time. I was twenty-eight and everybody told me I was too old. I'd only gone to the Winfield School at Magny-Cours because somebody told me about it. I wish they had before.

'Prost was small, he was *sympa*, quiet and immediately he was quick, immediately. He understood the science of racing as if he had been doing it for a long time. I supposed that that came from his years in karting although I think it's a gift you're born with. I kept finishing second behind him which certainly wasn't bad but there was no way I could beat him. That didn't exactly encourage me and, as I say, I was twenty-eight and I had the pub to run. What I have kept is happy memories of it.'

The irony is not just that Watelet won at Magny-Cours and retired there but that if only someone had told him earlier his life might have been radically altered. Slender threads always. Suppose André Prost had not taken Alain to The Siesta but had gone to the beach instead? Maybe this book would have been the Frederic Watelet story . . .

On the strength of the first three wins Prost was invited to run a Lola in a Formula Renault Europe race, the next rung of the ladder, at Dijon. He took pole from Didier Pironi, something only the naturally gifted could conceivably do because he hadn't had time to be anything but naturally gifted.

Jeanette Chabot watched at Dijon enchanted and astonished. 'He dominated everyone even though this was a higher formula than the one he was in. He was gifted, he was a boy who drove very properly – just as he does now – he was a boy with his head firmly on his shoulders. Some people have mad years when they are young. He didn't. He was very aware of what was happening and every time he didn't win it was the car, not him.' Dijon is an excellent example. Prost made an awful start – the car wasn't right and he estimates he got away ninth – but actually caught Pironi, leading, before a fuel leak stopped him.

Back in Formula Renault he won and won, reeled them off no trouble.

'I was doing Formula Three', Hughes de Chaunac will say, 'and I watched the drivers in Formula Renault who were up-and-coming so

I observed him during his first year and I was immediately surprised by how seriously he was taking it. He didn't have a big team, it was him and his mechanic. I spoke to him a bit. I'd been in motor sport a long time, I had experience and then we started to speak often at the circuits.' De Chaunac, a debonair-looking man famous in France for running racing teams – he is instantly approachable, instantly likeable – would continue to watch and talk to Prost until the point where it was quite clear they needed each other and a partnership would be born.

Prost won all the first twelve races, a statistic so stark and memorable that people still recall it effortlessly. He did not finish the final race, at Imola, and the circumstances remain unexplained. Some talk darkly of sabotage, itself unproven and unprovable although it does move de Lautour to muse, 'Why not?' and it does provoke Prost to say: 'There is always a reason for my anger in public. I was in the lead and I stopped at the end of the fourth lap. There was oil in the distributor and we saw it was sabotage. I believe sabotage practically never happens in Formula One or in the rest of motor racing but that day it did. That's why I was furious. And when you win twelve races and you can do the grand slam, which I believe had never been done at that level, it's a pity.'

Quite who would want to commit sabotage is unclear since, all else aside, he had won the twelve races and was building a reputation so powerfully that whatever came to pass in number thirteen had no relevance except to take the grand slam from him. Was it spite, envy, revenge for some previous incident which impelled some unseen hand to tinker and nobble? Or was it a genuine case of a malfunction? Probably even Interpol couldn't find that out now. The evidence is all gone.

In 1977 he moved naturally up to Formula Renault Europe, again with a Martini-Renault. 'I was an admirer of his approach to driving and at the same time our relations were friendly and also close – that is to say, there were some moments when we spoke seriously about motor sport and some moments when we spoke of other things – we laughed together', de Chaunac says, and, echoing the description we have heard before: 'He was someone who was timid, reserved, who didn't express himself very much but who had a quality when you got to know him and that quality was a will to succeed. You could feel that very strongly and the motivation that he had was enormous.

'For me it was fascinating. Something was happening which was quite different to other drivers I'd known, because before I'd run Jacques Laffite, Patrick Tambay, René Arnoux and Didier Pironi [cumulatively these people were French racing], but Alain Prost was of a later generation. Laffite and I were the same age so he was a chum who drove and I was a chum who occupied himself with the team.

'Pironi, Tambay and Arnoux? We were very near in terms of age but when Prost came there was an age gap and this was the first time I began to discover a different driver-manager relationship. I wasn't exactly like a father to him, more like a big brother. From that point on we had the means of establishing a relationship which we could develop together.'

This is obvious but do not be misled by that. De Chaunac quite naturally began with drivers of his own era who hardly required him to inform them how to make racing cars go around circuits properly; now here was one needing his wisdom.

That summer of '77 Prost, still running his own little team, found himself competing against Bousquet from karts. 'It was exactly the same in cars. The rivalry between us, which we had never been able to communicate about frankly, remained. When you are adversaries it creates a wall and you can't go out together in the evenings and have a laugh. The nature of racing is that you don't want to. So it was adversary–adversary but at no moment during the races could you say he did anything incorrect. I have no reproach to make about that. He never sought to win by any unfair means', Bousquet says.

'You could see his gifts when he discovered a new circuit. I remember Hockenheim [the third race of the season]. I'd raced there before but he hadn't, so the place was completely unknown to him and we didn't have a free practice session so he could learn it. Come the official qualifying and within forty-five minutes he had done a very good time and he often did that sort of thing. He learnt fast and that's a sign, isn't it?' Prost was fifth in the race.

At the next, Magny-Cours: 'We crashed. It started right at the beginning of the race. We had the same time, I believe, anyway we were on the front row. He made a better start and got away but I overtook him on the first lap. The surface of the track was a little humid and I slithered on it during the second lap and he re-took me. Immediately I tried to take him back but at the instant I thought

I had, he squeezed me, I bumped into him and had to abandon the race. I think I gave him a mouthful after the race [chuckle] in order to tell him that what he had done wasn't correct. He said nothing. But . . . no, it was me who made the mistake . . . no, really, I have no reproaches to make . . .'

A round of the Championship accompanied the French Grand Prix at Dijon in July, only the second time Prost had attended one. He had seen others on television but, 'I wasn't a fervent supporter. I was a little bit more interested in bikes.' He did follow rallies and any races in and around Lyons. He would get on his moped on a Sunday morning and cover as much as 150 kilometres to see them. The Formula One passion came stealthily, little by little.

Prost became Formula Renault Europe champion with six wins out of sixteen rounds and Bousquet, whom he beat, remains phlegmatic as well as enigmatic about that. 'He won the Championship, I didn't win the Championship. It's difficult to explain. It is true that we drove together, true that we did the Championship together, it is true that I can find 10,000 reasons why I didn't win but that is without interest now. It is the results which count.'

Prost's reputation had grown so quickly that he was asked to drive a couple of races in Formula Two in a Kauhsen-Renault and Formula Two was within touching distance of Formula One itself, the last staging-post. At Nogaro he was tenth, a place behind a certain Keke Rosberg. The Finn, a bristling and sometimes prickly man, would take away no memory of Prost at all. He was just an anonymous kid at another race, and that race was won by Arnoux, Patrese second, Cheever third, an Italian Bruno Giacomelli fourth, Pironi fifth. Prost had begun to bridge the generation gap by competing against these guys, each one of whom would be in Formula One either later this season or the next.

At Estoril in October he qualified third slowest out of twenty starters in the Kauhsen-Renault and on lap 19 lost a wheel – for a moment it looked like a bad crash. It was not. *Autosport*: 'Alongside Elj Elgh on the grid was Michel Leclere in the lead Kauhsen-Renault. The other two were handled by Alain Prost and local Formula Ford driver Mario da Silva. The latter didn't look remotely like qualifying but Prost got in.' This was not of course Ayrton Senna da Silva, nor (I presume) even a relative of his.

(*Far right*) Champion of the world for the very first time – in karts, and after a stormy championship.

(*Right*) The cartoon that Tony Jardine drew. Little Napper (alias Napoleon), one of a sequence which upset John Watson so much.

The crucial race to get Prost into Formula One. Here he wins the famous Formula Three race at Monaco in 1979 – with the whole Grand Prix world watching.

The French connection (*l-r*) Didier Pironi, Prost and Jacques Laffite find common cause in humour.

Prost and Gerard Larrousse, dignified Renault man-in-charge and subsequently owner of his own team.

Dijon 1981, the day he learned that not only could he win but that he could do it again. And again.

The hard year of 1982. Team-mate Arnoux goes straight on at Tarzan. You could hear the impact for miles around, and this is the result.

(*Above*) The new team, and with a good, affable, talented man. Prost, Eddie Cheever, 1983.

(*Right*) Prost foreground, Jean Sage – most sympathetic of men (his name literally means wise) – in the background.

(*Above*) Monaco might have been made for Prost : close to the armco, but never too close. It worked. He won there four years in five.

(*Right*) A muscular gesture at Hockenheim to show the futility of fuel consumption. Prost makes a big show of pushing the McLaren towards the line. An eloquent gesture.

(*Right*) The emotions of victory, Paul Ricard, 1983.

The face of 1982.

De Chaunac knew that the time was now. 'We very quickly reached an accord that we must do something together. We began to prepare a season in Formula Three quickly. He had a very, very keen willingness to learn, he had this motivation not only to win but to examine everything you needed in order to win and to understand what he had examined: he didn't content himself with setting the car up the best way it could be done and then just driving it, he was looking around to know what you had to do to have the best team, the best mechanics, the best atmosphere in a team, the best car, the best technique for driving it and that's extremely rare. He went to the bottom of things. When he was driving for me he was looking to understand the human mechanisms of motor sport. Human is a very important word.'

Prost joined de Chaunac, driving a Martini-Renault MK21B, in 1978. 'It was the first year of the Renault engine in Formula Three and that was a risk, a delicate matter because since the engine was completely new it was clear the car couldn't win races straight away. That's normal for a team but for a young driver it is very difficult. On the other hand it was an investment for him to understand that you needed patience to get results.' At Zolder he was tenth and at Monaco fourth, whereupon he received a very interesting offer from an American, Fred Opert, to do one race in Formula Two in a Chevron-Hart. Opert had been a guest at Ricard the day Prost became *Pilote Elf* ('When he won the award I was asked to go. A lot of people went').

Opert had 'seen Prost in Formula Renault and now in Formula Three, I'd seen him around the pits. I'd known that Didier Pironi was going to be a top Formula One driver, although he had had the best team in Formula Renault, I watched Prost because I knew Pironi, I knew de Chaunac and what de Chaunac had done. They thought Prost was good. Elf thought he was good.

'Pau was a very important Formula Two race, it was a glamour race and it came a week or two after Monte Carlo. We had three drivers, Keke Rosberg, Elj Elgh and Boy Hayje, a Dutchman. They had separate sponsors. The year before Laffite had finished second and it was a very good car. We kept it as a spare although in those days you didn't really have spares. It was a works March. At Monte Carlo we spoke to François Guiter of Elf about it because for Pau we were only running two cars. Hayje was going to do a race in Holland which clashed with Pau but it was more important to someone Dutch. So should we run a third car at Pau? Elf were keen but said for whatever reason that they had no money in the budget.

'It cost 12,000 dollars a race to run a car but we really wanted Prost and we had seen – what shall we call it – star quality? We finalized a deal over the telephone, 5,000 dollars if he used last year's car, the car Laffite had had. Elf said OK. One of our mechanics went to Holland and the other four or five went to Pau. Fortunately there were split practice sessions, only twenty cars at a time, so we could cope. We had a French mechanic – Prost didn't speak much English – and we assigned him to Prost.

'In qualifying he went extremely well, he was very quick, he out-qualified Rosberg. We didn't know what had happened at the factory and the new car was not the best and it's a new car that everyone watches, don't they? So Prost was fourth on the grid and Rosberg wasn't happy.'

'I'd never met Prost and no, I wasn't happy,' Rosberg says. 'We in the team came up with the conclusion that the old chassis was working better on the streets of Pau, which it never would have done on a fast circuit, but it didn't make you happy to be beaten by someone you'd never heard of, it still hurt – but it didn't leave scars for ever because we thought we knew why it happened. If he had been in the same car as us it would have taken away all the excuses.'

Brian Hart prepared the engines. 'Pau is a special track and many drivers think it's better than Monaco. I hadn't met him before and I spoke to him of course about what was happening.' These conversations were inhibited by language but are nonetheless revealing because Pau was difficult.

Hart: 'How did you get on?'

Prost: 'Fine.'

Hart: 'Any problems with the engine?'

Prost: 'No.'

Hart: 'Did it pick up after the hairpin?'

Prost: 'Yes.'

'Other drivers tend to complain a bit,' Hart concludes, 'but even at that stage Prost was able to drive around some problems. I don't know if he'd seen Pau before. If he hadn't that was even more remarkable.' He had but only once, in 1977.

	FIRST SESSION	SECOND SESSION
Brian Henton	1:14.41	1:13.64
Patrick Tambay	1:14.57	1:14.03
Bruno Giacomelli	1:14.04	1:14.50
Eddie Cheever	1:14.09	1:14.17
Alain Prost	1:15.19	1:14.14
Jacques Laffite	1:15.57	1:14.21
Derek Daly	1:14.80	1:14.23
Elj Elgh	1:15.83	1:14.44
Keke Rosberg	1:14.83	1:14.47

(Times are given in minutes and seconds, e.g. 1 minute, 14.41 seconds.)

Jeff Hutchinson, a large, amiable and knowing journalist covering the meeting, wrote that Prost was 'delighted with his Opert Chevron-Hart B40, even if it was the ex-Alan Jones/Jacques Laffite/Gregg Young/Maurizio Flammini/Arturo Merzario/Elj Elgh and Tiff Needell chassis!'

'During the warm-up lap before the race Prost got squeezed over by someone', Opert says. 'Pau was street kerbs and he put two wheels over, smashed a front wheel, well, bent it but there was still air in it. When he got the car round to the grid it had become a flat tyre. The mechanics were in the pits but these were a distance away.' The mechanics in fact were grouped around Rosberg's car. He had complained that his engine was running roughly and when he revved it bits of the engine and oil spewed from the exhaust pipe. Exit Rosberg but enter entirely by chance a neat, brisk self-made man who would sometimes wonder if people thought him boring and who would, virtually, reshape Formula One with his bare hands. At Pau he was running Cheever in a March-BMW and was now to do something, literally, with his bare hands. He was called Ron Dennis.

Opert's mechanics immediately whipped Rosberg's wheel off and 'ran like hell towards the car dragging a jack but only 30 seconds were left before the green light. Dennis and four of his mechanics lifted the car by hand so that when my people arrived with the spanners all they had to do was change the wheel. There was good camaraderie in Formula Two, you see. There was a guy who made lunch for all the teams, there was an Italian who made coffee for all the teams, people helped each other, we were all mates. If you needed to borrow a gear and someone had one that's what happened, that's the way it was. My first year in Formula One with ATS, Lotus and

Williams helped. Of course when you started to qualify tenth and twelfth on the grid they didn't . . .

'Anyway the green light came on and halfway round the first lap Prost's fly-wheel went. It had been set low and damaged when he went over the kerb although no one knew. He'd done the two days of qualifying and then couldn't complete a single lap. It was very sad to see that happen to such talent.'

'I'd read his name in Formula Three reports,' Elgh says, 'but he had the old car and nobody really expected him to do anything. In qualifying he was quicker than Keke and me and it was rather embarrassing. We got our own back because on the warming-up lap he went over the kerb, which was unfortunate. Well, now [1991] I can say he was unfortunate but obviously it was good for Keke and me because we could turn round and say, "There you go, you put boys in with the men and look what they do, they lose it before the start," but really it was a bloody great relief. At that stage in your career [Elgh is talking about himself, not Prost] you are very selfish and you say things to yourself which suit yourself.

'It was obvious he was good. You just can't do what he did at Pau if you're not. One tries to find excuses, "Ah, yes," we said, "he's probably done so much Formula Three here he knows the track, maybe he was lucky to put in one good lap in qualifying," that kind of thing, but to me – and I'm sure I said it to those nearest to me, like my wife – I thought, "Bloody hell, this kid is really good."

'The difference in technique in driving a racing car round a corner can never differ so much from a very good driver to an incredibly good driver. We're talking about tiny differences, tiny margins. The big difference is in the head, concentration, determination, being single-minded in a positive way. You won't let the smallest fault pass you by, you want to oversee it being corrected. For somebody like myself in the situation I am now in [the Le Mans sportscar race, 1991] I just shrug it off and say we've got bigger problems than that, but if you have the will to become a Prost or a Senna you have to nail every problem to the wall no matter how small and solve them. I can see all that looking back at Pau.'

'We'd given a price of 5,000 dollars but with the French it wasn't quite like that', Opert says. 'We got 2,000 dollars and later on we got petrol coupons for the other 3,000. [This is Elf paying, remember.] The race was in May and in September they slipped us these petrol coupons. I wasn't complaining. We had big

Chevy V8 trucks which were thirsty and every time they needed filling out came the coupons.

'Elf wanted a French World Champion, which there hadn't been before. It was going to be Jabouille, then it was going to be Laffite, then Arnoux, then it was going to be Prost. Well, they paid us in petrol coupons but so what? They got their World Champion.'

'He was totally unnoticeable during the weekend apart from what he did in the car', Rosberg says. 'I didn't get to know him at all. He was the same guy who came in who went out again.'

All this time Prost was learning an entirely new discipline: to be a member of a team. The cosy days of himself, a mechanic and an engine man were long gone. Nor was this easy. At Monaco he had qualified a long way down the field but finished fourth despite a smoking engine, at Nürburgring the engine went, at Dijon he was tenth, at Monza fourteenth; then, Ricard. Fasten your seat belts for Formula Three.

Autosport: 'Johansson made a demon start down into the first bend, followed by Prost, Serra, Piquet and Bardinon but it took Piquet no time to get into the lead and by the end of the lap Prost was second as Johansson dropped back to third. After two laps Piquet had a second's lead. Behind him Prost, Johansson, Serra and De Cesaris were all close together. Serra began to catch Prost. There were two groups but the fast Coulon pushed them all together from behind and by lap 13 there was a five-car chain behind Piquet. On the last lap down into the sharp corner at the far end of the circuit Serra forced Prost into a mistake: it was nothing big but it allowed Serra to get alongside. The two went through the following corner together and their slower lines allowed the charging Johansson to rush up behind them and right into Serra's gearbox. Serra went off with a puncture and bent wing. De Cesaris was delayed and so was Prost because charging through the middle of them came Coulon. Prost salvaged third place for Renault.' Piquet was (and is) actually called Souto-Maior and if legend be true he raced under Piquet so his parents would not know he was racing at all. He would become a commanding figure of the early and mid '80s and would be constantly pitted against the kid from Saint Chamond.

Prost did not finish at Magny-Cours – engine trouble – and was sixth at Donington, where he qualified seventh and, echoing Bousquet, here was a circuit he had not seen before. There were some interesting drivers who had not yet qualified after the opening session including Johansson, Frenchman Jean-Louis Schlesser and

Satoru Nakajima. (Johansson said that 'if I don't make the race I'll sell the whole expletive outfit and go and buy some golf clubs.' He did and he did not.) Prost drove steadily to sixth 'and I have a vivid memory of racing him there', Olofsson the ex-karter will say. 'Prost had had a fairly good practice time, I wasn't as quick as him but I could pass him easily in the race. I finished a place in front but that I think was the beginning of the Martini-Renault-Prost era.' The team was not yet ripe – but nearly.

Three days later Prost was at Silverstone for another round on another new track and he qualified fifth. *Autosport*: 'On lap 3 Teo Fabi outbraked his way past Prost's Martini at Copse but was unable to pull away and Prost regained his third position four laps later at Woodcote in a fine manoeuvre that left the large crowd gasping in admiration. This battle represented all that is good in Formula Three.' Prost held third place to the end.

'He was already a good driver,' Teo Fabi, another ex-karter, will say 'but the Renault engine wasn't the best. I thought however that he was lucky to be involved with Renault because it would give him the opportunity to go into Formula One.' It was a perceptive judgement and a portent, too. 'Prost's team wasn't competitive because the engine was not as good as, for instance, the Toyota', Olofsson says. 'The Toyota was so bloody good you needed it.'

'Did I know him?' Fabi muses. 'It's difficult to have close relationships with other drivers because you go to the race, concentrate on your car and after the race you go off in different directions so we never knew each other. Sometimes you can be a good friend with your team-mate if you stay together long enough, but it's very rare.' Olofsson on the same theme: 'I had no contact with him, he's always been polite if our paths happen to cross, there will be signs of recognition but that's all.' This is not criticism, just how combatants conduct themselves.

At Jarama, Madrid, he took pole, his first of the season, Derek Warwick, then an up-and-coming Brit, alongside him. At the start of the race Jan Lammers (Holland) muscled Bobby Rahal (USA) and Rahal did not budge, thank you. This confusion left Warwick in the lead, Prost hard behind him and after twelve laps Warwick had to slow – a car had broken down – and Prost nipped through. 'Prost overtook me under yellow flags', Warwick will say, 'and wasn't black-flagged. I thought: "Each to his own . . . "'

Prost quickened his pace and stayed in the lead for the remaining twenty laps. This was Renault's first Formula Three win since 1973.

A. Prost (Elf Martini-Renault/Gordini MK21B)	44:2.54
A. Olofsson (Ralt-Toyota/Novamotor RTI)	44:8.99
D. Warwick (Ralt-Toyota/Novamotor RTI)	44:9.62

'We were a little bit upset', Olofsson says. 'The Renault engine hadn't been so competitive before during the season. At Jarama there was no official checking of the engines, no checking of the compression for the air-inlet system – which was the normal way to check all the cars at that time. After the race we thought, not just the Swedish drivers but all others, that they were cheating because his engine was running so well but . . . the difference was Prost! I'm sure they didn't cheat. He was so good that people looked for other reasons to explain it. On the straights it was not such a big problem to pass the Renault engine but they'd improved the settings on the car and . . . then there was Prost!'

One race remained, Vallelunga. By now Bousquet had virtually retired and I include his reasoning because it demonstrates how some young drivers fall by the wayside while others like Prost continue with gathering impetus. After Formula Renault Europe, Bousquet had not moved into Formula Three. 'I drove under very precise conditions. I didn't want my career to descend before coming up again as it might have done, I wanted it to be vertical. I would have been able to find the finance for Formula Three but I didn't want to. If I hadn't had a job to go to (his family legal firm) my reaction would have been the same. To raise money is a different talent. It was different then, there were no special agencies doing it, sponsorship in racing was new and complicated and for me looking for money was a deviation of the spirit. I stopped driving.

'Prost was partnered by someone who I think was rich but I can't remember his name [it was Patrick Bardinon], he was injured and de Chaunac contacted me to take his place at Vallelunga. We were on the same row of the grid, mind you, Prost and I. In the race the bloke in front of me couldn't start his car, I covered ten metres, found myself blocked and that was that.' Prost didn't finish either – engine trouble.

Prost was ninth in the Championship. We shall not meet Bousquet again, so I propose to let him reflect from the vantage point of June 1991, when I interviewed him: 'I say Alain Prost hasn't changed, that he has an incontestable talent as a driver and for me he has lesser qualities in defeat. It's easy not to have a bad side to you in victory: you win, everything's lovely, everything's easy. When someone loses you see the difference in them and on those occasions Prost shows a side which is less likeable. He doesn't tolerate it. Perhaps more than defeat he can't tolerate the person who beats him. Like Senna . . .

'It's not just man against man, that's not the problem, it's a question of temperament. At the bottom of him is the idea that it is not possible for someone to beat him in a straight fight and sometimes that obscures his judgement. It's then that the complications and problems begin.'

Prost now had to make a decision. Logically he should have moved into Formula Two, the last step before Formula One itself, but Formula Two was weak at that time and neither Renault nor Elf were involved in it. Prost had to balance the deep desire within himself to move upwards, always upwards against the risk of staying in Formula Three and having, perhaps, another mediocre season. He listened to François Guiter and de Chaunac.

'He trusted my judgement to stay in Formula Three a second season. We talked about it a lot and for that second season I told him it was important to win races so that he would have the image of a winner. I said: "Before you do anything else you have first to win races." ' De Chaunac knew that ninth place in 1978 did not convey that image at all and hindsight would prove it because Prost had been headed by people going nowhere near the summit, Olofsson, Patrick Gaillard, Michael Bleekemolen, David Kennedy, Daniele Albertin . . .

The decision to stay was without question the right one. Normally race-by-race reporting is a tedious exercise, a recital of facts which are known, but in the case of Prost and the season of 1979 it is not tedious, and within it lie many moments which, when taken together, form a mosaic of a man moving towards Formula One and authentic greatness.

Vallelunga, 18 March. Michele Alboreto spun letting Prost into second place behind Piercarlo Ghinzani, Prost tracked Ghinzani but the Italian made no mistake and they crossed the line in that order, three-quarters of a second between them.

Österreichring, 16 April. Two heats, the combined time counting. In the first Prost 'cut across' the Swede, Slim Borgudd, 'forcing him into the pit lane' (*Autosport*) and ended it with a one-second deficit to Ghinzani which he more than made up in the second heat. Forcing someone into the pit lane? It wasn't quite like that. Borgudd, then thirty-two, was an extremely interesting man. He had spent two years as a merchant seaman before taking up drums and playing session music for, among others, ABBA. He had been racing for ten years. 'In 1979 Prost had big back-up from Renault, five or six engines. I was on a super-low budget, I didn't have enough money to buy tyres. I didn't have a mechanic, I did everything myself. I'd come into the pits, get out of the car, make some adjustments, go back out again but obviously I couldn't keep my lap times so members of Prost's team or other teams used to do that for me. Prost didn't know and if he had he wouldn't have been happy.

'A friend of mine used to bake Swedish bullar cakes which are like coffee cakes. I'd have like 200 of them with me at the races and they were very popular. I used to invite all the teams to come over to my little caravan for coffee and bullar and the French team liked them as well so there was a good relationship between us.' (This is a nice line in generosity as well as a way of getting your lap times done by the opposition.)

'At the Österreichring I made a very good start from behind. Prost came over to the right and I had to use the pit exit area. From the start line you have armco and then the pit exit which runs on for a little bit.' This effectively widens the track at that particular place: if someone moves over on you, you can move over on to the exit. 'I couldn't say for sure whether Prost was playing it hard or whether he knew I was actually up alongside him – but understanding how Prost is today, getting to know it through the years, I'm sure he was aware I was there because he always knew what was going on all around him. I don't think we even commented on it afterwards.'

The real point was that not only would Prost have known Borgudd was there but that the track was wider there, too. 'I raced wheel to wheel many times with Prost and he was very straightforward, very fair. In practice or qualifying or a race, in any situation – say, going into a corner – he always knew what he was doing, he could give you an inch to let you through or you could give him an inch to let him through but you didn't have to shut your eyes and cross yourself. I can't recall there were ever dodgy tactics.'

Zolder, 23 April. He led from flag to flag. 'I wasn't that competitive in England at that time, I don't think I'd been higher than sixth', Kenny Acheson, a merry Ulsterman, says. 'Anyway I went to Zolder. Prost had Elf backing, Renault, everything. There were heats in those days and we were the quickest against each other. Nobody had heard of me, a privateer in an orange car, and suddenly it was Prost and me all through the sessions and I got the feeling they weren't best pleased but it gave me a bit of a kick, I can tell you. In the warm-up lap my gear stripped so I didn't even start the race . . . '

By now a lot of influential people were watching, among them Jean Sage who was in the senior management of Renault's Formula One team. 'I hadn't met him before. The impression that he made was that he was very confident in what he was doing, very self-confident. He was trying to check everything, trying to organize everything around him.' Or, to paraphrase Hughes de Chaunac, to monitor and understand everything around him. Sage was impressed.

Magny-Cours, 1 May. On the warm-up lap two cars collided, at the start Michele Dallest was moving before the flag and that made Alboreto, on pole, swerve and Dallest struck Borgudd, went out of control and struck Alboreto. Prost, who had started on the front row of the grid, found himself with a 6-second lead by the time he reached the second corner. Goodbye. He won by 22 seconds.

Donington, 20 May. 'We had heats again and he qualified on pole, I was second quickest', Acheson says. 'We started the warm-up lap and I threw it into the barrier so I didn't race against him then, either . . . '

It was a wet race won by a New Zealander, Brett Riley, but 'with about eight laps to go Brett came up to lap John Bright and it took the leader more than a couple of laps before he found a way round. When Prost came up behind on lap 28 Bright again proved a difficult man to pass and as the Frenchman's car was proving a little difficult to drive it took Serra only a couple of laps to close up. Serra found his way past both Prost and Bright going into the last lap and while he pulled clear Prost could still not find a way by the local driver and had to be content with third place. After taking the flag he showed his disapproval by trying to drive Bright's March off the road at Redgate!' (*Autosport*).

'I had just picked up a sponsor,' Bright says, 'a bristly character called Tim Stakes and it was the first time he had been to a race. Conditions were so bad you just couldn't see. I think I'd spun earlier which was why I was a lap behind but as the track dried I began to speed up and I was lapping not far off the pace of the leaders – and that in a two-year-old March. I was not being bloody-minded, I didn't know who was behind. Prost was furious and on the slowing-down lap we banged wheels. He pushed me on to the grass but rightly so, I suppose, from his point of view.

'I got back to the little garages we were using. Prost appeared with de Chaunac and they were *both* furious. They were asking why I didn't get out of the way and de Chaunac kept pushing me on the shoulder, prodding me. "This is very important," de Chaunac said, "you're slow" – but I wasn't and nor was I usually a wanker. A big argument developed and then Stakes started to push de Chaunac backwards. Eventually it all died down.' (This story is to be continued, and with a happy ending.)

Prost had now driven five times, won three, been second once and third once. Monaco was on the supporting bill to the Grand Prix and in de Chaunac's evaluation 'obviously the most important race. Everybody was there and it was a rendezvous not to be missed. It was also very hard and truly at Monaco I was sure he would win. He was so strong in his mind, so strong in his mind it was impossible he'd lose it, impossible.' De Chaunac's repetition gives the full flavour.

The local police interviewed Prost about some prank or other, too. 'Yes', de Chaunac says smiling broadly. 'At Monaco before the race he was in trouble with the police. I remember the story but I can't remember what he'd done.' Neither can Prost but this is surely instructive: he was taking the racing very seriously but he was still a chirpy and mischievous fellow, too. Extremely normal, in fact.

'The race is always run before the Grand Prix, normally on the Saturday', Prost says. 'It's the most prestigious in Formula Three and sometimes the Formula One drivers and above all the team managers watch it because it's almost a legend that the winner will get into Formula One the year after.'

Monaco, scrutinized so closely by knowing eyes, attracted an entry of fifty-five who competed for only twenty places in the race and some useful drivers didn't make the cut: Eddie Jordan, Mike Thackwell, Acheson, Phillipe Alliot, Phillipe Streiff, Thierry Boutsen, Borgudd – 'A guy called Burger ran into my car, not the Berger you know [it was Hans-Georg Burger, a German] and *totalled* it so I had to take it back to England for repairs.'

In the first qualifying session Piercarlo Ghinzani was quickest, Prost a fraction behind but in the second Prost savaged the lap record by almost a full second and that was pole.

'The Russians have a proverb about a fish which jumps high out of the water', de Chaunac says. 'In his mind Alain had decided to jump very, very high. He had decided to win and he went very, very, very quickly.' I give you de Chaunac's repetition again. In the race there was an early multiple crash which eliminated five cars after Prost had made his start in what one contemporary account calls 'great haste'. Prost built up a lead over Oscar Pedersoli, an Italian, and was 'piling on the pressure'. He pulled the lead out to five seconds which is comfortable at Monaco and held it there to the end.

'At Monaco,' de Chaunac says, 'it was Prost who won it and not the car. He made the difference because I think that on the day we didn't have the best car, although it was a very good car. He was too strong for everybody else.'

A. Prost (Martini-Renault/Gordini MK27)	39:8.32
O. Pedersoli (March-Toyota/Novamotor 783/793)	39:13.53
C. Serra (March-Toyota/Novamotor 793)	39:20.70

'It was one of the greatest days of my driving career,' Prost says, 'because it was absolutely necessary that I won to have a chance of being in Formula One and I came to understand long after that the contacts I had in Formula One towards the end of the season came exclusively from this result in Monaco.'

Some of the watchers were sceptical about the true value of this victory, as we shall see in the next chapter. Formula One people ration their thinking very carefully and ask themselves all manner of questions which the ordinary spectator might not. Was the winner in the best chassis? Did he have the best engine? Best tyres? If he did he ought to have won, if he did not and still won that is much more interesting. Formula One people look for moments as well as victories. A chap way down the field in an awful car with a tired old engine is not the subject of derision because Formula One people know the context in which he is driving and if they see his commitment up at Casino Square, see him flinging it through, arranging it nicely at the side of the armco on the way down out of Casino, braking later than they thought he would . . . now that is interesting.

Prost's results were becoming so monumental that no sane person could doubt he was a rare talent. There was only one question: how good?

Zandvoort, 4 June. The timing computer malfunctioned during the second qualifying session, bringing chaos. It also brought another insight into Prost who, on the times the computer gave, had pole position. 'I don't want it because I did not do that time. Borgudd drove well and pole position is his.'

'I do not want pole if I have to protest to get it', Borgudd said.

Isn't it nice, nay amazing, to be able to set down these words, embodying, as they do, honour and sportsmanship; and while we are at it, Dallest locked Prost in a bedroom five floors up before the start of the race and Prost had to batter his way out. Good, honest prankmanship.

'Because I was repairing my car after Monaco,' Borgudd says, 'I missed the first session and only got there in time for the second. I nipped pole by a hundredth of a second or something from Alain and he was not very pleased. I don't think he thought I was capable of doing it and I recall his team went and checked with the timekeepers to see if I had actually done the time.' Once satisfied the team did behave honourably.

The race was over two heats and for the first the grid was constructed on the times from the first session, giving Borgudd pole. He led from the flag into Tarzan, the looping semi-circular corner at the end of the start–finish straight; on lap 2, Aris Luyendijk, a Dutchman, 'slithered' down the inside at Tarzan and relegated Prost to third. On lap 3 at Tarzan, Prost 'calmly drove up the inside and waved goodbye'. In the second heat Luyendijk made 'another electrifying start', Prost tucked in behind him and on lap 5 slipped through. On overall times he beat Mauro Baldi by 17 seconds.

(The Dutch Grand Prix was not until late August and Prost went there, as young drivers go to Grand Prix meetings, to put himself about, shake a few hands, gather a few telephone numbers and make an impression. He was dismayed that the moguls of Formula One ignored him but that is the way it is. If they want you they will be doing the telephoning, not you.)

Monza, 24 June. A wheel worked loose when he was in the lead – he and Ghinzani had disputed the lead at the chicane and collided.

Silverstone, 14 July. He qualified halfway down the grid. The track was slippery and he spent a while getting the car as he wanted it. Tambay was there (with McLaren in Formula One). 'The guy was winning everything in France. I took a journalist by the hand and said, "Come on, let's go over and see Prost the future French World Champion." I don't know why I said that. Maybe it was just kind of a joke . . .'

Prost jumped the start and was penalized a minute, accepted he could not win and stopped for a new rear tyre. 'When he came out he ran two seconds quicker than in practice although he was just running on his own back down the field', Acheson says. 'I know there were murmurings about "how come he is able to do this?" There has always been talk of "how come the Renault engine was that good?" when the year before it was pretty useless and the year after it was useless.' The answer was . . . Prost! As Acheson puts it, he was 'very, very good'.

Knutsdorp, 5 August. There was 'chaos' at the first corner with Prost 'being clobbered under braking. By the second lap however he was back up to second although hampered by a badly buckled front wheel which made the car unstable. Even so he closed on the leading Olofsson and went by on lap 17.' (*Autosport*). He won it by 3 seconds.

'In 1979 I was only doing Formula Three occasionally', Olofsson says. 'Knutsdorp was my home circuit and I was actually in the lead and then he suddenly outbraked me at the end of the straight. I was ten, fifteen metres in front and I didn't expect him to dive for the corner from that far back. He controlled me a little bit: he braked so bloody late and came on to my inside and then I realized it was too late to close the door – but that showed his judgement and his balance with a car. I remember this very clearly because you do expect the person behind to try an outbraking manoeuvre but I was watching in my mirror and I simply didn't expect it at that moment. I thought he was too far behind.

'What he's got is a total balance. His body tells him, his body gives him better information than the average good racing driver about where the limits are and how to drive quickly, not only in late braking but taking the corner at high speed, getting a good exit. It's a combination of many things, of course, but it is his car balance which seems to be so exceptional. That was evident at Knutsdorp, a difficult circuit for any foreign driver but he didn't have any big problems with that. When he is behind the steering wheel the whole package is so complete: he is aggressive but in control, he doesn't do desperate things and that's another of his strengths.'

Mantorp Park, 12 August. In the first heat – the final was over two – he was far in the lead when the engine went. He had been losing water through the radiator cap from the beginning.

Between Mantorp and the next, Jarama, FISA announced that the scheduled round due at Brands Hatch had been cancelled so that with only two races left Prost automatically became European Champion.

Jarama, 9 September. Prost took pole although a handling imbalance made him spin several times. At the flag he was leading decisively by the first corner and contented himself extending it a second a lap. He won by 22 seconds.

La Châtre, 15 September (non Championship). Pole, flag-to-flag. 'I was sure I had pole,' Borgudd says, 'but I didn't. I started second and it was very, very close. There were around five laps to go and I made an attack on him on his inside and my rear wheel came off because the axle broke. He just cruised to victory.'

By now his name had filtered into the gossip columns of the motoring magazines as a potential Formula One driver. In those more sensible times the fabled 'silly season' of who-goes-where? did not begin in earnest until September. Within a few years it would traditionally begin in August at the Austrian Grand Prix and then successively advance itself until the whole of a season became silly.

In September 1979 one rumour suggested that if Patrick Depailler left Ligier to join the Ensign team, Ligier would be out trawling for a Frenchman, Pironi or Prost. It demonstrated how much Prost's stature had grown. There may have been no truth in the rumour whatsoever but that is to miss the point. People judged him a candidate.

A season of Formula Two would have been logical but, 'Alain hesitated about doing that,' de Chaunac says, 'because there were not good solutions for him there and when it was proposed that he should test with McLaren I said, "You must and if they are successful you must do Formula One." That I think was a good choice . . . '

Since this was the silly season rumours abounded that McLaren had offered James Hunt three million dollars to make a comeback, that McLaren were talking to Clay Regazzoni, that John Watson's seat was not necessarily safe and that they might run a third car in the USA-East Grand Prix on 7 October for Elj Elgh. Teddy Mayer, who ran McLaren, denied that and said he had never had any intention of 'running a third car over there'. The significance of these words will reveal themselves soon enough.

A Formula Three race remained, *Albi, 22 September*, incorporating a round of the French domestic championship. Alliott took the lead but only held it for a hundred yards or so. Prost outbraked him into the first corner and goodbye. 'Albi was a little circuit', John Bright says, 'and it was an invitation race. The Brits went and I was in the two-year-old March, the same car I had had at Donington. Prost won and I was third so it proved I was competitive. He was cordial afterwards so the incident at Donington was not a problem. I suppose it was just French temperament.

'Prost was wearing a sponsor's anorak but he was so small it came down to his knees. I remember my girlfriend had gone to the race with me and she said: "Who is that little guy?" My memories of him are that he was very quick and, well, just the best driver that year.'

In late September, Prost flew to Montreal to watch the Canadian Grand Prix, put himself about again, shake a few more hands, gather more telephone numbers and the rumours persisted that he spent much of his time around the Ligier team. He went on to the next race at Watkins Glen and left, according to one rumour, with 'a smile on his face'.

A week later Pironi got the drive.

It scarcely mattered. These autumn days Tambay was leaving McLaren to do Can Am racing in North America which meant that McLaren had that most interesting commodity for 1980: a vacancy.

This is how Borgudd assesses the candidate. 'He was always a competitive guy, he was always unhappy if he didn't get pole. It's not pure luck that you get somewhere in motor racing. You create your surroundings. Elf were with him for a lot of years and through that he managed to get good equipment, which is essential. The combination of him, how he could set the car up and the backing gave him virtually an unbeatable year. We all come from different places. I always wanted to learn about mechanical things by doing them myself, that's my way and maybe he came from another background. Sometimes it's an advantage if a driver hasn't got knowledge about too many details. If he can just tell what the car is doing and then drive it that's fantastic but you can get too emotionally involved if you know everything which is going on mechanically and what the technical answer is. That confuses you. Maybe it was a strong point of Prost's that he didn't.'

Michael Korten, who had raced against Prost in karts and Formula Three, voices a commonly held view: 'It's not difficult to be in front if you are in a good car but the way he drove – victories, pole positions – it looked like his way was straight into Formula One.'

As an ironical postscript Fabi says: 'When drivers have the first offer to go into Formula One most of them take it and I made the same mistake. Normally it comes from a very poor team and really you destroy your reputation. Then it's very difficult to build it up again.'

Salutary words.

5

NO LAUGHING MATTER

> McLaren also took the opportunity to test a couple of other drivers. Kevin Cogan was apparently disappointing. Alain Prost on the other hand did a very impressive job.
>
> *AUTOSPORT* 15 NOVEMBER 1979

Memory is selective, memory can be misleading, memory isolates what you want it to isolate adding its own brushstrokes so that some aspects of what really happened may be softened, sharpened, others may disappear altogether. Memory is your own personal painting, not a photograph.

What really did happen at the Paul Ricard circuit in late autumn 1979 and subsequently across the season of 1980? The characters in the painting scarcely agree about anything except the most obvious aspect of all. At the age of twenty-four and from the first time he eased himself into a Formula One car Alain Prost was visibly no ordinary driver.

Even the invitation to take part in a test with McLaren remains softened by the brushstrokes. He says he went to watch the Dutch Grand Prix at Zandvoort in August 1979, was introduced to Mayer who offered him a drive at Watkins Glen in the United States Grand Prix, last race of the season, in a third car. Mayer already had Watson and Tambay as regular drivers.

Mayer, a small, neat man came from a wealthy Pennsylvanian family and had studied law but he loved racing and joined McLaren as a director in 1964. If he met Prost at Zandvoort he has forgotten and he certainly does not remember making any offer. In any case it may have been a misunderstanding, perhaps Mayer sounding Prost out in a vague way and Prost, who had had no reason to master English, assuming it was something else. Prost did go to North America to watch.

'I first saw him at Watkins Glen', Mayer says. 'He came there more or less as a guest of Marlboro having won the French Formula Three Championship and I was introduced to him. I didn't think much of it, to be honest. Paddy McNally of Marlboro said, "He's a promising young French driver", I thought "That's nice." I shook his hand and he didn't speak very much English and that was sort of that.'

Certainly when a young driver meets team managers for the first time and he is looking for the main chance, maybe any chance, he is liable to place great importance on every word they utter. The team manager finds a steady progression of young drivers coming to him and does not regard these meetings as momentous, except possibly in retrospect (if only I'd signed him then . . .).

However Prost understood it, he felt sure Mayer had offered him a drive. He refused it, a refusal which has taken its place in the mythology of Formula One. 'Yes', he says, the people at McLaren 'were surprised but it was one of my best decisions. Already they had two cars for Watson and Tambay and I had never driven a Formula One car. I told them I thought the arrangement would be bad for them and for me. Instead I asked them to let me have a test at Paul Ricard.' The idea of a chap at the portals of the Temple of Dreams reasoning it out in this way instead of grabbing with both hands is extremely instructive about Prost and extremely unusual in modern Formula One, which is why it is in the mythology.

Actually Prost was very nearly into Formula One the race before Watkins Glen, Canada, by chance. Niki Lauda took the Brabham out in the Friday untimed session, had a strange inner feeling which manifested itself in a question – what am I doing here? – brought the Brabham into the pits, got out and walked away from Grand Prix racing surely for ever . . .

Almost immediately the loudspeakers around the circuit began to echo a curious message. '*Would Richard Zunino please go to the Brabham pit as soon as possible.*' Zunino, an Argentinian, had one priceless asset that Friday morning. He was instantly available, although like Prost he had come to watch. He donned Lauda's helmet and overalls for the timed afternoon session which persuaded many in the crowd – who didn't know – that Zunino was indeed Lauda himself. Right car, right helmet.

It is one of those tantalizing little moments when history itself might have been irrevocably altered. Alain Prost was instantly available, too, and there had been evidently brief talks about putting his name out over the loudspeakers, not Zunino.

As it was he watched Alan Jones win and a week later Gilles Villeneuve win at Watkins Glen. The racing season was over.

'It was November and we were testing drivers', Mayer says. 'We'd promised Marlboro we'd give Alain a drive, which we did. We had Kevin Cogan [an American] scheduled as well. Watson came down and drove the car and did a time of whatever it was [1:6.3] and maybe spent an hour getting the car set up and then Alain got in it. On not more than his third or fourth lap – it was the first thing I noticed – he was doing his initial hardish lap and at the hairpin on the short straight he fishtailed. The next lap he didn't do that, he'd sorted that out, tidied it up and after about another four or five laps he'd done the same time as John or maybe even a bit quicker. By then I was convinced. Anybody who can do that that quickly is obviously a hell of a talent and I basically went round to the boot of my car and got out a contract.'

Tyler Alexander, a senior member of the McLaren team, was at Ricard too. 'Teddy's comment was that before Prost got back to the pits he had the contract and pen out so he was going to sign him up before he even got out of the car. That was when he'd done the first half dozen laps or whatever. On about the sixth lap Teddy ran back to his briefcase, got out the contract and waited for him to come back to the pits. Teddy didn't come over to me and say, "Prost looks good". I don't think he needed to. I mean you're all standing there and you're watching what's going on. To think any other way would have been silly.'

'The first time I actually met him', Watson – an Ulsterman known as Wattie – says, 'was that day at Paul Ricard when there was the test for two drivers as potential partners for me. [Tambay was almost certainly leaving.] Prost was the choice principally of Marlboro and Cogan was Teddy Mayer's choice. Prost was better known in Europe because he'd won everything he'd entered in the junior formulae and was obviously talented. He'd won in Formula Three in Monaco and although it is very much less so today at that period it was certainly considered an important part of your repertoire.

He came along to the test, a little, short French guy, quite quiet, obviously strong in self-confidence.'

So Watson drove, Prost drove. Now enter Cogan, who Mayer describes as 'a bit fresh-faced, typically American who hadn't travelled much and he wandered into the garage and stood looking at things and Prost, who could barely speak any English at all – he knew what Cogan was there for, obviously – sidled up to him and in very broken English said, "Well, the car is very nice to drive but you must be careful. It's a bit tail-happy." The next day Kevin spun five or six times in twenty-five laps. I was terrified. I mean, it was quite a decent car and I didn't want it written off and he looked very ragged and I really believe Alain was preying on his mind. I'm sure of it, convinced of it.'

Prost psychs Cogan? Alexander says, 'That's very true, that's Prost's way and it still is. I was there and Cogan didn't stand a chance, Prost had him stuffed before he ever got into the car. I know the scenario, I know Prost talked to him, Prost said the car's very twitchy and difficult to drive etc. Prost was working on the guy mentally before he ever got in the car. What else can you say? You can feel sorry for Cogan, sure, but if Cogan was the match for Prost he wouldn't have let it bother him, he'd have told Prost to clear off, got in the car and done a better job.'

Cogan remains baffled and not a little bitter about all this. 'I was twenty-two, I'd just finished a season in Formula Atlantic and I wanted to do something else. I was offered a contract by Shadows to drive right after the test I'd done with them.' That had been at Silverstone earlier in November and *Autosport* said, 'In the course of only twenty-nine chilly laps Cogan got down to one minute 18.5 seconds and Shadow were well pleased with him, particularly bearing in mind that this was his first drive in an F1 car and his first visit to Silverstone.'

'Shadow didn't want me to leave the office until I'd signed but I stalled them. At the time Bernie Ecclestone of Brabham said he'd like to run me [there was the Lauda vacancy to fill]. He'd watched me at Silverstone. He was very straight with me. He was negotiating with Hector Rebaque and he said if Rebaque came up with the money he'd take him. Bernie told me to hang on, he contacted a couple of teams who had vacancies and one was McLaren. Looking back I wish I'd signed with Shadow.

'I got to Ricard a full day ahead of when McLaren had asked me to come. A couple of people were upset I was there early. I thought

I was showing enthusiasm. They acted like they didn't want me. I'd got there early because I wanted to watch John Watson in the car and hear him talking about it. I didn't realize Prost would be driving. When I got there they showed outward displeasure. I was really shocked, it was really weird. A career for a twenty-two year old, especially an American in Europe, is a very delicate thing.

'Alain never spoke to me, definitely not. I didn't say anything to him except, "Hello, how do you do?" I didn't know who he was. He was quite shy, he wasn't comfortable speaking English.

'I spun once or twice but they had already made up their minds. Alain got two days, maybe three days. I didn't fit very well into the car and nobody seemed to care about modifying it. I thought that was very strange because before I even drove the car I realized I wasn't going anywhere. Imagine Prost getting out of the car and me a foot taller getting in. My feet kept hitting the steering well, I couldn't use the pedals properly, I even cut the tips of my shoes off but I needed about four more inches of room with the pedals.

'I did a few laps, I asked to drive John's car because he is nearer my height. John went into the truck to find an old pair of his shoes for me because they were smaller. I was trying anything I could. The first day Prost was in the one minute 11 seconds, then he got down into the one minute 10 seconds. I did a low one minute 12 seconds in a car I didn't fit in. I did some twenty laps, the car needed the modifications but they said, "That's all we wanted to see, thanks."

'I told Teddy I didn't think it fair and right that Prost had had the two days. I was basically slapped in the face for doing nothing wrong. In my opinion they had already made up their minds. I knew the deal with Prost had been done, it was so obvious it was pathetic. Nobody was doing a good job of acting to hide it. It didn't help me at all Teddy Mayer going round saying I wasn't ready. He said that to justify his decision. I'd heard Prost had Elf money and maybe that helped.'

Whatever the circumstances we might spare a little sympathy for Mayer who had without being able to fully anticipate it just seen a superb talent in Prost unfold before his very eyes and then had the potential embarrassment of having asked Cogan all the way to Ricard, and here Cogan was.

'Prost drove, then Cogan drove and the difference between the two you could tell before they even left the pit lane, and certainly once they were on their laps', Watson says. 'You can tell by the affinity a driver has with the controls in a racing car, the way he opens the throttle, selects gear, the way he looks in the car, his demeanour in a car – and Prost had all the demeanour of being a great driver before he ever became a Grand Prix driver. At Ricard he had the ability to cope under the pressure of having a test with what was then ostensibly a top team and driving a car which wasn't a bad car but which certainly wasn't the best car.

'I don't think Prost was worried about Cogan, he had such belief in himself that he wasn't concerned about Cogan. As soon as you saw one driver and then the other it was very evident to me – and I hope I understand racing cars and driving them – that Alain had this ability to do it well: change gear not fluff gear changes, he knew where the car's strengths and weaknesses lay, he had good feedback when he came into the pits. He was able to recall and convey what his impression of the car was. It didn't take anybody with a Mensa IQ to see he was something special.'

'I'd come to Marseilles from England', Cogan says, as a sort of touching little postscript. 'I'd a hire car and I basically took off in it.' One Formula One 'career' had ended just as another was beginning.

'I read', Cogan continues, 'a long interview by Prost some years later and he said he had gone faster than Watson. That's just not true. He was not quicker than John.' This does not seem a particularly heinous thing for Prost to claim and would certainly be a forgivable distortion of memory. He was after all a young man who had been out for the first time and made a profound impression on people who knew their business. The problem is . . . Prost is right.

McLaren had taken two cars to Ricard, the M29 which they had been using during the latter part of the 1979 season and a revised version. Watson did about thirty laps in the former with a best time of just under one minute 9 seconds, moved to the latter and brought the time down to one minute 6.3 seconds. Prost went out in the M29 and did one minute 8.4 seconds so the direct comparison is to Watson's time in this same car, one minute 9 seconds.

'Tambay was unhappy,' Prost has said, 'and did not come to the tests so there were two M29 cars, one for Watson, one for Cogan and me. The tests were to last three days. I was chosen to drive the first day and a half; on the first day I managed one minute 9.4 seconds and on the second one minute 8.4 seconds. For that car, the 1979 spare, I think it was a good time. I was very uncomfortable in it, banging my legs, and poor Cogan was a foot taller, the engine was tired and the tyres worn out. Teddy was judging our driving and judging the adjustments we made rather than our times. I had a spin [the fishtail?], but I made the right adjustments and made the car go quicker and quicker. Cogan had several spins, he tried too hard. Teddy did not beat about the bush, he stopped Cogan testing after 200 kilometres.'

Prost has also said, making a more general survey of what it had been like: 'The easiest thing to understand is the power. You have to drive according to the power, just as in Formula Three you have to drive taking into account the lack of power. It is the same problem but diametrically opposed.' It is also authentic Prost reasoning.

That was November. Tambay had not yet said definitely he would *not* be staying with McLaren in 1980, then 'ten days after the test Teddy phoned to say it was 99 per cent certain I would drive for them and invited me to the factory. On my arrival it was really heartening to see they had built a car for me. The atmosphere was good from the start. In spite of the difficulties I had expressing myself in English everyone listened to me closely. They took me seriously. It gave me confidence and somehow everything became easier. I told myself, "They take me seriously", over and over again. I could not believe it.' The deal was done at the beginning of December, one year plus a further one-year option for McLaren.

The opening race of 1980 and thus the opening race of Prost's Grand Prix career would be in Argentina on 13 January just six weeks away.

'I started at McLaren at the end of 1979 as assistant team manager', Tony Jardine – now firmly in the embrace of Press Relations and known as Teach – will say. 'I'd been head-hunted from Brabham where I'd been an administrator for all the spares and so on and I filled in as team manager when Herbie Blash broke his jaw. I knew a lot of the guys at McLaren, in fact I'd shared a house with a few of them. I arrived after the initial testing at Ricard and everybody was talking about this guy Prost but nobody really knew much about him other than he had been competitive at Monaco in Formula Three.

'That wasn't given much credence and the reason was because when British and other non-French teams went to Monaco – well, there were only three makes of tyres and if you weren't on the Michelins like the French you didn't have any chance. So the general feeling was it had been just a French victory and no one knew how good he was until he got into a Formula One car. When the people came back from the test at Ricard, Teddy

Mayer particularly said, "This guy's quick", Tyler Alexander said the guy was consistently quick and they were all making hand gestures when they said it which meant let's sign him. I think Marlboro were very keen on him, too.

'Don't forget we are now talking about a time when McLaren were going down. We were in the post-James Hunt era, Wattie had taken over as number one, 1979 had been a disaster with designer Gordon Coppuck's first wing car. It flattered to deceive in the first few races but it went totally the wrong way. He made the M29 halfway through 1979 and the car continued through the first half of 1980.

'Before the first race I'd only met Prost briefly at the factory. We were at St David's Road, a trading estate just near Heathrow Airport. My office was in the apex of the roof. You could touch the planes' wheels as they came in to land. I reckon if you'd have got on to the roof you'd have seen skid marks. If you happened to be on the telephone when Concorde took off you had to say, "Hold on a minute", until it had gone . . .'

This background is not irrelevant. McLaren has become the touchstone of how a modern team should be run, their factory at Woking looks like NASA ought to inhabit it and the building adjacent where Gordon Murray (ex Brabham) designs the much-vaunted production road car is called McLaren Towers. I am not joking. The contrast in locations underscores the team's situation then.

'My first impression', Jardine says, 'was his incredible conk! He had little piercing eyes and my immediate thought was of his small stature, like a jockey. We weren't sure how he'd go until we went off to Argentina.'

Between Ricard and Argentina, Prost drove another test and when Jardine first met him had come to the factory for the traditional and necessary seat fitting. In that testing Prost covered 1,300 kilometres and proved to be quicker than Watson so that 'arriving in Argentina I felt I was John's equal. How did John react? He was puzzling. It was difficult for me to know what he was thinking.'

Watson, ruminating, says: 'It probably wasn't stated in black and white but I was the senior driver, let's say, and he was the junior driver; but Alain is one of those very special people who you see maybe once or twice in a decade who are instantly good, like Senna after him. He wasn't someone who took a period of acclimatization.

'It was at a period in the life of McLaren before it became McLaren International, before the Ron Dennis–John Barnard partnership [which we will meet in due course], it was the ghost of what became, at the end of 1980, the new McLaren team. It had gone through a difficult period in 1979, especially the M28 which was a total disaster. Technically the team were not as contemporary in their thinking as Brabham, Ligier, Williams.' That is extremely relevant.

In the first session for the grid at Buenos Aires Prost was eighth, again very impressive, Watson only fifteenth. 'I remember after that session', Mayer says, 'the Renault people slid up to me and said, "See, we knew he was good", and I have always suspected we were just being used as a "farm team" for Renault. They wanted to give him some experience at our expense and that had been the plan all along. Maybe that's just being paranoid but they were certainly interested in him and for one thing he was French . . . '

The track was uneven and with the temperature merciless it began to melt. Prost, sixth row of the grid, made the only sensible decision. He would drive to stay out of trouble and see what happened. A lot happened. Of twenty-four starters only nine were running at the end and of those only seven were classified. Prost was sixth, a lap behind the winner, Alan Jones. 'I gained more satisfaction', Prost would say, 'from achieving my aim – to finish – than I did from a lucky sixth. Of course I was happy to have a point but I was not proud of it.' Authentic Prost again, and amazing Prost again, too. No driver had finished in the points on his début for seven years (Georges Follmer, South Africa, 1973) and none would again for nine years (Johnny Herbert, Brazil, Jean Alesi, Ricard, both 1989).

'Prost just kept persevering and persevering', Jardine says. 'He'd already blown Wattie off, he came through sixth, a championship point – fantastic. He did it with ease, you could see it never looked to be a major effort, the car looked like it was on rails. Everybody had problems with massive understeer and the heat and the biggest key to it all is that he got out of the car fresh. Others like Pironi were covered in sweat.'

At Interlagos, Brazil, two weeks later he qualified on the seventh row, Watson on the last, drove to stay out of trouble again and finished fifth. 'Even then', Mayer says, 'he understood that you have to finish races . . . '

'Argentina and Brazil?' Alexander ruminates about that. 'He was a rookie but so what? The kid was good. I think to be honest he was the same sort of chap then as he is now [chuckle] in that [long pause] he was just using us to go on to better things, and when the opportunity came to go on to better things he did. He was very nice really, a genuine guy, he was interested in doing a good job in the car. He seemed a team player. At the time he finished fifth we were scoring some points. We'd been through kind of a bad patch the year before, we were making progress and years later I read he made some comment about we were all goddamned idiots because we were as happy as hell he'd finished fifth when you're supposed to be winning races.

'I kind of think that was a pretty [expletive] comment really because we were trying to claw our way back from the bad patch, points are points and they're hard to get, very hard to get. We were pleased at his progress and I find he considered we were just a bunch of wankers for being pleased we finished in the points instead of concentrating on winning. Well, we were concentrating on winning. Sure, OK maybe the technology or the people involved or the car wasn't good enough to win races. OK, well hell, that's life in the big city.'

Mayer adds perfectly to this. 'What sort of a chap was he? It's very hard to know because his English – at the start, anyway – was pretty bad. He learned quite quickly to make himself understood even though maybe it wasn't totally English, it might have been pidgin a bit but he was very ambitious, yes he was. We had some problems with the car and to be honest the design team we had at the time wasn't the best in the world and he took it very hard. He was really very upset by this.'

Nor was he alone in being upset; John Watson, too, and for a quite different reason.

'Alain had brought the car home fifth in Brazil', Jardine says, 'and it was only a midfield runner, it was sort of a makeshift car. McLaren were renowned for their camaraderie, British, Kiwis, Australians, Americans and what we had was this incredible humour. It was a tradition. When for example Bruno Giacomelli drove in 1977 and 1978 he became Jack O'Malley, etc., etc.

'In Brazil there was a big chalk board in the garage. I'd come originally from being a teacher in Kuwait. I was also a cartoonist on the *Kuwait Times* although I used to sign them Hamish because I didn't want anybody to know I was moonlighting. Paddy McNally was then Marlboro's PR man, he knew about my cartoons and he said, "Come on, put it to good use." The circuit at Interlagos was very, very bumpy and everyone was complaining. It was a crude old circuit. At the corner after the pits you'd wait to see if a driver would go through it flat out at 170, 180 miles an hour. The driver went in and hoped his body would stay with him as he went through.

'You'd listen to the engine note and know if a driver was flat. Within four laps Alain was, whereas Wattie would be complaining about the bumps. We'd had problems with the crown wheel and pinion so I did a picture of a McLaren crossing a bumpy surface with a triangular road traffic sign warning of bumps and the car taking off on one of them. Wattie was into tennis in a big way at the time and the caption to the cartoon had Wattie saying, "I'll show you how to play tennis, that's easy as well" – having been crunched by Prost in his first two races. Prost found it a bit unkind to Wattie but everyone else loved it, the whole team did (except Watson).

'A groupie was chasing Wattie round the globe and every place we went to there were red roses. He was embarrassed. If he got to them he'd try and burn them but we generally managed to be first and put them across the car. Prost used to help us . . . '

Watson began to sense something else. 'He was instantly fast and instantly gave good feedback. He hadn't any experience of Formula One cars or ground effect cars, he was just very good. The consequence was that the team more or less started to focus on him from the technical standpoint and less on me. It was a particularly difficult period. I'm not saying that the information I was giving was accurate or inaccurate. I conveyed what I felt. Prost did the same but maybe the team felt that what Prost was saying was better. Anyway, the emphasis very quickly focused on Prost and I got left behind.

'Undoubtedly some of that was my fault, some of it was the team's fault. The team didn't get the best out of me and certainly I didn't get the best out of the team. They looked to Alain to be the cure to the car's problems rather than the problems being with the car itself.

'Fundamentally the team had not recognized the importance of certain aspects of ground effects in detailing the underbody, the importance of the aerodynamic side of racing cars. In hindsight these things were even more important than mechanical considerations. This was certainly within the knowledge of Williams, Brabham and Ligier, and it outweighed the traditional way of making a car handle, which was springs, roll bars, wings front and rear. Now you had underbodies that brought the car down and the team did not fully understand how that worked, how you could control it and what you needed to do. In reality it was something a driver could not do either because the information was orientated round a wind tunnel, you had to get it right in the wind tunnel.

'What the driver can do is say, "At this particular corner the car is doing this, at that particular corner the car is doing that", and I know Alain is very good, no, he's outstanding at it. During 1980 McLaren went to Robin Herd amongst other people – he was at March – and Herd assisted in various elements in the underbody's shape and the car did improve.

'At the same time Alain's stature was growing. As part of his character Alain is very, very singularly minded and ambitious. Quite right, too, or what are you about in motor racing? That is a strength, it's not a weakness, but his situation in the team was that he was getting the new stuff, the better stuff, first and I would get it second, which was really the team saying, "Well, we've got Watson, we'll have to put up with him, our future's with Prost, he's the man we want."'

Already, then, tensions are opening up, positions are changing, stresses are beginning to hurt. A Formula One team is a fragile gathering of economics, egos and equipment and when they function well they are so potent they take your breath away; when they do not it is immensely difficult even to re-establish harmony, itself a very fragile commodity among the jostle of egos; and behind all this there lurked another stress. Marlboro, who were paying the cash and whose name had become synonymous with McLaren, were not happy about 1979: seventh in the Constructors' table with 15 points (Ferrari top with 113), Watson ninth in the Drivers' table and he had earnt all of those 15 points, Tambay none.

'Yes, we were under pressure, absolutely', Mayer says. 'We'd been under pressure from them for some time because we hadn't been doing particularly well but that's motor racing. The sponsor wants action. What some sponsors don't understand is that you very seldom can take something that isn't right and make it right overnight. It's putting in place a series of things that long term will solve the problem and if you think you're going to take an unsuccessful team and turn it into a winning team – well, I don't care who you hire, you get John Barnard and Frank Williams and Ken Tyrrell and everybody else and put them in there and it won't happen. It might take two or three years. Does it put more pressure on the manager? That's not an unusual situation . . . '

This pressure could have devolved on Prost, now clearly the hope, the salvation and the lifeline to make Marlboro happy to keep the cash coming to keep the team in the manner to which they had been accustomed.

'Then', Jardine says in his chirpy way, 'off we went to South Africa . . .'

Yet another stress emerged and it did devolve down on to Prost. It was a very alarming stress. Doubt. Not about himself – about the car. In the free practice on the Wednesday 'something went wrong with the front suspension accelerating up the hill to Leeukop', the right-hand loop as you turned towards the long straight. Prost's left leg was gashed.

This crash meant that, as *Autosport* reported, on the Thursday 'he was forced to use the old original M29 for the first day's qualifying. Prost was running well but his practice came to an abrupt halt when the rear suspension broke going into the fast esses. The car launched itself off the kerb and into the barrier on the other side of the track, the wheel snapping round and twisting Prost's wrist as the car landed. It was repaired for the second day's qualifying but unfortunately for Prost the accident had broken a small bone in his left wrist and he was unable to race. "It ached after the accident but by 8 p.m. in the evening my wrist had swollen up and I could not do a thing with it", said Prost, who was back at the track to watch Friday's proceedings.' The writer of these words, Jeff Hutchinson, can scarcely have realized their significance; to him it was something he had seen many times before and would see many times after, a crash, nothing more. The significance however would grow and grow, and that is why I have dwelt on the minutiae.

'The net effect after Argentina and Brazil was that when we went to South Africa we all expected Prost to finish the race', Jardine says. 'In qualifying he went straight on into the bank and I had to take him to hospital. We had to check his leg: he was limping and hobbling. They kept him in overnight. That's when he started worrying about the car.' (At this point during the interview Jardine searches for the report in the *Autocourse* annual, finds it and a photograph of Prost. 'There, left leg in plaster, wrist in plaster.')

Prost began to ask himself questions about the safety of the car although being so fresh into it he wondered how much validity there was to doing that.

He remembers that Watson himself helped and advised and consoled. 'Yes,' Watson says, 'I did help Alain and whether it's a strength or weakness in me, on a working level with Alain in 1980 we got on very, very well, as good as I've done with any team-mate. I like him very much and the problem was not with Alain – because he was only doing what I would have done – but with the management of the team.

'In South Africa he had a shunt, he went off in practice, he hurt his wrist, it got more and more painful and Marie-Claude Beaumont, who was the PR lady at Renault, said, "Look, John, his wrist is really painful, please help him, can you take him to hospital?" Nobody in the team had done anything. Their view was: put a bandage on it, he'll be OK. I took him to hospital and to me he was like a little brother and it turned out he had broken or fractured the scaphoid, which is a very difficult bone inside your wrist. It's a real mess if you break it, it takes a long time to heal. I was there when he was told he'd broken his scaphoid, so he's got an affinity to me.'

You may well ask yourself how, even allowing for memory's distortions, both Jardine and Watson were able to take Prost to hospital and the explanation would seem to be as simple as that fastest lap at Ricard during the testing: namely not quite what it seems. He went to hospital twice, after the free practice on Wednesday (gashed leg, chauffeur Jardine) and after the qualifying on Thursday (wrist, chauffeur Watson).

Mayer remains convinced that 'the crash in South Africa was definitely his fault. He hurt a bone in his thumb. That was definitely driver error, yes, and I think Alain would say that. Basically you have your thumbs in the steering wheel and the kick-back just got him. The car was hardly damaged.'

Apart from the hospital visit there was another sense of affinity with Watson which Prost would remember. He did not of course know most of the circuits at all. 'I did deliberately sit down with him and say, "Now look, this is Kyalami", and I had no problem whatsoever in doing that,' Watson says. 'I enjoyed doing it'. Prost has not forgotten the kindness: 'He gave me a lot of practical advice. He agreed to drive in front of me to show me the good racing lines, he was like a big brother to me.'

'He made some mistakes during the time he drove for us', Alexander says, 'and we made some mistakes. Those things happen. South Africa was one of those deals where did he make a mistake or did something on the car break? We don't know and I don't remember us blaming him.'

Prost missed the next race, Long Beach, where McLaren hired a promising young Englishman called Stephen South. He was slowest in both practice sessions and did not qualify for the race. 'That showed us', Jardine says, 'how bad the car was because Wattie was at the back of the grid' – the second last row, in fact. 'It was a major disaster for Marlboro in the United States because we only had one car in the race and worse was to come at Monaco . . . '

Between Long Beach and the Principality lay Belgium at Zolder, a featureless place nobody particularly liked. It was famous then for the quality of the Belgian chips and mayonnaise available in the paddock and precious little else. Prost qualified a place in front of Watson but only four cars were slower. Prost's brakes went on lap 29 when he had been lapped by the leaders and Watson limped home running but unclassified twelve laps behind the winner, Pironi.

The first Monaco qualifying session was wet and all twenty-seven drivers in it knew that their times would be meaningless if the second was dry because everybody would go quicker; and all twenty-seven knew that only the top twenty were admitted to the race. The guillotine cut deep. (As an aside Watson was decisively out-qualified by Prost, ninth against eighteenth.) The second session was dry and the leaders were more than 20 seconds faster. Watson simply could not get the car into the top twenty and it cannot have helped that Prost was tenth.

'Monaco stands out in my mind', Jardine says. 'Prost had gone quite well in practice considering the car and considering everything but Wattie didn't qualify. A load of Irish fans had come to watch him and they were all outside the motorhome. "Teach," he said, "you've got to go and tell them." They said in their Irish accents, "We've come 1,000 miles to see John and he's not in the race!" So again it was one car in the race and Marlboro were pretty unimpressed by that.

'In the race, Derek Daly (Tyrrell), way behind Prost, tried a demon out-braking manoeuvre at Sainte Devote, he missed his braking point totally and using his team-mate Jean-Pierre Jarier as a launching pad his car flew, it seemed to be accelerating as it flew over the top of the field, it just missed Piquet, it hit Giacomelli, it hit one of the Alfa Romeos, it went over Prost and took his rear wing off then landed in front of him in a big heap.

'Prost went round with his rear wing missing and the car was retired. I'm not sure but I think the feeling among the boys was to bolt a new rear wing on and send him back out and Prost being Prost he'd have got some points. It was only the rear wing that was off. You see what I'm saying: after the two shunts in South Africa if there was any damage to the car he'd rather not drive it. In other words he wasn't going to do a Villeneuve and drive it whatever.' (Gilles Villeneuve remains revered for many reasons. One was when, in a race at Zandvoort, he drove virtually a lap with a rear tyre completely gone to get back to the pits to try and rejoin the race; the image of this Ferrari, the whole shredded tyre distended and flapping and flailing, the whole car tilted and Villeneuve making it move as fast as is humanly possible, is deep in the folklore of Formula One and so vivid that many people can replay it in their minds without any video assistance.)

Jardine is making a sharp point. The doubts about the car were growing. Nor was the cartoonist's pen stilled. 'After South Africa I did one of Prost as Napoleon with his arm like this [tucked into his tunic], one foot in the car like this wearing a uniform and saying, "to *Little Napper* from us all". It was carefully coloured and took me six nights to do. It was done with Teddy Mayer's approval – he gave me the money so we could have it framed to present to Prost. He told me after he's still got it in his guest loo. There must be a reason why . . . '

'Prost has said I took the cartoons well', Watson says. 'I had no choice because the management acquiesced in it. They thought it was very funny as well and that was part of the reason why I consider the management to be poor because no serious team should countenance that type of humour – let's call it that, humour – from team members working for me or for Prost or for the team. That was weakness and total callousness. The cartoons may have been considered funny but they should not have been. If you have two drivers in a team there's no way that situation should arise. At McLaren today Ron Dennis would have a cartoon like that off the wall in one second . . .'

Teddy Mayer is trenchant. 'The cartoons? There would have been a riot if we had taken them down. I'm definitely the man in the middle and I have to disagree with John. That kind of thing you have to learn to live with. If you can't live with that I don't think you're a man, and I do think John is a man. I'm surprised that he felt so strongly about it although he is sensitive. Did we focus on Prost even though he was a rookie? That's true and the cartoons did demonstrate that, of course they did.'

Mayer means that you 'always focus on the quick guy and like all great criterions there is an element of truth and an element of pain in it – this business of "you're the number one driver". I don't care how many pieces of paper you write, the guy who's going quick

Marlboro
Marlboro
1
Shell
Shell

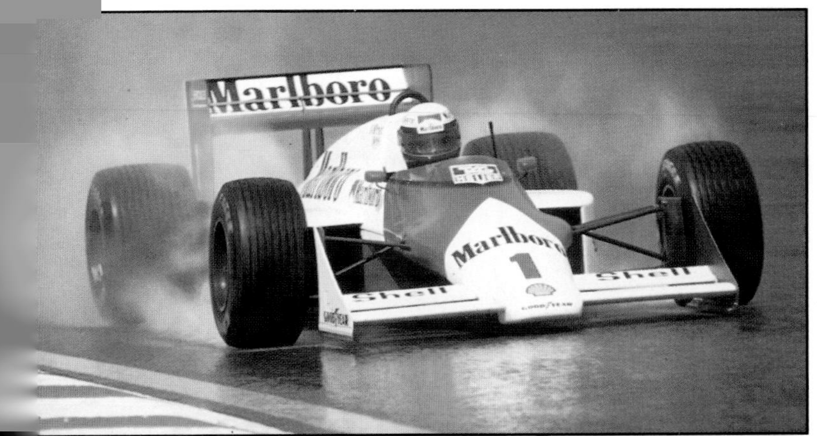

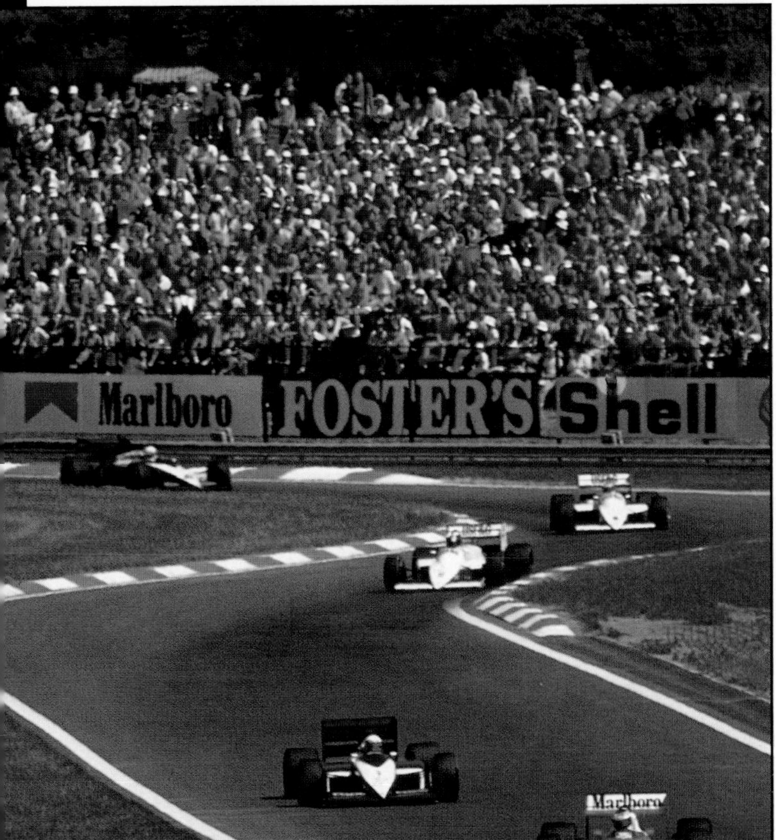
Marlboro
FOSTER'S
Shell
Marlboro
2
Marlboro
1

Powerhouse. (*l-r*) Marco Piccinini (Ferrari), Bernie Ecclestone, Jean-Marie Balestre and Prost, all smiles, 1987.

(*Top right*) Over the bridge at Monaco in 1987.

The new team, (*l-r*) Senna, Prost and Dennis; across 1988 and 1989 it would dominate Grand Prix racing absolutely.

Marlboro
Shell
Marlboro
Shell
BOSS
Marlboro
HONDA

The speed of the man going for it at Monza.

(*Insert opposite*)
A rare moment of relaxation in the sun. There aren't many.

Now listen, this is the way it is, Ayrton.

A rare moment, Prost off during qualifying at Monza in 1989.

The controlled flurry of the pit-stop which would help him to second place in Rio, 1989 – behind Mansell.

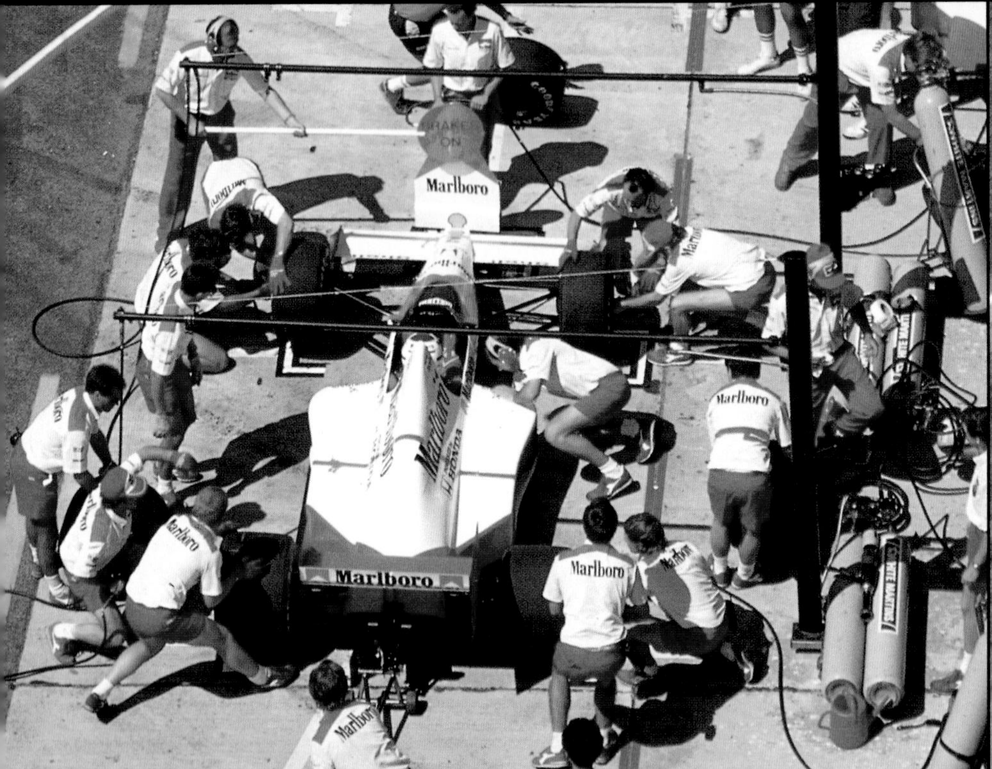

The moment the team-mates fell out. Prost claimed Senna broke their accord by overtaking him at Imola.

Optical illusion: finding a path through the trees at Monaco although he couldn't catch Senna this time.

on the day is the number one driver that day in any race team in the world and that's how it is. Why drivers can't understand that I don't know. You cannot say on a piece of paper what isn't true. But if one guy has a chance of the World Championship and the other guy hasn't then you're justified in doing it' – making sure you get the pit signals out to inform both drivers which order they should finish a race in. This is a very contentious subject and in many ways it violates the basic ethic of sport. Within a couple of years when another team held out a pit board to inform Prost and his team-mate of exactly this, it convulsed France.

'Otherwise,' Mayer continues, 'it's every man for himself, it's crazy, yes, but the way it is. We were under pressure from Marlboro, we had been for some time . . . '

Memories of mid-summer 1980 from Jardine: 'He had a fantastic sense of humour.' And: 'He did a rally for Renault. I was really into rallying and he was pretty good.' And: 'Anne-Marie [his wife] hated the races but she came to the French Grand Prix. I got on really well with her, she was a fantastic lady.' And: 'We had a cricket match, Tyrrell v McLaren at Ockham where Tyrrell are based. I asked him to play in that. I spent half an hour on the phone trying to explain what cricket was and he had never heard of it. In the end he said in his heavy French accent, "*I don't zeenk so.*" Then he said, "*I play boules, you know.*" We'd have batted him number one.' (Of course the man who bats number one bats first, so that the bowler clutching the ball – so hard that when delivered it can break fingers, arms, shoulders and noses – is inevitably fresh and fast. In refusing, Monsieur Prost was demonstrating that he was no bad judge of a situation.)

And: 'Leading up to the first Grand Prix we used to play all the other teams at football and he was very keen. He loved to have a little kick-around with the mechanics. We had a match coming up against Brabham and I'd called him up about something or other and said, "D'you fancy playing?" and he said, "Yes, yes, great." But unfortunately he had to go somewhere else and couldn't.' Truly the football career was a non-career now.

'Sometimes when he'd come over to the factory it was my job to go and pick him up at the airport. I enjoyed that. One time my old banger was in hock so I had to borrow my wife Janet's 2CV, what we called The Old Orange Puddle Duck. It was late at night and she had to come with me. I said, "Sorry about the state of the car", but he said, "No problem, at least it's French."

'Each time he used to try and persuade me not to take him to Teddy's house at Weybridge. He just wanted to be relaxed, I suppose, in a country that was still fairly alien to him. The first four or five times he came over he did stay with Mayer. I think Teddy was doing a number on him – "looking after my driver, he's new" – he knew he'd got a good 'un. I think it was like, "You will stay with me", and Teddy was Managing Director but Alain used to say, "Teach, Teach, can I stay with you? I don't want to go to Teddy's." A couple of times I did say to Teddy, "Let him stay with me", because I knew the guy, I knew he wanted to relax a bit.'

All this is eminently understandable. Mayer was acting in a sensible and magnanimous way, getting acquainted with his new driver, letting the new driver get acquainted with him, talking, talking motor racing. Mayer had a lot to impart. He had been in it a long time and was, of course, managing McLaren on the famous day at Mount Fuji when James Hunt won the World Championship – to take but one example from Mayer's career.

Prost, young and in this alien land, must have felt as awkward as you or I would have done staying in the boss's house; he and Jardine were about the same age, both laughed a lot, Jardine was the most relaxed and engaging person and if he cannot speak French he mimicks languages and accents so well that you think he can.

'I always used to carry his pocket money for each race and we got into this lovely routine [and, yes, as he recounts this Jardine moves inevitably into the French accent], "Teach, Teach, where's the money?" He'd snatch it, count it and run off . . .'

Prost's memories of that mid-season? Here he is, vintage 1980. 'I try to practise well but in the races I lack experience. The standard of driving is as I imagined, nobody seems bothered to keep within the safety margins. What shows up clearly is the difference in handling between the cars. If your car does not work well you cannot hope for a result, one tenth of a second lost is impossible to make up in Formula One. In Formula Two and Formula Three you can make up for the car's poor performance but in Formula One it is out of the question. I want to drive Formula One very quiet – smoothly.' And he would, he would, so smoothly that even fellow drivers wondered how it was done.

6

ONE OF THOSE THINGS

> You know, when you're in motor racing your relationship with the driver who's driving for you is very strong. The minute he stops it hardly exists. That's the way it is.
>
> TEDDY MAYER

The Spanish Grand Prix at Jarama on 1 June 1980 was subsequently declared non-Championship. It was the opening broadside in a struggle between FISA, governing the sport, and the Formula One Constructor's Association (FOCA). We shall not concern ourselves with that here, save to say that on the track Prost had another moment in qualifying.

Autosport: 'The two Brabhams were split on the grid by a brilliant Alain Prost who had another eventful practice with the McLaren team. The team's spare chassis had been modified at the front with revised suspension pick-up points taken off a fabricated box section, glued and riveted to the sides of the monocoque. Prost was asked to test the car on Saturday morning and after two slow laps he began to run hard but got only as far as the second hairpin halfway round the circuit. There he braked hard down from around 140 miles an hour and the new pick-up point ripped away from the chassis and the car rode up over its own front wheel.

'Fortunately for Prost the corner which previously had very little run-off area had been extensively modified by the organizers and after clearing the first row of four-feet-high catch fencing he had room to continue his high speed accident through three more rows of fencing before slamming into the low barrier, half-backwards. He climbed out of the wrecked chassis and limped back to the pits with no more than a bruised shin. Then the gutsy little Frenchman climbed aboard his regular chassis, went back out and lapped faster than he had all weekend. "If you stop and think about it you don't drive again", said Prost, who was third quickest on Saturday and one of the few drivers to improve.' He finished sixth in the race; and he was thinking about it, thinking about it . . .

At Paul Ricard after Jarama he outqualified Watson again, seventh against thirteenth but went out early with a transmission failure. He had been as high as sixth. Qualifying at Brands Hatch was a re-run, seventh against twelfth. He made a mess of the start, was twelfth after the opening lap but worked his way up to sixth – and in the points again, of course – by the end.

McLaren meanwhile were working on a new car. 'After the M29 they had the much-vaunted M30 which was going to be the answer to all our prayers. The trouble was the car was designed by committee, it wasn't actually left to the designer', Jardine says. 'I mean, I was doing drawings of the body work. It was a great team feeling but I think it's been proved that to be successful you need a dictator.'

'The new car was a little bit better but still not brilliant and we didn't really have a good aerodynamic programme at the time. We were struggling a bit for finance and we built the car in a hell of a hurry', Mayer says. 'In those days you didn't have big organizations where you can say to one group, "Look, go off and develop this car while we struggle with what we've got." Basically if you built something new you took it to the racetrack and tested it there. That was what you were set up to do. Absorb pressure? That's principally what a team manager is there for and no, it ain't easy although it's part of the challenge, it's one of the things that makes motor racing interesting.'

'I did some testing with him when we were trying to get the [old] car better – which we did', Alexander says. 'There were some things about the car which I'd just as soon not say. They are kind of criminal but in some ways the car wasn't too bad. He worked to improve the thing along with everybody else and he is one of the best guys to work with. Sure he's a hero now, then he was just someone who was going to become a hero, a superstar, whatever you want to call it . . . '

The new car was due to be launched at Zandvoort. Neither Prost nor Watson got points in the two races before, Germany and Austria. By now Prost had married Anne-Marie, his childhood sweetheart, and they set up home in a flat in Saint Chamond.

Mayer's words about testing at the racetrack are amply borne out. Prost conducted the 'shake-down', a term used to denote the very first, tentative running of a car, at Goodwood, a small circuit in the south of England, and Brands Hatch. It was a sure sign, as he realized, of the confidence the team had in him. Then the car went straight to Zandvoort.

The stresses broadened. In qualifying, Watson in, of course, the old car, was ninth, Prost eighteenth, and in the race, when Watson's engine let go on lap 18, Watson was seventh; Prost slogged on to take sixth place.

'During the course of 1980 the M30 was being designed and it was going to be the definitive McLaren. That car appeared at Zandvoort and of course Alain was going to have it so I was left with the M29. Two things happened and this just shows you the face of Formula One, how quickly swings between loyalty and disloyalty can happen. Alain got the new car and the management believed that this was going to be a significant step forward. I had a brake failure in practice, I had a big shunt at the end of the straight so I had to drive the spare car. The M29 had been gradually improving, it was getting better; now at Zandvoort I had the car that Alain had had in Germany and Austria [being used as the spare].

'I got it to work quite well. The M30 was actually proving to be not as good as this M29. I outqualified Alain and I had a good race [until the engine went]. We went to Imola for the Italian Grand Prix and I consolidated the performance of Zandvoort.' It was true, Watson halfway down the grid, Prost slowest of all; Watson in the points when the brakes went on lap 20, Prost profiting from retirements to take sixth place but a lap behind the leaders.

'From Zandvoort my position in the team suddenly elevated again,' Watson says, 'and Alain started to bad mouth the car – not bad mouth, that's not the right word – he started to complain that the car is no good, the team is no good. He was right, he was absolutely right.'

By now Marlboro had made up their minds. Canada was on 28 September, the United States East Grand Prix at Watkins Glen a week later. They were the last two races of the season. We must meet two men who would dominate Formula One, John Barnard, the designer people have already spoken about, and Ron Dennis, who had helped lift Prost's car at Pau in 1978. Dennis, arch-organizer, had hired Barnard for his team, Project Four, with a view to building their own Formula One car. As the teams gathered in Montreal history was taking deft and delicate footsteps. Prost would win two World Championships in Barnard cars, add another to make it three under Dennis – but that was years away, almost in another life.

'The driver has to protect himself', Watson says. 'Good teams will support their drivers, good drivers will support their team but at that time Teddy Mayer and Tyler Alexander were fighting for the survival of their company. They stood to lose Marlboro, the sponsors they had had since 1974. John Hogan and Patrick McNally were Marlboro employees and it was a tremendous disappointment to everybody because the M30 turned out to be such a "dog" – unfortunately, because Gordon Coppuck the designer is a really nice guy. Why it was a dog I don't know but that was a fact. Marlboro had invested substantial sums of money in the team and one would have assumed that McLaren – who had built good and successful cars and had had World Champions – would have moved forward into the ground-effect era but they hadn't.

'Ron Dennis had had a long association with Hogan and been sponsored at different times through people Hogan had been associated with, Ron was pushing to get into Formula One. In the middle of 1979 Ron thought he could get in by employing John Barnard in conjunction with BMW. In effect Ron took a flyer and hoped he would get Marlboro sponsorship and BMW engines for his team, Project Four. But Marlboro had this long-standing commitment to McLaren so Marlboro's concept was: we'll bring Dennis and Barnard into McLaren, the existing structure is there. That package was put to Mayer and Alexander and they steered it away, called Marlboro's bluff, basically they said if you do that we'll walk out of it and you'll have nothing. At that stage Marlboro backed down and it was put on the back-burner.

'In 1980 the biggest ray of hope that Marlboro had was Prost, and then the reality of the situation dawned on Mayer and Alexander, it was reviewed again and they accepted the fact that Ron was coming, Barnard was coming. It was an uneasy partnership.'

'We'd been talking for several months', Mayer says, 'and Ron had something we needed. He had John Barnard. We needed a designer. My big mistake, I suppose, was a year before. Barnard had come back from America where he worked with Jim Hall at Chapperal and I knew he was upset with Jim Hall because he claimed some, if not all, the credit for designing the Chapperal when he had absolutely nothing to do with it. John came to us and I think if I'd been willing to get rid of Gordon Coppuck and take John on as chief designer instead of just offering him a job as someone in the design department we could have had him. My mistake was being too loyal to Gordon. Ron brought other things to the team, too, he was a good organizer and he was partially responsible for convincing Marlboro that we were under-financed.'

'When Barnard came and started to engineer my car in Canada,' Watson says, 'things that he did had instant and significant results in the handling. Downforce was suddenly there where it wasn't before. All he did was make some very simple ride-height changes because he understood what ground effects and downforce were all about.'

'Ron and I went to Canada and Watkins Glen just observing', Barnard says. He did not observe for long. Barnard was his own man, sometimes maddeningly stubborn, prey to volcanic outbursts and yet affable, too – and a genius. He had already been working on a revolutionary composite car and, his mind full of restless enquiries for absolute information, was doing testing in the wind tunnel at Southampton University on 'the aerodynamic side of it.' In Canada, 'We fundamentally changed the set-up of the car, ride-height, chassis-rake and so on – changing the centre of pressure to make it more driveable. Those were the things you could do quickly and which had an immediate effect. It seemed to make quite a difference.

'Obviously Ron and I wanted to keep Prost. I can remember having breakfast with Ron and him and we said: "Are you going to stay, are you going to stay? There's new stuff coming, we're really going to turn the thing around." He more or less said then, "No, I don't think I'm going to stay, I've had enough, I'm nervous about the car, bits have fallen off." ' Barnard understood. 'There had been one time when they were trying some suspension or something and it was put on in the most God-awful way, just literally pop-riveted on the side of the chassis and it just pulled straight off [Jarama]. He'd had a few of those sort of things which really disturbed him.

'I remember Ron saying at that breakfast – the impression was coming over that this guy was going to leave, it wasn't cut and dried but we weren't going to keep him whatever happened – "I'll tell you Alain, you're going to piss blood, one day you'll piss blood", and that stuck in my mind.'

Watson, still in the M29, qualified seventh, Prost in the M30 twelfth. In the race Prost crashed – he had been holding Riccardo

Patrese (Arrows) at bay and Patrese, then at a very impulsive and impetuous stage of his career, flung the Arrows inside at the hairpin and knocked Prost into the air. Watson finished fourth.

The circuit at Montreal is on the Isle Notre Dame and the artificial lake for the rowing at the 1976 Olympic Games runs along behind the pits. 'Canada', Jardine says, 'was a significant point. It was very clear that McLaren wanted to keep Prost, everybody knew what his driving was like but it was no secret within the team that Prost wanted to go because he didn't believe the car was commensurate with his talent and by the time we went to Canada, Renault were openly and actively wooing him.

'It was in one of those old boathouses where they had the skiffs right at the end of the lake and I said to Teddy, "Renault are chatting up Prost [it seemed to be Gerard Larrousse and Jean Sage, very important people]. Do you want me to go and stop them?" Teddy said he would deal with it himself.'

Mayer says: 'We knew by then Renault were after him. I don't remember how I knew it, but we did. There wasn't any doubt that that was what was going on.' Mayer did try to deal with it himself.

'He said to Prost,' Jardine remembers, ' "Why are you doing this, why are you doing this?" Prost obviously felt pretty jingoistic about it, Renault were really emerging as the team to win the World Championship . . . '

Of Canada, Alexander says: 'Then the merger happened with John Barnard, who was the best guy around and I think Prost took a liking to him.' And of the race: 'Prost ran over Patrese's wheel but he had been going well then something broke at the front and it was our "fault". OK, well sure, except earlier he had had the front end of the car about five feet off the ground when he drove up over Patrese's tyre and banged it on the ground. We didn't say: Alain Prost crashed the car, but he said, "The car broke and I lost all confidence in it." The mere fact that he'd ridden over somebody's wheels earlier had no bearing on the thing [to him], and it's sad because those are things that sometimes happen. You can be mad at it for the moment for sure but then you've got to get over that and get on with it. To hear him still talking about it years later, I don't know, to me that's just rubbish. Why bother?' Alexander is not, of course, apportioning blame for the incident, only pointing out that it happened.

'When you lose confidence in a car, it's finished', Prost has said. 'When I sign a contract, I mean it. When I give my word I mean it. Whatever people say I did not leave McLaren because it was convenient, because I had received a better offer. After Montreal, with one race left, I did not know what to do. Because of my contract I felt I should stay with McLaren but I admit I was getting more and more worried about suspension failures all the time – you reach a point where you expect the car to break, you are waiting for it to happen and in those circumstances you can't drive properly.'

Only Watkins Glen remained, Alan Jones had won the World Championship in a Williams at Montreal and superficially the final race might have seemed – if any motor race ever can – a stroll through the pastures of Upstate New York.

'Now enter Ron Dennis', Jardine says. 'We already knew he was joining and being made a director and of course behind that was Marlboro. They knew exactly what they were doing. We understood about five days before that Ron would be coming to North America. We'd seen his name on all the lists, the movement schedules and so on. None of the existing team knew if we would be in the new set-up, this amalgam of the two. At Watkins Glen, Ron was looking after Prost but there was this uneasy atmosphere.'

(In the midst of this necessarily heavy stuff we might pause for a genuine smile, however irrelevant to Prost's own story. 'We stayed at Seneca Lodge, that was the place to stay', Jardine says. 'It was described as "*a log cabin colony set in the natural order of the universe.*" The reality was we had little gas fires, it was rotting, it had woodworm. It had been the scene of great triumphs with James Hunt dancing on the tables with a belisha beacon strapped to his head. He was brilliant, Hunt was brilliant. I don't think Prost came near the place . . . he stayed at the Glen Motor Inn, which was just up the road . . . ')

The first qualifying session for the United States East Grand Prix was on Friday, 3 October. It was cold but sunny, a crisp autumnal day. Prost was tenth, Watson sixth.

Of the untimed session on the Saturday morning *Autosport* would say: 'Alain Prost was very lucky to escape a high-speed shunt when the suspension failed on his Marlboro McLaren M30. "I don't remember much other than that the car went straight on and I tried to crouch down in the cockpit. I think it was the front suspension that failed. I had no steering," Prost said a few hours later after a visit to the local hospital for a check-up. A fence post gave him a nasty bang on the head and a bruised arm.'

'He had a top rocker or something break', Barnard says. 'He wasn't hurt but I took one look at him and I thought: "This guy's out, there's no way he'll stay."'

'I was on the hospital run again . . .' Jardine says. 'He was taken to the medical centre at the track. I couldn't get in. Ron Dennis had got there before me. I hadn't spoken to Ron because nobody knew the situation with the amalgamation and we were all being very careful. I remember it very clearly. Ron said, "Some oink had him off." He was taken to a hospital where there was a small private surgery and I went down to see him there. He was lying under a sheet and they were checking him out. He said: "I don't want to know about McLaren, I'll never drive that car again." He was very, very upset.'

'The final thing was that shunt at Watkins Glen', Watson says. 'He was my team-mate, luckily he wasn't badly injured, he'd got a bit of a knock and the shock was quite severe. To my knowledge nobody from the team went down to see him in the medical centre.' This statement is not of course a distortion of memory but a question of timing. When Watson arrived it was naturally after the untimed session because he, Watson, had been driving in it; Ron Dennis had already been, Jardine had failed to get in, and quite possibly others had been too; I have only used Watson's statement because it underscores, I believe, his vision of the deterioration of the team.

'I walked down to see how he was', Watson continues. 'He sat there on the bed in the medical centre and he said, "John, I'll tell you one thing now, you will be the number one driver at McLaren next year, there is no way in this world I will drive for this team next year." He had a two-year contract, Renault had come along and were making all sorts of noises, money, whatever. He has said subsequently that if McLaren had held him to the contract he wouldn't race and I believe he would have walked away from the whole thing. [In a solid part of France like Saint Chamond, a man's word is his word, remember.]

'Certainly with the M30 there were a number of incidents which he puts down to mechanical failure. What the team says or how they assess those failures may be different because ultimately they were shunts. The team might say, "Ah, but he hit a kerb and that could have led to the shunt", but whatever the cause or reasons ultimately there is the fact that he lost confidence in the car and the worst thing for any driver is not to have that, to come to a racetrack and not be sure that the thing isn't going to fail.

'I assure you a mechanical or structural failure will never happen at a point on the circuit where it's safe, it always happens where you are at your most exposed and of course Alain had something in Canada, the shunt in Watkins Glen and the combination of those factors plus his ability to see through the management and the opportunity to go to Renault . . .

'There had been a full swing from Prost the blue-eyed boy getting the latest and greatest equipment to me with the old car – well, Wattie can have it, forget about him. I was the one who was performing and Prost was complaining, "Oh, the car's no good, this car's rubbish." There had been the mechanical failures and he was very critical of the car, critical about the management prior to Watkins Glen.

'Alain is a very, very bright man, extremely intelligent, he does not suffer fools gladly and he has got self-belief and self-confidence; and he was being courted by other teams. Ferrari, I think, were after him [there had been persistent rumours and an approach as early as March], Renault were certainly after him and here's this young guy in his first season in Grand Prix racing and major teams are trying to get him to drive for them. He saw through all this slightly sycophantic hero worship. Then things started to swop around through no fault of his own or my own. Circumstances brought this about. That's why Alain and I remain friends. He respects that and the fact that I did something for him.'

Prost remembers the Glen like this: 'What really made up my mind to leave was the accident. I got back to the pits to find that people in the team were talking about driver error, going too fast on cold tyres and things like that. I said, "OK, if you want things like that, it's finished. If you won't release me I stop Formula One, I won't drive." People say that I went to Renault because of money. They paid me about half what I could have got if I had stayed with McLaren in 1981 so the question of money never came into it.'

Prost duly went to the circuit on Sunday morning because he had qualified for the race with his Friday time. He decided he was not well enough to take part in it.

'I know later on he said some things – that Teddy was nasty because Teddy asked him to drive – and that's another of those things: I mean how did Teddy make him drive? Teddy said, "We'd like you to drive." All Prost had to say was, "I can't see", or whatever and he wouldn't have driven', Alexander says. 'What these guys tend to forget is that life is a two-way street. He did a couple of laps,

I assume to see if he felt all right. That's what you do, then you stop and say, "I can't do it, forget it", and the team says OK. It's obvious – so it's funny [peculiar] the recriminations, the garbage in this business. It's kind of sad.'

'Watkins Glen? The car broke, yes it did', Mayer says. And Prost's confidence in the team? 'By then I'm pretty sure he wanted to go to Renault and this was just a way of getting out of the contract. Yes, the car did break at Watkins Glen, he wasn't dreadfully hurt that's for sure but he was mildly damaged. The only guy who can really say he was dizzy was him, I can't, and we didn't pressure him to do so either beyond saying, "Are you really sure?" You cannot force a man into a racing car, absolutely not. We made no attempt to do that.'

'I didn't see him again after the States until he was a Renault driver', Jardine says. 'The funny [peculiar] thing is I'm still friends with him today, he still comes up and says, "Hello, Teach" despite what he might feel about my cartoons of Wattie.'

Renault? Oh yes, it happened. But didn't McLaren have a one-year option on Prost for 1981?

'It was the time', Mayer says, 'when everybody found out you could break contracts. You could just walk away. We went to some lawyers and they said, "Well, you may get some damages and you may not." That was probably the first time people found out. He told me he was leaving, I don't remember where. My response was to do what I had to do and tell him he couldn't leave, that we had a contract and that we would take legal action. It got unpleasant, it's not a good relationship to have with a driver but you also have a responsibility to the company and the sponsor so you have to do these things.

'Since then we've found out a lot about personal service contracts and they don't really hold water. If you want to walk away there is very little that can be done. It was quite a shock when the lawyers told us that. What the law says is that you can't stop a man from earning his living and if he doesn't want to drive for you or design for you or whatever for you, you can sometimes – depending on how things are written – get some damages but you can't stop him doing it for somebody else. But you get over those things.'

The situation at the end of 1980 was, Alexander emphasizes, 'a) we had a contract with him and b) we knew the French guys wanted him and that he was French. What were we going to do?

You can't force him to stay and drive so you can end up in a huge big legal thing.

'Contracts aren't exactly contracts. Some of Carl Hass's dealings with Mario Andretti in the States have been handshakes because the handshake might actually be better.' Better, I wonder, because it confers a moral obligation? That makes Alexander smile broadly. 'There are no moral obligations in this business but I know what you mean. The inference is you might just as well shake hands as have a twenty-page contract. If you're not going to do something afterwards, you're not going to do it. That's what the Prost thing boiled down to. It was a chance to drive for Renault, for France. How are you ever going to stop him?'

Watson, experienced in the ways of it all, broadens that: 'It was a fantastic opportunity to effectively become the number one driver with Renault and have a turbo-charged car – McLaren didn't have that, they were going to run with normally aspirated engines in 1981.

'You're a young driver, you're ambitious. A driver has to think of himself in a very singular way. He has also to think of the team but in a different way. You don't win World Championship points out of sentiment. You have to be as hard-headed and single-minded as the people who are in control of the teams. If you're not they will eat you up, they will use you. Someone equated racing drivers to light bulbs: you take one out and you put another one in. That is the mentality they have. I understand that mentality because they are in motor racing from a different perspective. I helped him because I liked him. He was beating me but my contribution wasn't just to help him, it was to help myself and in helping myself you talk as a team. You have to. You cannot be an island in a team.'

There are some final reflections on 1980.

Tony Jardine: 'As a chap he was very genial although it was a two-way street. [That phrase again.] He was as keen to get the most out of you as the team was of him. Drivers have either got it or they haven't. There's no real halfway post. If you start going to yourself, "Hmmm, I'm not sure", when you are watching, then forget it. You just know when the star quality is there. I'd watched him win at Monaco the previous year in Formula Three and the car looked like it was on rails, but you ask yourself what that means: French driver, French team, French tyres – the best Michelins – and you still ask, the way you do: can the guy drive? [In other words, he had got it but how much of it did he have?] Let's be honest, in 1980 the McLaren chassis wasn't the best but he flew whereas in certain circumstances Wattie struggled and Wattie has always been one of the most gifted but unlucky drivers. Prost, straight in, had Wattie sussed up very, very quickly. And Wattie did help him, Wattie ever the gracious man recognized his talent.'

Teddy Mayer: 'I was a little bit surprised at how demanding he was on himself, the car and the team, although obviously he was an exceptional talent. You could tell that all along. Even at that stage he thought he was good enough to be demanding – he screams and yells at Ferrari now like a banshee [this was, of course, before he left, late 1991], he lays down the law and sometimes I think he goes overboard. It's difficult to know how the Italian press finds out it's being done but they seem to know and I suspect if they do it hasn't been done in the most private and tactful way possible. I think he makes a mistake there. Going back to 1980, I could see the seeds of that, absolutely.'

Mayer pauses, reflects, rummages in his own philosophy. 'There's never any point in looking back except to learn lessons. There's certainly no point in having regrets because what happens happens and it's the same whatever you're doing. Would I have given John Barnard his head? I would hope so but you never know now what you'd have done then under those circumstances. John had a lot of talent which would have stood us in good stead over that period of time.' He would of course have designed a state-of-the-art car which would have been nicely ready for the 1980 season and the arrival of Prost and that would have altered the story of motor racing through the 1980s, that would. The deft and delicate steps of history which didn't happen. You notice the conditional tense all the way through the paragraph.

'It's understandable I was loyal to Gordon Coppuck but I should have done it.' Was the management not strong enough? Mayer pauses for a long time. 'It's difficult to say. We were under-financed and it's hard to be strong when you don't have much money. In 1980 it was a pretty good field, we'd been there a long time and people may be right: I wasn't strong enough to say let's send Gordon off and put Barnard in there. I should have done it and I knew that several months later. But you're learning.

'I applied it when I went to Penske [in the States] for example. I had a look around for a month and I said, "We need to have a new designer, this guy's a nice guy, he's a friend of mine but he ain't gonna do it, got to get rid of him right now." And we did; but it's a hard thing to do. Motor racing takes hard things. It doesn't encourage sentiment a lot.'

This was a lesson Alain Prost had learned. He would need it in the years ahead; and sometimes need it badly.

John Barnard: 'He didn't know Ron and I and what was going to happen. Although I'd been in racing for twelve years or so I hadn't really mixed it with the Formula One people, I hadn't been, let's say, responsible in Formula One. He wasn't comfortable at McLaren and that came across. He had the chance to go to Renault – given all the circumstances there is no question which way anyone would have gone if they'd been him although I would like him to have stayed. The main thing was that he was quick. Wattie took far too long about setting the car up, he was hopeless qualifying but he was a bloody good racer, a fabulous racer and Prost could just blow him off. He was that much quicker but at the same time I was thinking: what can the guy do? He's French, it's Renault, they've a turbo engine and it was obvious you had to have one, all of France will be behind him, the guy's got to go there.

'It's fairly difficult for me to make strong associations with people and probably likewise in the reverse – people find it difficult to know me quickly; but it was one of those things, we tried to keep him, we couldn't and he moved on. We had no idea that we would ever be able to get him back.'

7

NON, JE NE REGRETTE RIEN

If there was a chance for him to win the World Championship . . . in the last race perhaps I would have played for the team – but I say perhaps.

RENE ARNOUX

Jean Sage hauls everything down to six words: 'We wanted Prost, Prost wanted us.' During the weekend of the Grand Prix at Watkins Glen, Sage said, 'At the moment we have approached no one but Alain Prost about driving for Renault in 1981 but if nothing is settled soon we shall have to speak to other drivers as well. Obviously we would be interested in Carlos Reutemann. We are not compelled to run a Frenchman and you know Renault sell very well in Argentina.'

A week later Ron Dennis was saying, 'Marlboro and McLaren International have exercised their option on Prost and will take the necessary steps to make sure he stays with us. I must say that as a newcomer to Formula One I expected to experience more gentlemanly conduct over such matters. I am very disappointed that a major manufacturer and major sponsors are acting in such an unethical way. The guy has a contract and their actions have been just blatant enticement. People say that Prost doesn't want to drive for us. But if our car goes quickly in testing and he's on pole for a Grand Prix we'll be the greatest thing since sliced bread. All drivers are the same. When things are going wrong it's always the team's fault.'

By early December Prost had joined Renault to which Dennis said, 'We are evaluating our position with a view to legal action and financial compensation.'

Gazing back on this now, Sage – a stooping, rather benign patrician figure who began watching motor racing in 1950 and Grand Prix racing in 1959 – sets it all in to context. 'I first saw Prost when he was driving in Formula Three in France with a Renault engine and he won the Championship. This engine had never been competitive but when it was in Prost's car it started winning. I was already working for Renault and that's why I met him.

'Teddy Mayer may think we used McLaren in 1980 as a 'farm team' but no, nothing like that was planned because we already had Jean-Pierre Jabouille and René Arnoux and there was no question of firing one of them to take Prost. But we did look at him.'

Jabouille told Renault he was leaving to join Ligier-Talbot for 1981 then, 'He had this very bad accident in Montreal, he had two broken legs and for sure he was not going to drive: but he had signed just before so it was bad luck for him and for Talbot.

'I don't remember when we decided to go for Prost but it happened just after Jabouille had his accident. It was around then. Were we talking to Prost in the boathouse there? We had been talking to Prost all year, he never stopped calling us complaining about McLaren. He had several accidents, parts broke during the season so Prost was not completely wrong. When he was hurt in one of the accidents – well, I have a picture of him with his arm in plaster and he was with us, he was eating with us, he was always with us.

'We wanted Prost, Prost wanted us but before Jabouille signed with Talbot there was nothing very precise. Jabouille's leaving had nothing to do with Prost – Prost had been talking to us since the beginning of the summer but not about a contract. He was talking because he felt better around our team than at McLaren.'

For 1981 Renault now had two hot ones, Arnoux and Prost. 'Yes, but one much more intelligent than the other. I didn't say which. Having two French drivers happened by chance, you could say, because we didn't have to. They were quick, they were good and there was no reason to have somebody else, but it could have been an English driver or an Italian driver or whatever. It was not imposed on us to have two French drivers, it was clear we were free to take any driver from any country where Renault had a market.

'I think Prost and Arnoux didn't like each other from the beginning. They had different characters and they had never been friends.

Life was hard because it was very difficult to keep them together. We did it until July 1982 . . .'

René Arnoux, then thirty-two, was more experienced than Prost. In 1978 he had driven for Martini Ford and Surtees Ford, joining Renault in 1979. In 1980 he won Brazil and South Africa and was sixth in the Championship with 29 points. Up to Formula One his career had been uncannily like that of Prost. He won the *volant Shell* (of the same cachet as *Pilote Elf*) at Magny-Cours in 1972, was Formula Renault Champion and European Formula Two Champion. In simple terminology, a winner.

There is another context to be examined, that of Renault itself. In May 1976 Gerard Larrousse, newly appointed Competitions Director, announced they were going into Formula One with a turbo-charged car, the first people to try (or risk) it. The car, sponsored by Elf, had a 1.5 litre engine, Michelin tyres and Frenchman Jabouille to drive it. It was a package as Gallic as garlic and no doubt you could smell garlic here and there around it. (For non-technicians, a turbo engine utilizes the waste gases a normal engine emits, thus increasing its efficiency and power, but naturally it was complicated.) The début was Silverstone and the British Grand Prix in 1977 but the turbo went on lap 17. This was to become for Renault and the others who tried (and risked) it a familiar, tantalizing problem: reliability. But by 1979 the turbo was fast, finishing races and soon enough there would be a rush for them.

The context has to be widened to the implications of what Renault were doing. France had never had a Formula One World Champion and there was a vast harvest to be gathered in terms of publicity alone; with the converse that the company was spending a lot of money and if it failed the publicity became adverse on the same scale. This created yet another situation full of inherent tensions.

Nor was Prost's baptism an easy one. In his first race, Long Beach 15 March 1981, Andrea De Cesaris (Prost's replacement at Marlboro McLaren) nudged him at the start, he spun and was out. Already.

In Brazil two weeks later he qualified fifth fastest, Arnoux eighth but it was a wet race. On lap 20 Prost moved out to take Pironi (Ferrari), Pironi moved out of the way, spun in a puddle and punted Prost off. He was eighth then.

In Argentina two weeks after that his luck changed. He was third, 49.98 seconds behind the winner, Piquet (Brabham), but got nothing in Imola, nothing in Zolder, nothing in Monaco, nothing in Spain where Villeneuve tapped him early on and he ran third with the front of the car disfigured – 'superbly', as someone noted – until even he could control it no longer and he slid off. The French Grand Prix at Dijon was next, centre-point of a season for Renault except the race, wherever it would be, where they won the World Championship later on . . .

Arnoux took pole, then Watson, then Prost and the start was unique: Arnoux claimed that the light went to red, flicked to green, flicked to red again, flicked to green again. He responded to the first green, braked at the second red and was engulfed by the pack. Prost tracked Piquet and was seven seconds behind when a cloudburst stopped it. At the re-start Prost vanished into the distance winning it on aggregate from Watson by 2.29 seconds.

'To an outsider this victory could seem to be the best but not to me', Prost says. 'It was certainly the most important for the rest of my career. I often say that the one I've just won is the most important but some are more important than others. After this first one I knew I could do it again, my mentality changed and from that day every start was taken with the objective of winning.'

This is a significant shift in any driver's thinking and the most astonishing example remains Nigel Mansell who drove seventy-three times before he won (Prost had taken nineteen). Suddenly in Belgium in 1985 Mansell (Williams) was second, won Brands Hatch three weeks later and South Africa two weeks after that. Peter Warr, Mansell's team manager when he had been at Lotus, has a theory about this: when you have done it once you have also learned how to take the pressure, control a race and there is a psychological point, too. You have proved all this to yourself, answered questions about yourself and you do not have to worry about that any more. You know how to do it again. If Prost felt any need for confirmation he did not have long to wait. He led in Britain, Germany and Austria and then won Holland, won Italy, was second in the final race, Las Vegas. He ended in sight of the Championship itself:

Nelson Piquet	50
Carlos Reutemann	49
Alan Jones	46
Alain Prost	43

Arnoux was ninth on 11 points, which can hardly have lessened the tension.

The season of '82 was drawn into many dimensions, tragedy and bitter, brutal pathos threaded through it. Arnoux took pole in South Africa but Prost won, Prost took pole in Brazil and won, Lauda – lured back to McLaren by Dennis – took Long Beach (it was not a turbo track), Pironi took San Marino from Villeneuve in dubious circumstances – Villeneuve, the number one driver at Ferrari trusted Pironi not to nip by at the end when Villeneuve could not respond. The old number one and number two driver tension again. Two weeks later Villeneuve was dead, killed in qualifying at Zolder and many who knew and treasured the man have never quite recovered from this. Patrese won Monaco, Watson won Detroit, Piquet won Canada where a young Italian, Ricardo Paletti was killed at the start, Pironi won Holland, Lauda won in Britain; and they came to the French Grand Prix at Paul Ricard, 25 July. This race lives on in bitterness, dispute and controversy. No other words will do. It also lives on in contradictory statements.

'Arnoux didn't keep his word', Jean Sage will say. 'Arnoux proposed that OK if I am leading the race and Prost has more points than me in the Championship [he did, 19–4] and has still a good chance to win the Championship I'll let him win. He said that in front of Larrousse and me and that's why I personally put the pit board out towards the end to remind him. I stood there holding it because I didn't understand what he was doing, because he wasn't keeping his word. We did not impose this on Arnoux, it was his proposition.'

René Arnoux is vehement. 'I think that you have to understand that when you're talking about a sport and also two top drivers in the same team they must work together to make the team progress. It is in the interests of both drivers. If one driver doesn't accept having at his side another driver who is as fast, who can win races . . . well, you can't ask the team to tell the other driver to let you past. For a driver to reach Formula One he must have won all the disciplines before, Formula Renault, Formula Three, Formula Two, he must be a winner and then all of a sudden you say to this winner: tomorrow you let the other guy pass you if the case is this or if the case is that. It is a major error on the part of the director of a sporting team.

'That is not the case if you have a number one and a number two but Prost and I were engaged with the same status. At Ricard I didn't propose anything, they asked me if the case eventually arose to let him past – but nobody could imagine I would have a thirty-second lead by mid-race.'

What happened is starkly simple: Arnoux took pole, Prost alongside him on the front row, Arnoux got away in the lead but was swamped by Patrese and Piquet in the Brabhams, Prost running fourth. Patrese's engine blew but Piquet pulled away from Arnoux at a second a lap until his engine blew, too. That was lap 24 of fifty-four and Arnoux led Prost by ten seconds. Worst for Prost he had lost a side-skirt and that directly affected the pace he could sustain.

Lap	Arnoux	Prost
25	1:44.359	1:46.265
26	1:44.170	1:44.637
27	1:44.103	1:44.578
28	1:44.351	1:45.536
29	1:44.052	1:44.950
30	1:43.651	1:44.198

'I showed René a signal to let Alain through on *five* occasions – ten, nine, five, three and two laps before the end', Sage said immediately after the race. The count-down:

Lap	Arnoux	Prost
44	1:44.264	1:44.004
45	1:44.027	1:44.088
46	1:44.470	1:43.752
47	1:44.832	1:44.290
48	1:44.725	1:44.126
49	1:44.979	1:44.244
50	1:44.403	1:44.174
51	1:44.664	1:44.894
52	1:45.336	1:44.371
53	1:45.254	1:44.907
54	1:46.679	1:44.842

Arnoux crossed the line 17.308 seconds ahead of Prost and it was a very popular victory. Arnoux had an earthiness about him, the common touch almost, which made people identify themselves with him, he had had a long run of ill-luck – he had not actually won a race since South Africa in 1980 – and in terms of merit on the day had done it squarely, no nonsense. There was fallout at varying levels.

The great world beyond Formula One was frankly puzzled, imagining in its innocence that races were supposed to be won by the fastest driver who got home first; for Arnoux the situation became untenable and he would not stay for 1983; Prost meanwhile, filling up his car at a petrol station on the way home, was mistaken by the attendant for Arnoux. The attendant congratulated him and said, in effect, 'That shows that so-and-so Prost.' Prost did not dare proffer his credit card – it had his name on it, of course, and all would have been revealed – but paid cash instead and fled.

The irony is that Prost himself neither instigated the supposed agreement nor would have done. He says that a senior member of Renault's overall management and Larrousse 'without me asked René Arnoux if he was leading the race that eventually we'd do a team race and he'd let me win for the perspective of the World Championship. René Arnoux said yes and during the race we were first and second, they held out a pit board and he refused to comply. Perhaps I didn't react very well that day from the media point of view.'

'No, I don't regret anything about Ricard,' Arnoux will say, 'and if I was driving again tomorrow it would be the same. Me, I'd like to say something personal. If I had a place close to the heart of a team I would never go to the Sporting Director and ask that another driver should help me to win the Championship. Never. I know how a driver's mind works and on the day when he can win a Grand Prix he will. OK, if there had been say three races left to the Championship that might have been different but it was only mid-season, there was a chance for him to win the Championship but it was minimal. If there had been a situation for the last race perhaps I would have played for the team – but I say perhaps. People don't know what happens deep within a team and it's not always rosy. It's difficult to say, "OK, I'll play a role for Renault" [rather than yourself] although we were being paid by Renault. You would also need to do a season in harmony, correct in terms of human relationships, for you to accept it and if all that doesn't happen it is harder to accept. The situation became intolerable and I left.'

'Immediately after,' Sage says, 'it was a complete split between them. It was very, very, very difficult to hold the team together and the problem is that after the race I made a big mistake – but I don't regret making it. I went to Prost and I said, "I'm sorry but you know the situation exactly, you're not happy and I agree with you but there's nothing which could be done", and Arnoux saw that and it was not only a split between Prost and Arnoux but between myself and Arnoux. Arnoux started to be very aggressive to me on some occasions.

'Arnoux starting talking to Ferrari. I discussed many points with Marco Piccinini [of Ferrari] about Arnoux leaving us to join them and one time Arnoux said, "It's not true, Sage never discussed anything with Ferrari", but I did. Arnoux said, "I did it all by myself and Sage should stay with his frying pans" – something very rude.'

The harmony, if it had ever existed in any meaningful way, was gone.

And now tragedy stalked Formula One again. We come to Hockenheim, to the untimed session on the Saturday morning, to a circuit under heavy rain, and to Didier Pironi doing a sequence of the fast laps which drivers often did to prepare themselves and their car in case the race on the morrow was wet, too.

Pironi was on his fourth lap and coming down the straight towards the stadium which is a snakelike uncoiling of the track between heavy concrete stands originally constructed for Hitler's rallies. But he was still on the straight, emerging from the chicane halfway along it. Cars churned spray and amongst it Pironi saw the Williams of Derek Daly to the far right of the track. Pironi made an understandable assumption: Daly had seen him and moved over there to allow him safely through.

Pironi was wrong.

Prost was on the left of the track concealed in the spray and slowing to come into the pits at perhaps 120 miles an hour. Daly had moved right to overtake him. Pironi could not see Prost at all and went hammer down for what his assumption led him to believe was open space on Daly's left. He may not even have glimpsed Prost's Renault at all because he was doing at least 165 miles an hour, maybe more. Pironi's left-front wheel hit Prost's right-rear, the Ferrari was pitched into the air striking in its trajectory Prost's crash helmet.

'I felt helpless', Prost would say. 'Didier was going much quicker than me and his car actually overtook me *in the air*. It landed gearbox first in front of me then bounced away somersaulting down the road. It was terrible. I was worried about hitting him because I had hardly any braking. The right-rear corner was gone from my car.'

The Ferrari was destroyed, Pironi was trapped and one of his feet almost severed.

I remember the ethereal quietness which settled on Hockenheim that morning, of how people spoke in whispers or an excited gabble, pursuing the latest rumour and nobody knew, nobody really knew. Sports journalists are entitled to wonder quite why they have chosen to cover this sport and journalists are not risking their lives. For the drivers, coming after Villeneuve and Paletti, it was as if they were living a long nightmare. It altered Alain Prost.

'I can guarantee you', he would say almost a decade later, 'that Pironi's car went straight on into the air, almost *thirty metres* up. It landed on its rear then on its front and it was cut in two. It was absolutely atrocious and since that day I have guarded an incredible memory of what wet conditions mean.' In the years to come it would guide him to withdraw from at least two wet races and say very publicly why he had withdrawn.

Tambay won Germany, De Angelis won Austria, Prost was second behind Rosberg in Switzerland, Arnoux won Italy at Monza – and made a great show of stirring the crowd from the winner's balcony because they knew he was coming to Ferrari and, from the noises they were making, seemed to regard this Renault victory as really theirs – Prost was fourth in Las Vegas, Rosberg fifth to take the Championship from Pironi and Watson.

Las Vegas was of course Arnoux's final race for Renault. In the first qualifying session he was quickest, then Alboreto (Tyrrell), Cheever (Talbot-Ligier), Prost. 'Suddenly,' Sage says, 'two minutes before the end of the second session, Prost did the pole lap from Arnoux and I said, "Oh yes, this is fantastic." Arnoux came and grabbed me by the lapels of my jacket and said, "You won't agree, but you like Prost more than me." I said, "Just think for a moment. We were first and fourth, now we're first and second – so you'd prefer to be ahead of Prost but only in second place rather than have Prost in first place for the team? Are you joking?" If it had been Arnoux on pole it would have been the same. He was very, very aggressive.'

Before we leave 1982, a couple of reflections. The first is from Arnoux, who began my interview by saying, 'I will not speak of Alain Prost because I spent that year with him at Renault and I can't say it passed well, unfortunately.' I pointed out that in Prost's book he says all this has healed and their relationship is one of 'comradeship and mutual respect.'

Arnoux replied: 'Our relations are good morning, good night and it stops there. He certainly doesn't want to have me for a friend. I don't say I detest Prost but he is someone who doesn't bring anything to me and I don't bring anything to him. I've known him for a long period and I regret nothing. There are people who like me and people who don't like me and it's the same in all walks of life.' However, at the conclusion of the interview Arnoux said: 'Alain is a very great driver with a strong character – because if he didn't have that he wouldn't be where he is.' A nice tribute and an accurate one, too.

Keke Rosberg, who can bristle about all sorts of things and who, detaching himself from the tragic undercurrents of '82 to discuss the racing part of it, says, 'When Alain was at Renault we were frequently racing against each other, don't forget we "met" each other very, very often. People tell me it was a bad season of racing but it wasn't. The maximum amount of wins that season was two [Prost 2, Lauda 2, Pironi 2, Arnoux 2, Watson 2, Patrese, Piquet, Tambay, De Angelis, Rosberg, Alboreto all 1]. You went to the races and a lot of people could have won them and that's what it's about. I always got along with Alain.'

As the man said, some people like you, some people don't.

During the close season skirts were banned. These skirts, invented by Colin Chapman, were simplicity itself and yet fundamentally altered Formula One. A thin strip was fixed to each side of a car running front to back and this strip trailed along the ground. Air rushing at the car was compressed under it because it could not escape through the sides: the skirts acted as a seal.

The air *sucked* the car to the ground and the faster the car was travelling the greater the suction. This became so great in corners that steering the car through by touch and feel was no longer possible. The driver aimed the car and it stayed exactly there. Suspensions vanished, which gave the drivers the sensation that they were rock-breaking; cornering speeds alarmed everyone, particularly drivers who hoped to God they had aimed the car in the right place. If they had not it was too late. The skirts were alarming in another way. If a car left the ground the seal was broken and they acted in reverse, forcing it further up. The driver became a pilot.

'Now the skirts have gone the pleasure of driving has come back', Prost said in 1983. 'For me the cars are more difficult to drive because they demand more concentration. They are more . . .

amusing. It is better now because it is the skill of the driver which counts.'

This was one aspect of the season and there would be many others. Prost would now be partnered by Eddie Cheever, the 'sour-faced' American we originally met in karting. Cheever had first driven Formula One in 1978 and reached Renault via Hesketh, Osella, Tyrrell and Ligier. Looking back on the relationship Cheever would say, 'Prost is stunningly fast, an exceptionally talented driver and a very hard worker. Among the people I've been associated with there's no one who even comes close to him. Watch him through any slow corner and it's like he's bedding in the brakes. There's hardly any change in the car's pitch or attitude because he's so unbelievably delicate on the throttle.'

'Cheever is a very nice man,' Sage says, 'but I think we made a mistake because he was one second slower than Prost, one and a half seconds and Cheever never accepted it. They had exactly the same cars – exactly the same cars. You'd open the gearbox after a race. Prost's was perfect but Cheever's destroyed. And when he was breaking the car – because he had many, many breakdowns – he said, "You are not giving me the same car as you are giving to Prost." ' Tensions again, tensions, tensions, tensions.

Prost was seventh in Brazil, eleventh in Long Beach, won France, was second at Imola, third at Monaco, won Belgium. He led the Championship with 28 points, Piquet 24, Tambay 23, Rosberg 16. Cheever, joint seventh, had only 8 points. France had begun to anticipate its first World Champion and the package remained very Gallic, French car, French engine, French tyres, all put together by a French team back by Elf.

In the background, in great secrecy, there was another tension. Prost had what are described by a former member of that team as 'personal pressures, private problems'. The law of privacy is rigid and terrifying in France and even when the secret was out no word was written about it. We come back to the question posed in the opening chapter of this book: how far, in painting a portrait of a man, are you entitled to pursue him? To the bedroom door or beyond?

I believe that, as Canadian Prime Minister, Pierre Trudeau, once said, 'the Government has no business being in the nation's bedrooms', and precious few other people have either; but when this has a direct effect on a man's career, a material, almost measurable effect, it must become a legitimate subject. How else can you evaluate the career, paint the portrait if it is not to be warts and all?

There is another constriction. The biographer can hurt bystanders by describing such things and what about their rights? As with car crashes, innocent people feel the full impact, too. In the paragraph which follows the innocent are, I hope and trust, fully protected.

Some time in the summer of 1983 – probably June or July – Alain Prost became involved with a person close to the team. At first virtually nobody knew and assumed, as the pressure inevitably increased after mid-season when the run-in to the Championship began, that it was this which was affecting him. No doubt it did. It affects every man in differing ways and in differing degrees; what compounded it were the 'private problems'. To what degree this affected the run-in we shall never know but many do not question that it did. End of paragraph.

He genuinely disliked Detroit and finished eighth there, the car was down on power in Canada where he brought it home fifth, he won Silverstone, won Austria. Prost 51, Piquet 37, Arnoux 34, Tambay 31, Cheever still seventh but now on 17.

Holland was a head-to-head, Piquet on pole cleanly away, Prost easing past Cheever and following. It stayed like that until lap 42 when both cars approached the horseshoe corner called Tarzan, a favourite overtaking place because it was at the end of the start–finish straight. Whoever got there first or had the guts to dive inside took the corner.

Prost made what he describes as a 'classical attack'. Piquet moved towards the middle of the track, Prost hugging its rim did dive inside. He was virtually alongside Piquet. The Renault hit a bump, rose a fraction at the rear and as he braked the rear wheels locked, the car twitched, he held that with opposite lock and now the car twitched the other way, into Piquet. The specific point of contact: Prost's front-left wheel.

By now wisps of smoke were coming from all four of Prost's tyres, momentary wisps from Piquet's front tyres and both cars plunged straight ahead, out of the horseshoe. Prost was on the other rim of the track somehow holding the car but Piquet was pitched across the wide run-off area, struck a tyre wall and came to rest out of the race. Prost continued but the car was damaged and he plunged off himself a few moments later. 'It was my fault with Nelson,' Prost would say, 'but I don't understand why it happened. He gave me enough room and I was not braking extra hard.'

The admission of guilt (Prost was genuinely 'upset' about what he had done) stands as evidence of the frankness we have come to know so well; and stands as a rebuff of Tyler Alexander, too. What astonished Formula One was that Prost had actually made a mistake. It was so rare as to be memorable, so rare that it is still discussed and in its context then it had a strong bearing on the World Championship because if he had won that was 9 points, Piquet 6 for second. Now neither got anything except a walk back to the pits.

Other tensions, too. Renault were not at all happy about the fuel Brabham were using.

Three races remained, the next at Monza. Arnoux, a firm favourite among the Ferrari faithful, had moved into second place, Prost 51, Arnoux 43, Piquet and Tambay 37. All four could win the Championship but Monza, a place of raw emotion which drew some of the baser elements of Milan to witness it, would always be a specific pressure-point. The legacy of Prost and Arnoux at Renault in 1982 remained and those events had not necessarily endeared Prost to France. Now Arnoux chased Prost for the Championship in a Ferrari at Monza.

This is what Sage told me at the time of a test session at Monza a few weeks before the Italian Grand Prix: 'It's going to be bad for Arnoux because the crowd is so excited. He told me he was afraid of the Italians' (presumably in case something happened which made them riot). Sage added that the crowd had thrown bottles at Prost's car and laid straw on the track to try and make it skid off. I found it difficult to believe. He assured me it was true.

Prost started to receive threats to his life, threats of kidnapping. The President of France's bodyguard, three very rugged gentlemen, were brought to Monza to protect him for the Grand Prix and despite the team trying to pass this off in a jocular sort of way (they would, wouldn't they?) Prost was clearly feeling it. A memory of that drifts back: one bodyguard, sheer as a cliff-face and seemingly constructed of boulders, walking side by side with him, and him unshaven, withdrawn, lips pursed and I thought: "People who win World Championships do not look like this." There was too the factor of the 'private problems' and no reasonable person could avoid making the judgement that they did not help.

Renault began to try and 'shield him' (Sage's words) from anything and everything except actually driving the car. At Monza – anticlimax. Prost's turbo went while Piquet was winning the race and Arnoux finishing second. Prost 51, Arnoux 49, Piquet 46, Tambay 40.

At the European Grand Prix at Brands Hatch, Piquet won again, Prost 6.571 seconds behind, Tambay's brakes failed so he was out of the Championship while Arnoux, who spun and limped in ninth, had only a mathematical chance. Prost 57, Piquet 55, Arnoux 49.

Tambay had signed to replace Cheever at Renault for 1984 and during the run-in of 1983 was savouring the prospect. This is Tambay's tribute to Prost. 'He bites his finger-nails so deeply that it must be very painful for him but he cannot stop it. I mean, he's just concentrating on his job all the time. He has an approach to everything – as Senna does, but in a different way – which triggers everybody up to another level of intensity; he has a way of approach which creates pressure in other people, a way of looking at things, analysing things technically which is completely different to other people.

'I was going to be in the same team as him, I was really looking forward to that because I would have learnt a tremendous amount from him. I could feel this during the last months of 1983 when we were talking about being team-mates. He was calling me up every other day, every three days and we were already discussing technically what the next car would be and he was already working on his relationship with me on the phone. His approach was completely different to any team-mates I had had up to that point,' (and Tambay had been in Formula One since 1977, not counting racing in the United States too).

But now, moving towards Kyalami and the South African Grand Prix, 15 October, Tambay faced an ambivalent race, his last for Ferrari where his present team-mate Arnoux still clung to that mathematical chance. Prost faced no ambivalence and neither did Piquet. Nor did Arnoux. All needed to win the race.

The day before qualifying, the Formula One world gathered at Kyalami, a track set in bleached countryside a comfortable drive from Johannesburg. Prost was there still looking haunted, hunched at a table under an awning talking urgently with some technicians.

Sage, seeing us (I was walking by with Derick Allsop, another British journalist), rose and hurried to us and said, '*Please* don't bother him now. *Please* leave him alone.' It was a poignant if understandable moment, since neither Sage nor Prost nor indeed the rest of the Renault team were reclusive by inclination. Looking back on it now Sage says, 'I tried to protect him all the time. Yes, of course there was much, much pressure but not from the Company. There was pressure from the situation itself: of being in a position to win or not win the Championship.'

We motored off to a nearby hotel called the Kyalami Ranch where people had draped themselves round the pool and surrendered to the sun. 'Where's Piquet?' we wondered. A photographer jerked a thumb up towards the first-floor windows. 'Having a nap', the photographer said. And that was the second poignant moment.

By this time just about every French journalist who could put pen to paper was either at the track, searching for his luggage at Jan Smuts airport or in the air on their way to it. There were rumours that Renault had pre-purchased full-page advertisements in just about every French periodical to salute the victory and all that that would mean; certainly, as Prost would tell John Barnard at a later moment, they expected to win and that was the attitude they took. Here is Barnard: 'It was interesting listening to Alain's views. Flying down to South Africa they'd already won. They were talking about, "We'll sandbag it through practice, we'll just hold back a bit in practice, and then when we win we'll cross the line in a certain way and this is how it's going to be." This was their concern. Typically French, I suppose.'

It wasn't the impression I was getting.

Journalists can easily miss matters of moment, though, and to demonstrate this on the first day of qualifying Arnoux stopped somewhere on the circuit – an electrical fault – clambered out and persuaded the marshals the Ferrari was in a dangerous position, please push it out of the way. They pushed it over his foot. A little while later I was making my way through the pit when I saw him seated with the foot in a bucket of cold water. I had no idea what had happened and when I enquired after his health he said something very rude indeed. Arnoux however would start the race.

Qualifying, day one: Tambay, Piquet, Prost, Arnoux. Day two: Piquet, Patrese, Tambay, Arnoux, Rosberg, Mansell, Winkelhock, De Cesaris, De Angelis, Prost . . .

He was not unduly concerned. The Brabhams and Ferraris had more power down the long straight in qualifying but the race would be different. Sandbagging? Maybe, maybe not. The race was not different. Piquet, on half-tanks for initial speed, vanished into the Veldt and crossed the line to complete the opening lap two seconds ahead of his team-mate Patrese, Prost fifth; and Piquet turned the screw, stretched the lead, stretched it, stretched it. Prost, his boost pressure falling, was helpless. He cajoled his way up to third when the race was nearly ten laps old but surrendered even that to Lauda (Marlboro McLaren) on lap 17, would regain third when Lauda pitted for tyres on lap 33 and cover no more than two further laps. The turbo had gone. Piquet cruised to the Championship comfy as you like, allowing Patrese to win and De Cesaris to finish second. Third place was ample. Arnoux had long, long gone, lap 9, engine . . .

There was a rumour that BMW in Munich started making telephone calls to just about every French periodical saying, 'We understand you have recently vacated space for full-page advertisements. We'd like to place one for Piquet and Brabham and the World Championship – oh, and BMW . . . '

The fallout was as sharp as shrapnel.

'It was really bad for everybody,' Sage says, 'because the year before we had nearly been World Champions. If only we had finished the Austrian Grand Prix of 1982. Alain had been leading all the race and four laps before the end the electrical engine on the fuel pump broke. You look at what a difference nine points would have made in 1982 and then you think that Keke Rosberg only won Dijon because a skirt broke when Alain was leading . . . so you can imagine after Kyalami in 1983 it was really bad.'

The mistake at Zandvoort and the three points over Piquet was costing and hurting that night of 15 October. Final table: Piquet 59, Prost 57, Arnoux 49, Tambay 40, Cheever sixth, 22.

Prost flew back to Paris, John Watson flew back to London – Watson who was still with McLaren and had had a strange season finishing equal with Cheever.

'There had not', he says, 'been any negotiation, any discussion about the following year except on the plane coming back from South Africa when McLaren's only comment was: "Well, I suppose we are going to have to sit down and discuss it with you." [These are not encouraging words.] I said, "Yes, anytime you like." After that it was fate if you like.'

The week after Kyalami, Renault fired Alain Prost.

8

THE COURTESY CAR

> If you said to Alain, 'Listen, I really need to talk to you all of the night', you've got it, no problems.
>
> JOHN BARNARD

The Rat was suspicious. He need not have been. 'I've had fantastic relationships with John Watson, with Keke Rosberg, with Stefan Johansson and with Niki Lauda certainly but the only one who taught me something, who dominated his subject, was Lauda.' Thus Prost on The Living Legend, known to one and all as The Rat because somehow his face looked like that.

Lauda had begun in 1971, survived an horrific fire at the Nürburgring in 1976, survived four seasons at Ferrari, won the World Championship in 1975 and 1977 and in Canada in 1979 had suddenly walked away. Prost, who was there, might – as we have seen – have inherited that Brabham seat for the race and the next, Watkins Glen, but didn't.

Ron Dennis persuaded Lauda back in 1982 but McLaren had no turbo and except for rare moments he and John Watson panted along behind picking up what they could.

Sometimes it was frankly bizarre. At Long Beach in 1983 Watson qualified twenty-second and Lauda twenty-third and this on a street circuit where overtaking was not, let us say, easy. Watson won the race from Lauda and only Arnoux was on the same lap. (I chanced upon Watson in his hotel afterwards and before I could say anything he said, 'Don't ask me, I don't understand it either.') This was the

The face – and the eyes – of 1984.

The photographer's favourite vantage point, and an image famous all over the world: the harbour at Monaco. Here Prost is moving towards a third place in 1983.

(*l-r*) Ron Dennis, Prost and Niki Lauda, and no pictures now please, although here it is.

In 1984, he won Hockenheim from Lauda by 3.149 seconds. They were given wreaths then, before sponsors objected that wreaths obscured the view of the logos on the driving overalls...

The place where the nightmare is strongest, Monaco in the wet. This is how Prost coped in the McLaren in 1984, the race which remains controversial.

The carcass of the McLaren at Zolder in 1984, the last Belgian Grand Prix to be held there. Prost's distributor went after only five laps.

(*Insert opposite*) The European Grand Prix at Brands Hatch in 1985 where he was fourth – enough to give him his first World Championship.

The full contour of Druids horseshoe, Brands Hatch 1985 – and to savour it, look at the car behind him.

Rio 1985 and a mountain to climb all season long to his first World Championship.

Leading Lauda in 1985 – 'a fast son of a bitch,' Lauda would say.

Prost, just taller than four tyres, 1986.

Preparing for action with the mighty Detroit Renaissance Centre looming behind.

Victory at Monaco in 1986, his 'hat trick'. And an irony, too. Both Senna and Keke Rosberg would be future team-mates.

The majesty of Monaco, 1986, but don't book into the hotel behind unless you've as much money as Prost.

man who on the flight back from Johannesburg had heard those disquieting words about re-signing for 1984.

'We'd had these situations like Long Beach and Wattie just streaked past Lauda as if there was no tomorrow', Barnard says. 'With all these things in his mind he ended up after the season saying, "Niki's getting three million dollars or whatever and I'm not even getting a million, what's going on? I've raced as well, if not better, in many cases than Niki. I want the same money."

'But then you get into it, it's not just how you drive a racing car, it's who you are, what sort of name you are and that's very, very difficult. Lauda's Lauda and Watson's Watson and it's almost impossible to explain that to somebody without hurting their feelings. In a way it's like stardom. What makes a star? Who the hell knows? But once you're there you're there. This wrangling was going on and then suddenly Marlboro in Switzerland phoned and said: "Alain Prost just walked into our office, he's not working for Renault any more, do you want him?" The reply was, "Yes, please."

'In those days Marlboro used to take care of the drivers, it wasn't part of the team budget so you couldn't pass up a deal like that. He had turbo experience which was very valuable and you've got to remember that all these guys need some time, they need experience to read the race properly – to understand when they need to push, how they need to push. You've got to remember the times like at Zandvoort when he tangled with Piquet, all these things he had been through. He didn't just turn up as Professor Prost, he'd been a wild kid at some points but he had an unbelievable talent and now experience.'

Watson is not and can never be bitter because it is not contained within his nature. 'I came back from South Africa on the Saturday, Alain did also, he was dragged into a meeting on Sunday in Paris with Renault and was told he was fired. On the Monday he speaks to Marlboro and says: "Can you get me into Ferrari? I've been fired." They said: "Bloody hell, no we can't but maybe we can do something at McLaren." Alain said, "But you've got John and Niki at McLaren." They said, "Niki is there under contract but John's contract is up. We can get you into McLaren."

'I think Renault was a very destructive period for him. He won lots of races but he didn't win a Championship and he ought to have done. The marketing division of Renault basically wore the guy out, he was having to do far, far too many things and it was at the time when motor racing was becoming demanding: testing was more and more important, the evolution of the cars was equally important.'

Renault, incidentally, are vehement about how much promotional work Prost was actually asked to do and one of their employees made the careful calculation that during 1983 he did three sessions of one hour each and no more; but that because he felt he was being overloaded they produced 'huge posters' and plastered them all over France bearing the legend 'All the Company is behind the driver', as a way of getting publicity while taking the pressure off him; and that when the posters went up Prost was not asked to do any more.

However, 'When he was actually booted out he came to McLaren and he was punchy', Watson says. 'It took him the best part of a season to unwind as a person and as a racing driver and then go on to become truly great. I think Ron Dennis would have had a bargain with Prost whatever he cost. My statement is: he got a bargain with Prost. He got my place, yes, but that is a motor racing fact of life.'

'It was a shock for me, yes, because it was a drawback', Tambay says. 'What is very strange is that at the end of 1983 he may not have become a megastar. Why it happened is very awkward [the 'personal problems']. It's something that is very strange, why he was kicked away from Renault. There is a hell of a night going on in Lausanne [Marlboro] where Prost is all day there dumping on Watson. It was the end of Watson and the beginning of Alain Prost. I am sure he would not have created his forty-four victories without that little happening on the eve of 1984. I think it's very important to talk about that but I don't know how one can talk about it. But that's the real story, that's the way it happened.

'I wonder if Alain had been in the team with me during 1984 would he have been able to go the distance with the fuel just by being Alain Prost? [Renault had a chronic consumption problem and new regulations limited each car to 220 litres.] He would probably have been in the same situation as me because at the start of the season we were the best team to be in contention with McLaren but in the first race, Brazil, I ran out before the end, the second race, South Africa, I ran out six laps before the end . . .'

This is no more than a tantalizing footnote to the story of what might have been and what might not have been.

Now moving into 1984 McLaren had turbo engines (first run by Lauda at Zandvoort, 1983, with the comment, 'Thank God!') and now The Rat is casting his suspicious glances. 'I did not know him at all before 1984', Lauda says. 'I never had a problem with him and maybe that was partly psychological. I'd been at McLaren, I was developing the Porsche engine and it was my baby. Maybe too it was because he wanted to learn. But I think he's a difficult character to be honest. I've watched him over the years and he's a moaner, he is not a good politician, he has a lot of problems in his private life. I never had a problem with his character because we had – how do you say? – a different level of understanding. There was no friction. We were always intelligent enough not to fight because we talked to each other and we kept to that through two years, no aggravation at all but I know that many other people have had aggravation, his friends, his Ferrari team [in 1991] and so on and I don't understand it in a man of his class and speed and knowledge. It's unnecessary to moan because he doesn't do himself any good.'

'When they started working together,' Barnard says, 'they benefited from each other. For sure it sent Niki into a tizz because Alain always pulled half a second on him in qualifying and he just couldn't handle that. Niki said, "I don't know, I just don't understand this, I don't know how the guy does it, I must go away and think about it." That's what Niki said to me: "Jesus, I just don't understand this guy." For Niki, you could calculate how to do it. There had to be a set of circumstances, a set of vehicle dynamics which allowed Alain to go quicker and he had to figure out what that was.

'To be fair Niki did improve in qualifying during the second half of the season but he never quite got there. On the racing side Niki had the advantage of being a former World Champion, of always looking at the overall picture. He had the ability to say, "This is not my race, there's no point in risking the machinery and my neck for nothing." '

'He came into the team, he was good, he blew me off in practice every time and I could only win the Championship because of my experience', Lauda says. 'I decided where my limit was because we had this stupid turbo situation with 800 horsepower in the races but you qualified with 1500. He could adapt himself much better for one flying lap on qualifying tyres with that sort of power. He took more chances and he was doing the right thing and I wasn't prepared to – so he was the better man in that department, no question about it. After three races trying to outqualify him I failed and I said to myself, "OK, no problem, I concentrate on the races." I was using both practice days just to set my car up for the race, test the tyres and so on and he was qualifying like crazy.'

'I spoke to Alain a lot in the early McLaren days,' Brian Hart says, 'mainly in the era when he was able to outqualify Niki. He had what very few drivers have, this all-round ability. It was quite difficult to set up the turbo car and he did a very good job – it was a new car, the TAG engine, it was complicated and even worse when you had to concentrate on the engine as well, let alone the car. As an example, in the turbo era the biggest problem was the so-called boost lag because that seriously affected the car. Prost and The Rat quickly got it into a manner where they could compensate for that. They not only knew how to accelerate but what to tell the Porsche engineers.'

Prost began his reincarnated career at McLaren with a rush. He won Brazil – mentally important after the Renault trauma – and was second in South Africa, did not finish at Zolder, won Imola, was out of the points in France where Lauda drove 'my best race of the year. I drove like crazy and passed Tambay and stupid things like that. Prost developed in me the mood to take chances again.'

At Monte Carlo Prost was leading in a thunderstorm. We already know his views about running at all in the wet and his memory of Pironi's crash – Pironi still crippled this June day in 1984.

On lap 31 of seventy-seven of the Monaco Grand Prix, with Senna (Toleman) catching him fast and Stefan Bellof (Tyrrell) catching Senna, Prost was thinking of self-preservation more than places. Time and again he gesticulated as he crossed the line for the race to be stopped now. The man responsible, Jacky Ickx, did. A thunderstorm of its own broke. Ickx, as it seemed, had given the race to Prost by stopping it then because in another lap or two Senna would have been past him. Ickx's integrity was darkly imputed, though not by Senna.

'It was a controversial decision', Ickx says. 'Some people thought it was right, some people didn't. For a long time Senna felt it was a mistake because he thought he could win the race. I understand his disappointment very well because he was a master of the wet. He had the race in hand, he was sure to win it and suddenly it disappeared – so he was upset for a number of years. Now that's all gone, we can talk, it's over. Prost felt he was going to lose the race and had probably already given up when suddenly it was handed to him on a silver plate.

'Why did I stop it when I did? Have you been in the control tower at Monaco? You are sitting in a room with all the connections to marshals, fire people, doctors. You have twenty television screens, you can follow the Grand Prix on TV. You don't face the spectators, you don't face the team managers, you don't face the drivers: the only thing you can see with your own eyes is the corner by the swimming pool.

'But on the screens you see everything, people going off here, spinning there, having a major problem in another place and there is a moment where overall you have to judge if the race is safe or not. That is a personal judgement and that's why I was Clerk of the Course: not to follow the little rules and this and that, but the opposite – to have somebody experienced to decide whether or not you stop. I believe the most important thing for a driver is to have a career lasting twenty years. I am against the idea of having accidents freely, having people hurt and I don't even speak about killing themselves.

'I decided in the circumstances that was enough, that that was it. These questions – Senna would have had a go at taking Prost, Bellof would have had a go at taking Senna – did not interfere with my decision. I never had them in mind. I was only taking care of the fact that I could see on my screens a lot of spins everywhere, there had been accidents already. I could not see Prost gesturing to stop it.

'You will never know what could have happened. You can always say two laps later it would have been Senna, three laps later it would have been Senna, they would all still have been there on the track. I don't know. Formula One is terribly difficult to drive in wet conditions. Monaco is not so fast but it's impossibly narrow. The job of a professional driver is already dangerous. You don't have to push it beyond that. Prost and I spoke several times afterwards. He said to stop the race was a benediction.'

Monaco was to prove a mixed benediction. Only half points were awarded and that would cost Prost.

'It was a great season', Barnard says. 'We all had a good time. For me the problem was that in the middle it was virtually a foregone conclusion that Niki or Alain would be World Champion – didn't matter to me which – and I was already worried about what I was going to do for a follow-up in 1985. I started to step back from it because by mid-season you've virtually done all your modifications or they are already in the pipe-line. It began to play on my mind that I had to come up with another step.'

Finishing positions from Monaco: Lauda 2, Prost 3 in Canada, Prost 4 following Detroit, Lauda 1 at Brands Hatch, Prost 1, Lauda 2 at Hockenheim, Lauda 1 in Austria ('I had him right under control', Lauda says. 'I think after the first lap I was three seconds in the lead.'), Prost 1, Lauda 2 at Zandvoort, Lauda 1 at Monza.

'Towards the end', Barnard says, 'there was a little bit of one driver going off in this corner with his engineer and the other going off in that corner with his engineer. That was a thing we definitely didn't want to happen and we forced the situation very, very carefully to keep it together.

'Certain engineers with certain characters were susceptible to that kind of – what shall we say? – being sucked in by the megastar and stroked and worked on. Once you've got the split you've got a real problem because it doesn't end there, it goes right through the whole team. We didn't have a briefing afterwards when everybody wasn't there, drivers, engineers, but there were a few times when I had to come along and say, "*Hey, out of that corner, get back in.*" '

Two races to run, Europe at the Nürburgring and Portugal at Estoril. Approaching the Nürburgring Lauda had 63 points, Prost 52½. (This Nürburgring was hewn out of a part of the old circuit and was utterly dissimilar to it. It had been designed by computers as well as humans with an eye upon total safety and as such neutered. Of course newspapers made enormous play of the return of Lauda to the place where he had almost died in the fire so long before but Lauda being Lauda wondered what all the fuss was about, the fire was a different era, the track was a different track.)

Prost won the race, Lauda a cautious fourth after a spin and consequent damage to his tyres. Lauda 66, Prost 61½ with a bonus two days later when FISA announced that Tyrrell were being docked all their points so far for a car-weight infringement. Martin Brundle lost his second place at Detroit and that moved Prost from fifth to fourth.

Lauda needed only second place at Estoril, however. 'The most fantastic race for me was Portugal', Barnard says. 'Niki really cocked-up the qualifying and was eleventh, a disaster, while Alain was on the front row. That race was when Niki almost drove over the top, it was the one time I saw him go to the point where he was passing and taking chances which in my book were on the ragged edge of you can't do that and get away with it. Niki had the ability to change like that when he needed to and I think that's what Alain learnt.'

Prost won, Lauda, travelling like a man possessed, second, and that was The Rat's third Championship. 'Because I'd approached qualifying during the season in the way that I had,' Lauda says, 'most of the time I had a better race set-up so I could win it by half a point, simple as that.' In the mêlée after it – a wild scrummage of media hawks fighting each other to get near him (blows were exchanged) – Lauda was heard to say that in 1985 he would help Prost win it. The Rat did not say such things lightly.

'I must say he was very sad. I remember him on the podium next to me and he couldn't believe the whole thing,' Lauda says, 'because he had been ready for the Championship. I did not show my happiness to him, I stayed calm, I knew what he was feeling and I told him – before his eyes got wet – "Hey, you're good, don't worry, next year you're going to be World Champion." I took the heat out of him. I could easily have said, "Here you bastard, I've got you, I'm the Champion", but I didn't. And the next year he proved me right.'

That night at Estoril, Lauda would write in his autobiography, *To Hell and Back* (Stanley Paul), 'I finally managed to dash back to the hotel, change and keep a dinner date with Mansour Ojjeh, who had hired an entire restaurant. There were no speeches or other such formalities. It was all good fun. Prost – who had turned up from Monaco with Stephanie – started to relax again.'

It was the same Stephanie who had been there on 10 May 1970 watching the Monaco Grand Prix with her mother and father from the Royal Box, as it were, the same Stephanie who had now become a friend of the teenager who had been on holiday that day, there in a stand surrounded by those noisy Italians.

There were lessons from 1984. 'Drivers like Prost, I believe, think through the race on the Saturday night before it and the various permutations of where they'll be and it's all locked in their brains', Hart says. 'So by about lap 15 *he'll* drop out soon, *he's* hard on tyres and so on. It's just amazing. They'll probably never tell you but I believe that's how far ahead they think. Now Prost thinks the race right the way through. Niki was a strategist, as Prost would subsequently become. Prost learnt an awful lot that first year, that honed him, that completed the education. It took away the impetuousness. He thought: "Hang on a minute, The Rat wins from all the way back there", and then he started to do the same. He's a very special driver, a very special man.'

'He is very prudent now in the way he drives', Watson says. 'In overtaking he will not go for gaps which are not there. I remember watching in 1984 and thinking, "Bloody hell, what is he doing?" He'd be leading a race by an Irish mile and passing people and exposing himself to their mistakes, and that is what happens. It is not that you necessarily make a mistake but you rely on – and trust – the judgement of somebody else too much. What Alain has learnt is to keep himself out of trouble.'

These lessons absorbed, 1985 was no trouble – while Lauda had nothing but trouble. 'It was a really strange one', Barnard says. 'The Rat seemed to suck in Did Not Finishes like a sponge, it was just unbelievable. I really don't understand that. I think fairly early in 1985 he had made up his mind he was going to retire. Whatever it was, something went, something said, "That's it, I've had enough." '

Yes. 'It was a combination of various things', Lauda says. 'Prost drove a perfect season, there was no question. I had to take a decision whether to come to Vienna and work or not because Lauda Air was getting bigger and bigger, we'd bought new aeroplanes, so there was a transition in my life anyway. I took the decision to retire in the middle of the year. My best race was Zeltweg [the Austrian Grand Prix in August]. I announced my retirement on the Saturday morning there and on the Sunday I had no more pressure. Then you realize that when you are retiring all you want to do is stay alive, because the worst thing is to make that decision and then . . . '

'The 1985 car wasn't as good as the 1984. We'd had another regulation change over the winter and we'd all lost downforce, there wasn't a huge amount happening to the engine. There were new electronics, stuff like that, but not a fantastic step', Barnard says.

'On the 1985 car I tried to get more information on geometry and I played around with that in a fairly extreme way. This was the thing which kept changing on the car throughout the year. I started off with one lot of roll centres and anti-squats, things like this, and I moved along down the line. What I was trying to do – although I didn't actually tell anybody this at the time – was establish the effect of each individual thing. "Well," people could say, "why didn't you do it in testing?" But for me testing those sorts of things at one circuit is not good enough. You need a range of circuits, the street race, the fast track to get the full picture. I did formulate a picture over the year, I learnt a lot about car reactions versus geometry changes. We kept moving the rear geometry all the time but the basic package was still efficient, still a good race car in as much as we had turbo engines, we had a fuel limit, you still had to use tyres efficiently and that was another key: Alain was brilliant on tyres.

'He was brilliant looking after tyres, brilliant on telling you when a tyre was going off – in telling you after a ten-lap test that this tyre is going to be too strong for the race or too soft or whatever. His ability to separate the tyre feel and chassis data was unbelievable, to me anyway. I had never met anybody who could separate it that well.

'You just don't get the chance to do long runs. You say, "Fill her up and do ten laps", and that's fine, you know, ten laps will tell you X but the race might be sixty or seventy laps and you've got to know if the tyres will go the whole distance. Have they stabilized? Are they going to stay like that? At evaluating he was one of the best.'

The Rat meanwhile suddenly produced a storming race at Zandvoort, beating Prost by 0.232 of a second. They simply fled round nose to tail, Prost attacking, hammering, pressing and The Rat resisting. Thereby hangs a tale. 'I had a friend called Herbert Volker, who I wrote my books with', Lauda says. 'I think I was twelfth on the grid and Herbert is a dreamer but a very good journalist. He said to me on the grid, "You're going to win today." I said, "*Are you crazy? You must be. I'll try and finish as well as I can but I will take no chances because I have to stay alive.*" Herbert looked at me and he couldn't believe it.

'Piquet screws up his start and suddenly I was fifth on the first lap. At that instant I remembered Herbert's eyes and I said to myself: "OK, I give it a go for Herbert, simple as this." I raced. The problem was I got the wrong tyres during my pit stop. There was a mix-up and they gave me hard tyres, Prost had better tyres and I was handicapped by that at the end. I had to fight to keep him off. This was my problem: I had a hard tyre on the left rear instead of a soft one, I was driving like crazy but I still couldn't go as quickly as I wanted to. There were no team orders so it was logical that if I could win I would win – but I didn't want to anyway, I was finished with racing and really I only won because of Herbert. Otherwise I wouldn't have cared.'

Afterwards Lauda muttered that sure he would help Prost win the Championship as he had said, but not yet, surely? Five races remained and anyway he judged Prost good enough to win it for himself, unaided. Prost 56, Alboreto (Ferrari) 53, De Angelis (Lotus) 30 . . . Lauda 14.

Prost won Italy, Alboreto got nothing and they came to Spa.

'It was wet and dry, one of those deals at Spa,' Barnard says, 'and the car wasn't a 100 per cent and we'd played around with it, we'd changed the front bar on the line – this kind of thing – and in the end the car was actually going quite well. He finished third. You stand there watching the times lap by lap and you get the feeling, "Hang on a minute, this guy's cruising." Afterwards he said, "Look, I'm sorry. It was quite possible to win the race but I wasn't going to take that risk. I wanted the points for the World Championship so I thought: safe to finish third, I'll do that." So he was reading the season for the Championship and that was why he did it.

'It sounds simple but when you know these guys you know that when the old helmet goes on and they form up on the grid so many have nothing in their heads but the first corner and how they're going to blast past somebody and that's it. The good guys, they've got a little room inside the old head which is still chundling away thinking about the Championship, thinking about the race, thinking about how it's going to play itself out.'

Round Spa's undulating curves and sweepers Prost had demonstrated all the perspective and the prudence of The Rat himself. It is called self-denial and that inescapably involves self-control. When you add it to great talent you have an awesome partnership and it wins all manner of things, including World Championships.

The consummation was Brands Hatch at the European Grand Prix, the race after Spa. Alboreto's engine blew making enough smoke to suggest that a chemical factory had caught fire and Prost, who had had a desperate start, fourteenth after he took to the grass to miss Rosberg (Williams), motored home fourth. Prost 72, Alboreto 53 and with only two races left he was uncatchable.

As Fred Opert said all those years ago, France wanted a World Champion and they got one although, that day at Brands Hatch, Prost pointed out quietly that it had taken an English team (and a German engine) to get him there and added, mischievously, that he has no particularly strong 'nationalistic feelings' and was just as happy to win it in England.

The Rat retired and was replaced by a certain Keijo Rosberg (better known as Keke) for 1986. 'I always got along well with Alain. The link was that through my days at Williams I had a good relationship with Mansour Ojjeh [whose company Techniques d'Avant Garde, TAG for short, had backed Williams and was now backing McLaren]. So even when I was at Williams we spent some time socially although Formula One people didn't really get together that many times. But we did in Rio after the race, places like that.

'I got to know the fun-loving side of Alain. He was great. I don't know if he's still great [1991] – that's nothing to do with the racing or the pressures, it's just getting old. We've all changed, we're not hooligans like we were when we were twenty. It's the ageing process whether you're a racing driver or not.

'I wasn't going into a pressure situation at all in 1986. I left Williams, I wanted to drive for McLaren and I knew I was going to retire after one year. I wanted to see another top team, I wanted to work with McLaren, I knew Ron well, I knew a lot of people in the team, Mansour, Alain and so forth so to me it was fairly easy to go there – except John Barnard didn't really make my arrival easy, or didn't want to help me a lot; but then I didn't see much of him because he didn't go to a lot of races so it really didn't matter to me.'

Rosberg crashed the car in testing at Rio which did not exactly endear him to Barnard. 'I am not', Rosberg says defensively – or as defensively as he will ever get – 'very well known for crashing cars and I hadn't done many laps when it got away from me at the long corner because the car was just so different from what I was used to. If you ask me what my memory of my McLaren year was, it is understeer with capital letters. I got the chassis right three times, the Brands Hatch test in June, the German Grand Prix and Australia.

'I got on with Prost very well because I was naïve enough not to get into politics and look at what was going on. Afterwards I believe – without ever having discussed this with anybody – that I was testing all the management systems for the new TAG engine. I can't find any other explanation for why I didn't finish so many of the races and Alain did. I know we had some new sensors. I was running second in Austria and the sensors failed.

'I finished five races that year out of sixteen, Niki had finished three the year before and Prost wins the Championship both years. That didn't change our relationship because I was so convinced the team were doing the best they could for me except they wouldn't change the chassis the way I felt I wanted it and I would have expected a little bit more, not support, but guidance from Alain.

'Every time I asked him: "Would you go through there with a car understeering so much?" he said "Yes." I didn't do anything about it but he knew it killed me. That's a hard thing to say but every time he would be quicker. Alain is a very clever guy, which I had never been in that way, he did the right thing. I would never have done it. That's my problem.

'I was the new boy, he was winning races and when I said they'd got to do something about the understeer they didn't because Alain was still winning races. If Alain had said it they would have done it, so therefore you must be a little bit careful about saying it's hard. It isn't. Alain wasn't listening for it.

'There's another thing. Alain's driving style is unique. The way he entered corners, especially in the turbo-charged era, was completely different to anybody else. There was maybe one guy who used a similar technique and that was Niki. The technique was entering very, very deep into the corners, braking into the corners where the classic racing driver brakes on the straight, slows the car and flicks into the corner – you always brake in a straight line – but with his feel and confidence he would brake into the corner. The way I braked you couldn't turn the steering wheel, it wouldn't turn. He felt and fed the brakes into the corner, I'd hit them so hard they'd be just before the limit of where wheels lock. I once made a concerted effort to drive just like him but I couldn't, in the same way that I'm right-handed and I just can't write with my left. That's a similar kind of change.

'If a car understeers for you it understeers for you. You can try it backwards, forwards, sideways, whatever and it understeers for you. It was so dominant that I would say the whole year I only used 75 per cent of my potential in the car.'

We're back to the tensions.

'This', Barnard says, 'is Keke having a go at me. There was a time when we went testing at Brands and I said, "Right, I'm going to do whatever it takes to make it work the way you want." We went up and up and up on the front suspension. What Keke wanted was the front end stiff, not moving, enough bite aerodynamically to make it turn, yank the steering wheel fast and hard and the front goes pop, turns in and your boot is back on the power. It was very, very difficult to do that and keep the back end in. You could get the front to work like that but the back would step out and before you knew where you were you were going backwards into the fence.

'On top of all that I never felt it was right. I always wanted the car to drive off the back wheel. The thing that John Watson, for example, liked was a tremendously rearward centre of pressure and a car which was completely glued at the back, very sensitive at the front so you could come into a corner, turn the steering wheel and the car stayed glued while it turned in off the back wheel. With Rosberg it was the other way around: "I want to come in, brake as hard as I can, yank the front in and the back has got to follow." The way our aerodynamics had derived we just couldn't do it. Prost could drive it like that . . .

'Keke tried to copy Prost, that was the amazing thing. We talked about it and said, "Well you can drive it like Alain because fundamentally I think it's a better racing car the way it is." But Keke could not seem to cope with the careful turn-in. You get a Prost set-up car, a guy comes along tries to jam it into the corner, jumps on the brakes, down goes the front, whoops, the centre of pressure is immediately thrown to the front and round comes the back.

'Alain was able to lead it in, gently bring it in, turn the wheel gently enough. You've got to remember we're talking here about such fine limits, such fine changes that you could stand and watch and you'd have a hell of a job to see any difference on the track – but Alain was able to get it into the corner and then open the throttle, boom, and that's it, he was away, gone.

'I suppose the root problem was that I still didn't feel what Keke wanted was *right*: running a car with that much of a forward centre of pressure just to make the front end work, because you had effectively wrecked the car mechanically.

'It ended up with Keke and me in different directions. It's so personal, the whole thing's about interactions between people, driver to engineer, engineer to his engineer, to mechanics, the management, it's all about personal relationships. If a bloke says something has got to be black and you say you understand but it's got to be white, at the end of the day you can like the guy, you can have a good time, you can go out to dinner with him but fundamentally you think: that guy is wrong. And he is thinking: you are wrong. A compromise? This is the old problem, isn't it? How many compromises do you make in this business and get away with it? The less, the better off you are.'

Rosberg's plight was not helped by Prost winning Imola, Monaco and Austria, although both Williams drivers, Mansell and Piquet, were going very strongly and by Adelaide, the climax, Prost had to win the Australian Grand Prix and Mansell finish fourth or lower. Piquet was not so well placed. Wherever he finished, it had to be ahead of Prost, who comforted himself with the thought that Rosberg would fly round the streets of Adelaide and drive for the team.

'Ron had not spoken about it', Rosberg says. 'I went to Alain before it started and I said, "I'll race the life out of you because my car is fantastic but if you need me at the end I'll help you in every way I can." Those were exactly the words. No more were exchanged and I would have done it because the nicest way for me to leave Formula One was to be quick but also to show that I considered the Championship very valuable for my team. If they had asked me if I could have done a better job the answer would have been I could not. Who cares if you retire with X wins or Y wins on your list? But if I could go to the team in the evening and say, "Well, that's my last race for you and you won the Championship even though I had to finish seventeenth to do it", I could leave content.' This is the driver making an equation with himself: the final equation.

Mansell took the lead followed by Senna and Piquet, who both went by very quickly – Mansell could play the percentages, drive tactically – and before the end of lap 1 Rosberg went by too ... flying. As they crossed the line Prost was fifth. Now Rosberg attacked Adelaide. On lap 7 he overtook Piquet with savage, decisive ferocity while Prost slipped past Senna to position himself fourth: Rosberg, Piquet, Mansell, Prost. But Rosberg was driving away from the whole lot of them.

Prost took Mansell and closed on Piquet but that was a problem. Prost seemed quicker through the corners, was braking later and was certainly no slower than the Williams on the straights but lacked the decisive power to overtake. On lap 23 Piquet suddenly spun, gathered it – coming back on to the track in a thunderous rotation which nearly sent Thierry Boutsen (Arrows) into orbit – and set off again: Rosberg, Prost, Mansell, Piquet.

Rosberg continued to drive away and on lap 32 Prost limped slowly towards the pits. 'I got a puncture on my right front tyre. It happened on the long straight and gave me a small moment when it began to go down. Three laps before I had had a small touch with Berger (Benetton) when I lapped him at the hairpin but I don't think that caused the problem. It was simply a normal puncture.'

The history of motor sport, no less, would record this as the puncture with most abnormal consequences.

It was tricky to get the jack under because the car had sunk as the tyre deflated and the pit stop lasted 17 seconds. Prost emerged fourth but 20 seconds behind Mansell and Piquet and 50 seconds behind Rosberg. You cannot seriously hope to win a race never mind a World Championship from there. This posed a logistical problem for Rosberg which was growing into a moral dilemma. 'I had that lead and I was running 2.8 boost. Normally we used to run 3.2 so I was being very, very conservative. Our minimum setting was 2.8. I was thinking that everybody would be thinking Rosberg is going to run like crazy because it's his last race. I was also thinking to myself: You're crazy to retire if it's this easy because it's the easiest race of your life.'

While these thought processes were consolidating themselves in the interesting and combative mind of Rosberg, Goodyear examined the tyres which had just been taken off Prost's car and concluded that leaving aside the puncture which anything could have caused, the wear of the tyres would, should, enable the other Goodyear runners – Rosberg and Mansell and Piquet – to finish the race without making stops for fresh ones.

Rosberg began mentally rehearsing quite how he could contrive to get Prost to win. 'I was trying to work this out: if it comes to it *how* should I do it? Am I going to stop *demonstratively* in front of the line and *wait* for him and risk stalling the engine there? What then? So Alain goes by and wins but maybe Nigel goes by in second or third place and takes the Championship. I said to myself: no, no, oh, no, no this is *not* the way to do it. I would have had to stop there for half a minute. *Imagine* the situation and you know if the bloody thing *stalls* . . .

'So, much as I might have been tempted, I *couldn't* because it was too risky. I decided to slow down progressively and let Alain catch me at the right rate of seconds per lap while *making it very clear* that I was slowing down. That was part of the exercise.

'Then I was on the straight, sixth gear and anybody who's done a lot of work of crank cases and pistons and rods and stuff like that knows that when an engine goes it goes *grrrrr*, a huge vibration. This noise comes, I declutch immediately because I'm afraid it's going to lock the engine, I roll to a stop, take a big breath and I get out of the car. I look under it and I think *that's strange*, no oil like there would be.'

Rosberg, standing on the edge of the track near the car, gave Prost a thumbs up and walked away from Grand Prix racing after 114 races and a World Championship of his own in 1982. He would not drive again. But the consequences of his career were not over, not at all over.

A global television audience of several hundred million had seen what Rosberg had not. A rear tyre had broken up and the *grrrrr* was it flapping against the body of the McLaren. Goodyear, watching among the global audience, knew instantly that if that had happened to Rosberg it meant Mansell and Piquet were both vulnerable: mortally vulnerable.

Prost, with the advantage of new tyres, was catching the two Williams. Rosberg had gone on lap 63 and now Prost was with Mansell, probing, looking. A lap after Rosberg's exit he went through and was within sight of Piquet. That was academic. Mansell had an enormous cushion over Johansson in fourth place. Mansell could cruise it.

Along the straight Mansell's rear left tyre exploded and he was wrestling the car to save his life at 200 miles an hour. Somehow – in one of the great feats of car control – he aimed it into the run-off area at the end of the straight where, slowed now, its nose nudged a concrete wall. Piquet's on-board radio crackled: "Come in for tyres now, now, now."

Rosberg, all unknowing, was walking back to the pits.

Spectator: 'The same thing's just happened to Mansell.'

Rosberg: '*What, blown his engine?*'

Spectator: 'No, no, no, rear tyre just like you.'

Rosberg: '*Like me?*'

Rosberg (talking to himself): '*Hang on a second, the engine might have been running when I got out of the car!*' It was late for that now, too late. 'Don't forget with the noise of the wind and everything you don't *hear* if the engine is running while you're driving the car. *How can you?* And you ain't gonna check when you've stopped on the track because you're sure it's blown and you're gonna *get over the barrier fast*. Then you remember: *I don't think there was any oil*. I could have made it safely to the pits and probably finished the race.'

As Piquet peeled gracefully yet urgently on to the curving slip-road to the pits Prost surged by. Piquet was stationary for 8.38 seconds. It wasn't much, at this point in a race it was a hell of a good job by the mechanics, but it was too much. By the time Piquet had gunned the engine and was back out, the race had moved away from him taking the Championship with it. Specifically: after 67 laps the gap was 18.979. As if to emphasize it Prost went faster than he or anybody else had done in the whole race on lap 69 and now within a handful of laps a whole season would be decided. Piquet had to beat him.

Lap	Prost	Piquet	Gap
70	1:21.063	1:20.902	18.226
71	1:21.641	1:22.543	19.128
72	1:21.471	1:23.728	21.385
73	1:21.165	1:22.130	22.350

Later, from lap 78 through to the end, Prost would exercise all his caution and the gap tumbled down, 18.784, 17.394, 15.484,

11.114, finally as he crossed the line for the last time, 4.205. There was a reason, a nightmarish reason . . .

Rosberg: 'Everybody thought I was running *crazy* on fuel. Actually my fuel reading was the same as Alain's, they were both minus. We'd stopped disastrously during the season [Rosberg at Imola, both at Hockenheim] but I was running that minimum boost, 2.8, so I couldn't reverse the situation. Alain finished the race with minus five on the clock.' Prost's gauge had moved to zero two laps before the end.

At the instant of victory he slowed the McLaren immediately, clambered out, leapt clean into the air, danced a jig of delight – truly – waved to the crowd, shook his head in stark disbelief, plucked his gloves off and flung them on to the bodywork of the car as if to say: *Well what about that*?

'You know,' he would say, 'this was a special race in special circumstances. Normally I would have lifted off a little bit and taken care of the fuel but because of the Championship I thought: "OK, I go [smile], I win, or I stop and I let Nelson win." I think the computer was wrong [smile] and I finished with minus five. [Pause.] This is a fantastic Championship because 1982, 1983 and 1984 I lost by four points, two points, half a point, but it's really a shame for Nigel. I know how it is to lose by such a small amount.' It was well put, sincerely put and they were the words of a big man.

Piquet, exhibiting a prudence of his own, said that to pit for tyres was absolutely the right decision. He was after all still among the living.

Prost, looking extremely calm and with no trace of sweat even, murmured softly that he didn't think he'd made a major error all season.

Rosberg: 'Ron used to rent a disco at an hotel for the team on the last night of the season and we all went there. I'd given my wife a diamond-studded brooch in the shape of a helmet just after the race and said, "That's it." All that was left was to go home.'

Before Adelaide, Rosberg had given Nigel Roebuck an interview musing on leaving Formula One. In it Rosberg said Prost was the best driver he had ever seen. Roebuck queried that with, 'Are you really sure?' Rosberg sprang down Roebuck's throat thus: 'No, I don't think so, I know so.' Now in mid-season 1991 – when I interviewed Rosberg – he said: 'Overall as a professional driver, that is to say looking at it in all aspects, I still do. He was smart, a lot smarter than me in how to go about it in terms of what helps me, what doesn't help somebody else. He would take all those things into account but let's not forget I was retiring. I wasn't going any place but home and that makes the situation very, very different. I don't know where the hiccup came but I personally think it was John Barnard, who thought: *Who the hell is this Rosberg? Never spoken to him, don't know him. Why does he want to change my car?*'

Barnard himself was leaving too, for Ferrari. He was and would remain a Prost fan, if I may use such an undecorous term about a man whose cars dominated large tracts of the 1980s – courtesy cars in fact. This is his reflection and it is by no means a diversion, although it embraces other things: 'I don't think analytical ability is something you are born with and anyway I think it's determination, how hard you want to push yourself and everyone around you. It's this all-consuming desire: you've got to win, you've got to beat the other guy. All the other things follow.

'If you need to spend four hours thinking about the set-up when you get out of the car or five hours or all night – playing through your mind what you did five races ago when you changed this bar and that wing – that's what you do. It's not fantastically complicated.

'The ability to remember is a gift. The big thing with Alain was this: we'd go testing and quite often we'd take one step, one change to a bar or a spring – a close change, we're not talking about doubling the spring rate, we're talking about a 5 per cent change, very, very tiny – and he'd say, "Ah yes, this one does this, that one does that", and it was logged away. That was the important thing. In his mind all these little changes were separated from how the engine and tyres felt, were analysed, stored.

'There is always a point where you have to make a change and you have no real chance of testing it. The [dreaded] favourite is after Saturday qualifying and the car is still not a 100 per cent right so you have to make a change and that's it. That was Alain's key. "OK," he could say, "we make this change or that change and I know what the car will do, I know the car will be all right. I can tell you what the car is going to do." We'd make the change and we weren't worried because he wasn't worried. And it would work and he was right . . .

'He had this uncanny ability to store changes, it was almost like he had this little card-index in his head. Niki was a quick decision-maker. Almost before he got out of the car he'd focused his mind on what the problems were and what he was thinking of doing about them. Alain almost relived every metre of the track he had covered and the more laps he'd done the longer it took to relive it. To recall so many things which happened at high speed is a gift but it is also training. Training your mind.

'You have to have a natural skill to enable you to drive the car fast, then the mental discipline to separate one bit from another. All Formula One drivers can drive the car fast, they think they are putting their all in, they go through the de-brief, OK, have we finished? I'm happy to stay but really I'm off down to the beach or the hotel. That is the difference. If you said to Alain, "Listen, I really need to talk to you all of the night", you've got it, no problems.

'I suspect that Senna learnt that kind of approach from Alain and being Senna took it to the next step. "Ah, I can see how much recall he's got and, ah ha, I'm going to do more, I'm going to remember everything." That's all about the competition thing, isn't it?'

By winning the World Championship back-to-back, 1985 and 1986, Prost was now competing with history itself. Only two people had done it before, Jack Brabham (1959–60) and Juan Manuel Fangio (1954–5–6–7). It was the same Brabham who on that distant day in 1970 had hesitated over his braking at Gasworks Corner, Monte Carlo, and lost the race while the teenager in the stand was enjoying himself so much but dreaming of football.

For 1987, Prost was joined by Stefan Johansson, the affable Swede who cannot remember if he ever drove against him in karts but does remember he did in Formula Three. 'I don't have strong memories of him then because I didn't know him even to say hello to. I knew he was the man to beat on the Continent but I was racing in England and just doing the odd races there. I'd got to know him slightly in Formula One, we spoke a bit on occasions at the races. I didn't really get close to him until we drove together at McLaren. And at McLaren it was great.

'He struck me as very intelligent – well, maybe intelligent isn't the right word because I don't know how you define intelligence anyway, but his logic in the way he sets the car up, the way he treats the whole concept of driving is unique. I don't think Senna developed as a driver until he drove with Prost. I am sure he learned a lot just by watching, keeping his eyes open, seeing how Prost worked with the car. I certainly learned a lot and I improved in the way I set the car up, the way I thought about the car.

'There were all kinds of problems that year. Our engine was not performing as well as some of the others and because of that testing was minimized, especially chassis testing. It meant I personally did no testing whatsoever during the whole season, which obviously hampered my progress.

'As a team-mate he was totally honest. There was never ever, ever a problem about anything. I'm not holding any illusions about myself. I realize that I wasn't in the same category as him and I'm honest enough to admit that I wasn't. That didn't really take the pressure off me, no, not at all, in fact in some ways it made it worse because you tried to over-compensate: you try too hard, you make little mistakes here, little mistakes there which cost you half a second here, half a second there in qualifying and that's all the difference. You're not harmonious in your driving.

'It's difficult to single out one particular race when he drove like a master because he does it all the time. It's easier to pull a race out of your memory where he really didn't do a good job, and [reflective pause] I can't do that either! He does a good job virtually every race. I mean the guy's won forty-four races and he could have won another twenty or twenty-five if he hadn't had car problems and he's been so close to the Championship apart from the ones he's won that he could have been World Champion five or six times . . . '

There would be no hat trick in 1987. Prost won Brazil and Belgium early on, but the main body of the season fell away (it was a Piquet–Mansell–Williams year) and by Monza, Ron Dennis was announcing to the world that he had signed Ayrton Senna to replace Johansson for 1988 and that McLaren would have Honda engines.

The world would never be quite the same again.

Alain Prost was 'only' fourth in the World Championship of 1987, which did not prevent a poll in *Paris Match* placing him above Yves Montand and Jean-Paul Belmondo as the Frenchman they most envied. It was more than a consolation. It made him extremely and understandably proud. And anyway they only acted, he was for real.

9

THE TROUBLE WITH AYRTON

> Even before he joined McLaren I knew we were never going to be friends because our personalities are completely unalike. He is a very strange guy.
>
> ALAIN PROST

Mid-summer 1991 and Ron Dennis is seated on the first floor of the McLaren motorhome at Magny-Cours enacting what has become a ritual before the French Grand Prix. He is speaking to British journalists at a press conference which has two carefully constructed ground rules. These are that you can ask anything you want and the answers will be entirely governed by Dennis's own creed. That is, 'I will tell you the truth or I won't say anything.'

Question: Was it the biggest failure of your career when you couldn't make Prost and Senna live happily under the same roof?

Answer: I would go along with the biggest disappointment but I don't think I'd go along with biggest failure. [Self-deprecating smile.] I can give you bigger ones. But you're mixing issues here. If you're talking about the moment when they weren't going to work together then it is disappointing that it was not possible to have a more harmonious, stable relationship. Sometimes it was great, sometimes it was difficult, but don't mix that up with the period afterwards when they were going in different directions.

Question: Could any man on earth have held them together?

Answer: Any answer would be accurately perceived as pure ego on my part. I gave it my best shot and I'm not qualified to say more.

Ron Dennis, most rational of thinkers, remains slightly bemused, slightly unsure. Forgive him. We are in deep and dangerous waters in the company of very strong swimmers. Ayrton Senna joined Marlboro McLaren for the 1988 season and it was announced – as we have seen – at Monza during the 1987 Italian Grand Prix where simultaneously McLaren announced they would be powered by Honda engines. Although all this was done in a typically restrained way – Prost and Senna stood shoulder to shoulder amidst the trees of Monza's parkland smiling politely and any moment now everyone would say the right things – a potentially awkward epoch was being spawned which, in its culmination, would reach a wild, embittered, embattled siege of three men, Prost, Senna and Dennis, before it was finally and mercifully embalmed.

Foraging through memory you cannot find a parallel in any other sport because all else aside the consequences in racing cars are immeasurably greater.

You might cite the early days of Jimmy Connors and John McEnroe when Mr Connors was definitely not amused by the swearing, the shouting and the rest of it but they were, after all, only hitting a soft ball at each other; and that perhaps is a representative example of friction in other sports. Even in the infamous Bodyline cricket series when two England fast bowlers, Harold Larwood and Bill Voce, physically battered the Australians you have to remember that Larwood and Voce were on the same side and firm friends.

Perhaps the only true parallel in terms of potential consequences lasted 124 seconds on 22 June 1938 in New York. Max Schmeling, who was the Nazis' idea of an Aryan folkhero, had already beaten Joe Louis, a negro, for the heavyweight championship, this was the return bout and they do say that they found some of Schmeling's *teeth* in Louis's glove when it was done . . .

This is a pointed comparison to draw, Louis *v.* Schmeling and Senna *v.* Prost, but I do not shrink from it. There were moments as Prost and Senna moved towards their culmination when people genuinely feared catastrophe and once or twice that catastrophe was very close indeed. It would flow, perhaps inevitably, from this September day at Monza – although then of course people did mouth all the right things.

'I am sure you would like to know about the new partnership with Ayrton', Prost said. 'I think in the past we [McLaren] have shown we could have two equal number one drivers. I know that Ayrton is very professional and I will help him to integrate in the team. We have to work together but of course I will do my best to beat him on the track.'

'From a personal point of view,' Senna said, 'I am very happy to work with Alain: two top drivers working together can only make a team stronger.'

With hindsight you cannot miss the almost unbearable irony, although we have had plenty of irony in our story already. Who truly knows where it started to go wrong? Perhaps as early as the third race of 1988, Monaco. Prost won Brazil (Senna disqualified for changing to the spare car after a delayed start), Senna won San Marino from Prost; and they came to Monaco. Senna led comfortably until lap 67 when he had what motor racing calls 'brain fade' – his concentration lapsed and he banged the armco just before the tunnel, a mistake so cavernous to him that he felt it 'brought me closer to God.'

'I won', Prost will say, 'and at the gala that evening I made a small speech. I said it had been Ayrton's race but what had happened was all part of the game and I was very happy to win. Then Ron Dennis took the microphone and said that Ayrton had been fantastic and there must have been a problem with the car because he couldn't have made a mistake.' Prost felt this was over the top and also felt humiliated.

The very next race, Mexico, Prost decisively outdrove Senna to win by 7.104 seconds and this – although McLaren insiders have never been anxious to reveal it – had a profound affect on Senna who throughout his career had had to stretch his own credulity to believe that any man could beat him like that: fair and square. Perhaps there, too, it really started. Senna would dig even deeper into himself to make sure it did not happen again, this intolerable thing.

Around the two men gathered a form of tension which neither could avoid and most days it seemed to pursue them every waking moment: the Marlboro McLaren Honda was virtually unbeatable, Prost winning Mexico from Senna, Senna winning Canada from Prost, Senna winning Detroit from Prost, Prost winning France from Senna.

By Silverstone, Prost was insisting that he had to aim for perfection because Senna did, and Senna was insisting that he had to aim for perfection because Prost did; and however wary they were of each other was not revealed. No undercurrent had surfaced from the deep and dangerous waters – yet. Going into the British Grand Prix, Prost had 54 points, Senna 39. Senna won the race but it was so wet that Prost, who had handling problems, retired on lap 25; a voluntary retirement. 'It is', he said, 'my life and my judgement. I decided it wasn't worth going on.'

More privately Prost would expand on it, mentioning that the Open Championship had been stopped because of bad weather and if they did that for golf what was anybody doing letting racing cars go round in it? He explained graphically that you can see nothing and drive by ear, listening for the man in front to change down for a corner, hoping he reduces his speed consistently; memories in fact of Hockenheim and Pironi.

The French Press launched bitter attacks on him implying that his nerve had gone, his motivation – that all-too-common buzz word of Formula One – had gone too, although, as he says, 'I can live comfortably with people saying that.' His retirement at Silverstone underscored the man he had become. He had no fear whatsoever of saying it was too dangerous and he had chosen to leave the race and moreover he said it when he could legitimately have claimed the handling was the cause and no person except himself would have been any the wiser. But Prost is not like that; he was, and remains, his own man and as he has pointed out it is his life anyway, not yours. End of discussion.

Senna won Germany from Prost, Senna won Hungary from Prost, Senna won Belgium from Prost and now at Monza, Prost out-thought and then out-kidded Senna. The race would be tight on fuel, Prost had an engine problem from the start and sensed he couldn't finish. Instead he pushed Senna (who could not know of his problem) and forced Senna to respond, making Senna use more fuel than he wanted.

Prost did retire (involuntarily), while towards the very end Senna, markedly slower than the two Ferraris chasing him, had a crash with Jean-Louis Schlesser (Williams). No one has ever disclosed how much fuel he had left . . .

Portugal was a raw frightener but only after Prost had begun to apply psychological pressure. He put in a lap of 1:17.411 during the second session and promptly changed into civilian clothing, stood on the pit-lane wall with a purple pullover casually slung across his shoulders and watched the timing screens as if to say: there you are, Ayrton, beat that. Ayrton couldn't.

At the start of the race Prost moved over from the right and squeezed Senna who had to put two wheels on to the white rim of the track, and although Senna stayed on the power and took the lead at the first corner he was an angry man. Prost tracked him all round the circuit and they rounded the right-hander into the long start–finish straight. As they approached the line itself their speeds climbed towards 180 miles an hour. Senna was over to the left of the track. Prost darted to the right and Senna angled to the right, covering the move. They were now on the start–finish line and a milli-second after they had crossed it they were level but both over to the right of the track. Prost was squeezed, the pit-lane wall was a solid barrier running along next to the car and, in a sudden ripple-motion, everyone on that pit-lane wall sprang backwards. The cars were at the instant of colliding and worse, Prost seemed to hit a bump because his McLaren skipped towards that of Senna. For one frightful milli-second there could not have been more than 15 centimetres between the cars and quite possibly less.

They flicked apart, flicked together again but not so close this time. We are talking now about 30 centimetres between them.

They flicked apart again, Senna moving fast over to the left to get the best line for the first corner, Prost pursuing him there and once – another milli-second – made a feint towards him with the whole car, muscling Senna further over. Prost took the corner and the race, Senna sixth with handling problems.

Publicly Prost said: 'We didn't touch but we could have and then it would have been disaster. I don't understand manoeuvres like that. If we have to do things like that to win the World Championship frankly I don't care about it. And I'm going to tell him . . .'

Privately, in the motorhome, Prost beckoned Senna over and said very calmly and very quietly – which is the most devastating way to do it: 'Ayrton, I didn't realize you wanted the Championship that badly.'

But Ayrton did and by season's end Ayrton got it after a superb drive at Suzuka, Japan, although Prost was mercilessly punished for consistency, racking up 105 points (an all-time record) against Senna's 94. The deciding factor was that both drivers could only count their best eleven finishes and that left Senna with 90, Prost only 87. To put Prost's achievement into its true perspective here are the Championship winning totals from the start of the modern era within brackets the totals before deductions:

1950 Giuseppe Farina *30*; 1951 Juan-Manuel Fangio *31* (37, four best counting); 1952 Alberto Ascari *36* (52½); 1953 Ascari *34½* (46½); 1954 Fangio *42* (57); 1955 Fangio *40* (41, five best counting); 1956 Fangio *30* (33); 1957 Fangio *40* (46); 1958 Mike Hawthorn *42* (49, six best counting); 1959 Jack Brabham *31* (34, five best counting); 1960 Brabham *43*; 1961 Phil Hill *34* (38); 1962 Graham Hill *42* (52); 1963 Jim Clark *54* (73, six best counting); 1964 John Surtees *40*; 1965 Clark *54*; 1966 Brabham *42* (45); 1967 Denny Hulme *51*; 1968 Graham Hill *48*; 1969 Jackie Stewart *63*; 1970 Jochen Rindt *45*; 1971 Stewart *62*; 1972 Emerson Fittipaldi *61*; 1973 Stewart *71*; 1974 Fittipaldi *55*; 1975 Niki Lauda *64½*; 1976 James Hunt *69*; 1977 Lauda *72*; 1978 Mario Andretti *64*; 1979 Jody Scheckter *51* (60, four best from each half of season counting); 1980 Alan Jones *67* (71, five best from each half of season counting); 1981 Nelson Piquet *50*; 1982 Keke Rosberg *44*; 1983 Piquet *59*; 1984 Lauda *72*; 1985 Prost *73* (76, best eleven counting); 1986 Prost *72* (74); 1987 Piquet *73* (76).

Prost's 87 was more than any man had scored, even taking all the totals *before points had been deducted* except of course Senna himself this same season of 1988.

'What happened away from the track in 1988 was relatively normal', Prost will say. 'It was difficult but we did a season of sport without any real problem [except presumably Portugal]. You mustn't forget that it was me who let Senna come to McLaren, it's me who brought Honda to McLaren, it's me who discussed the contracts in Japan with Honda since the end of 1985 – and there are a lot of people who forget that. At McLaren I was living in a fantastic atmosphere. I had the possibility to say no to Senna coming but I thought that the team would need a driver of his talent when I stopped. I was had. On a human level it is difficult to accept that. What happened in 1989, before the start of the race at Imola, was that Senna said to me . . . '

What Senna said to Prost presaged the beginning of the end of the partnership and henceforth they would co-exist as strangers for almost a year and a half. Prost had been second behind Mansell in the first race of this season, Brazil, where Senna crashed, recovered and finished eleventh. Imola was next.

' . . . Senna said to me, as we'd often done before, "At the first corner let's both of us try and escape the others, neither of us will attack which one of us is in the lead and we'll start the race at the end of the first corner." Imola is a dangerous circuit notably braking after the start (for the first corner). He took advantage to overtake me since I was in the lead and thus he broke his word. I didn't go to the post-race press conference, I was fined 5,000 dollars for that by FISA, and for something where I felt I had been held up to ridicule.'

Imola and first and foremost the ghostly, nightmarish vision of Gerhard Berger's Ferrari losing control, churning itself into wreckage against the armco and bursting into a fireball. Berger survived with comparatively minor burns, something scarcely credible, and the race was re-started. Prost led, Senna took him under braking at the first corner and won it.

'At the second start,' Senna will say, 'he started a bit better than I did but I was in his slipstream, I gained speed because of that and I pulled out well before the braking point. My overtaking manoeuvre was thus begun, in my opinion, well before the first corner and as a consequence outside the terms of our agreement.'

In the matter of opinions, where we are back among the milliseconds, definitive judgements barely exist and rushing towards a corner at vast speeds you have to remember that one person's braking point may not be another's – and Senna has been called the last in a long line of demon brakers, meaning he does it later and more fearlessly. The corner was a right-hander but of more significance leading to a left-hander. Prost took the middle of the track before the right-hander and Senna went outside him, midway after the right-hander and by the left-hander Senna was full alongside but now of course the outside line had become the inside line. It was where you had an advantage for the left-hander.

On 23 April 1989, Senna finished the San Marino Grand Prix at Imola 40.225 seconds ahead of Prost. Between that and Monaco on 7 May, McLaren tested at a track in Wales called Pembrey. Dennis, who had known nothing of the no-overtaking accord, sought out Senna for an explanation and further explained that Prost had taken it very badly, was 'disgusted and wanted to stop driving'. All three met at Pembrey and Dennis 'exercised an enormous pressure on me [Senna]' to try and smooth things out. Senna did not find this 'correct but Ron insisted and said to me, "If you say sorry it's forgotten, everything's back in order." And I did it. It was stupid because it meant I had changed my mind on the concept of the accord and my overtaking move. I did it for the good of the team. The three of us were there with no other witnesses and Ron said, "This stays between us, we won't speak any more about it, OK?" And when I arrived at Monaco everyone was talking only about it. In acting as he did Alain wanted to make me culpable.'

What Prost did was give an interview to *L'Equipe* in which he said: 'I do not wish to drag McLaren into difficulties caused by the behaviour of Senna. McLaren has always been loyal to me. At a level of technical discussion I shall not close the door completely but for the rest I no longer wish to have any business with him. I appreciate honesty and he is not honest.' Prost had spoken to Dennis by telephone saying that although he wanted to stay with McLaren he thought it might be better if he joined another team or even stopped driving there and then.

Dennis, understandably on the defensive, confirmed that Senna had apologized at Pembrey and added the ominous words, 'The problem is now resolved.' Equally ominously, and retrospectively, Prost would say, 'A guy like Senna thrives on conflict.'

They moved uncomfortably through the season and by the French Grand Prix, Prost was clearly leaving. He did not 'lose any sleep' over the decision and now weighed several options including a possible drive for Guy Ligier, a possible drive for Jackie Oliver at Arrows, a foray into sportscars with Mercedes or, astonishingly, a year's sabbatical paid for by McLaren so that a) another team would not get him and b) he could come back.

At Monza, which Prost approached with 62 points, Senna 51, Prost began to make pointed complaints that he was not getting equal treatment. He was not mollified by the fact that he won the race: Senna had led to lap 44 of 53 before his engine blew and by then he had a lead of twenty seconds. On the podium Prost lowered the cup into the crowd so some unknown member of it got the ultimate souvenir to take home. Psychologically this was an interesting gesture, too. The Thursday before Monza Prost had announced he was leaving to join Ferrari.

'I must stress that this decision is genuinely the product of joint discussions between myself, Ron Dennis and Mansour Ojjeh', Prost said. 'As friends we have debted a range of options open to me for the future and have all kept each other fully informed.'

This cordiality was strained by Prost's assertions over equal treatment – Dennis himself was moved to mount a strong defence of the team's standards – and further strained when he lowered the trophy into the crowd because, as Dennis said, it did not belong to him; not to mention a further twist when Prost said his situation within the team had become impossible.

By Portugal, the next race, a statement had been hammered out which said bluntly, 'Alain deeply regrets the adverse publicity and the resulting embarrassment that have been caused by his actions. Honda and McLaren have accepted that these resulted from Alain's perception of his treatment by the team and were not made with malicious intent. Honda and McLaren have again reassured Alain, to his satisfaction, of their commitment to equality and will continue this policy regardless of Alain's move to another team for the 1990 season.'

Was this, and it is a question one is entitled to ask, a pre-emptive strike by Prost in case anyone, anywhere might seek to favour Senna but would no longer dare to do so because of the tidal wave of publicity Prost had already stirred from the deep waters? Was it simply that Prost was enraged (and suspicious) because Senna was faster? Prost answered that one himself by pointing out that while Senna might be faster he sure as hell was not almost two seconds faster, as he had been in the second qualifying session at Monza (1:23.720 against 1:25.510).

The thread in our story returns. Any suggestion of unfair play still enraged Prost as it had done all the way from karting. It violated something inside him.

That said, I will never forget the face of Ron Dennis as he leant against a wire-mesh fence at the rear of the paddock at Monza and explained, barely concealing his vehemence, how sophisticated the technology had become setting up a Formula One car for a driver, how each nuance was accommodated so that it was no longer a question of preparing two identical cars; but that each was prepared to the best of the team's ability for the man driving it. The whole good name of the company he had built to such a mighty force in motor racing was at stake, its ethos was equally at stake and there was no question of compromise in such matters; nor did Honda behave like that, nor – he was damn near hammering it out like Emile Zola himself – did Marlboro. End of discussion. But tensions, always tensions.

Paradoxically Senna collided with Mansell in Portugal, Prost finishing second and while Senna won Spain, Prost was third. 'This result was exactly what I was looking for', Prost said. He had 81 points, 76 counting, Senna had 60 and two races remained, Japan and Australia. Senna could fully count whatever he got in them, Prost dropping anything fourth or lower but that was hardly relevant. If Senna did not win the Japanese Grand Prix he had lost the Championship whatever Prost did or even if Prost did not bother to show up.

Interesting, that.

Before the start Prost said that 'many times before' he had left the door open for Senna rather than risk a crash but he did not propose to do it today.

Interesting, that.

Senna blew the start, Prost was off like a hare and it took Senna a long tract of the race to catch him. Prost knew as well as Senna that Senna had to win the race and Prost was not about to go back on what he had said.

When Senna did catch Prost he discovered that if two cars are evenly matched there is nowhere to overtake. Prost was steady, precise, controlled under the assault, Senna attacked each corner hard, wasn't afraid to slice into the apexes, hurl it over the kerbing – the line was totally different to that of Prost – and at each corner he would draw up a little, at the exit of each corner he would see Prost move away and the gap re-established.

This was the classical distillation of drama, one man pitted against another, one man's nerve against another man's ambition and it had moved too far and too fast to bear within it the nuances of give-and-take interplay between them. And like drama it was gaining in strength moment by moment – Prost seeming to skim the circuit, Senna seeming to bend the circuit in his hands – and somewhere into lap 42 or 43 or 44 it had become a hard thing, sheer and shorn and simple. The others, only twelve of them running now, might have been bit-players, might have had walk-on parts, might have loomed to be lapped and panicked, might have wrecked it; but they had been shed by the strength of movement and wherever they were on Suzuka's 3.641 miles they were not here, none of them as the two red-and-white cars hunted each other. It had a purity about it, the purity of isolated combat leading to something momentous. The anticipation gripped Suzuka like an iron fist.

On lap 44, Senna closed right up on Prost approaching the chicane. The approach: a graceful curve feeding them on to a very short straight feeding them into the chicane itself. The chicane: a 90-degree right, a flick into a 90-degree left and if you had the balls you might – might – find enough momentum from the graceful curve to slip inside just before you reached the mouth of the chicane. You would have to brake later, too, you would have to out-brake him. The reward: possession of the chicane, the race and very possibly the World Championship. This lap 44 Senna was close but not close enough.

Two laps later he was closer and flirted with the inside. Prost was over the left taking up position to turn into the mouth of the chicane. Senna could see in freeze frame: Prost a long way to the left and enough room – maybe, maybe, maybe – to get through if he had been even closer.

Interesting, that.

The problem: to get closer next time round.

Into the broad sweep of the start–finish straight they travelled, the strength gathering still, into the first curve where Senna was close, close, close, braking later than Prost again, through a left-right Senna tracking, the gap re-established, down through the undulating sweepers Senna closing again and at the hairpin Senna seemed to stab the snout of his McLaren towards Prost but Prost was already moving away . . .

Curves and corners and straights and rises and dips fled by, all seen in flickering images, channels of armco fled by, a timing device froze them at 0.520 seconds apart but that had no meaning any more. The gap was feet and inches, not time. And they came back to the graceful corner, Prost placing his McLaren to the rim of the kerbing to get round it, Senna riding the kerb hard – two wheels full on it. As he did a short, sharp shudder passed through the car from the kerbing; and they rushed at the chicane.

Prost moved far over left, left, left and the gap was there again. Prost angled the car towards the middle of the track, the turn-in position again, but Senna was coming hard at him, the distance between the two cars narrowing foot by foot, shrinking, vanishing. Senna moved full to the inside. He was travelling straight ahead. Prost turned in and the gap was gone. He turned across Senna. He turned across Senna very late. If he had done it twenty, thirty metres before, Senna would have had to follow him obediently through; but he hadn't . . .

Senna's gloved hands already had the steering wheel at an angle to follow the white-painted edge of the track into the chicane. His front nearside wheel was already feeling towards that white line.

The impact battered his car sideways, those hands now ramming the steering wheel the other way to try and straighten it, that front wheel already pitched on to the white line, a broken front spoiler rising like a shard of debris. The wheel was over the white line and on to kerbing, kerbing so high that it tilted the car at an angle; both cars were locked together, both helplessly flowing past the chicane towards a run-off area. One last time Senna churned the steering wheel to try and regain the track itself. It was too late. Five times Senna's yellow helmet juddered under the grind of running impact.

A gloved hand dipped to the gearknob and flicked it into neutral. They were travelling slowly now, were into the run-off area, were coasting gently to a halt. The gloved hand rose and touched the yellow crash helmet, a quite unconscious movement which might have meant anything, relief, anger, anything.

Prost gave Senna a wistful glance, unbuckled his seat belt and walked away while Senna now had both gloved hands out of the cockpit indicating for the marshals to give him a push. They did. They hauled the car back on to the track – itself an alarming moment, a motionless car bisecting the track and please God let none of the remaining twelve come at it now – they shoved it forward on to the run-off area again and the gloved hands were urging them to shove harder. Seven white-helmeted marshals did shove harder, a posse of them bending into the back of the car as they did it. The engine fired and Senna set off down the run-off area to rejoin the track at the far end of the chicane. Prost had his helmet off and, walking towards the pits at an even, purposeful pace, began to unbutton the front of his driving overalls. On his face: nothing.

Senna pitted for a new spoiler and set off to win the race. The moment Prost saw him go by – Prost still walking back – he wondered what was going on, was reassured when he was told that Senna had had a push, had rejoined beyond the chicane. Both were grounds for exclusion.

Senna was excluded, Senna reached for his lawyers and Prost said: 'I felt sure to win once I got into the lead and somehow I always thought the race would be decided one of two ways: either he would lead from the start or it would finish like this. I looked in my mirrors, saw where he was and thought he was too far back to try anything. He had been closer than that before and stayed behind. You know Ayrton's problem? He can't accept not winning and because of that he can't accept someone resisting his overtaking manoeuvres. Too many times he tries to intimidate people out of his way.

'A lot of times I have had to open the door, like in Canada or in Portugal in 1988 or Silverstone this year and if I hadn't we would have crashed like today. And I said before the race . . .

'The way he drives is very good and I must say he is fantastic, unbelievably quick but for me he is driving too hard and if you have

Stirling Moss, the old master himself, with the master of the 1980s. A portrait of two gentlemen.

Leading Senna out of the chicane at Suzuka in 1989, both drivers on their way to an infamous exit... at the chicane.

(*Above*) The new team-mate. Prost and Mansell confer at Hockenheim.

(*Right*) Making the sparks fly at Spa in 1990, where he was second to Senna.

(*Left*) Monkey business in Jerez, 1990, and pass the champagne please!

1

There would be a row at Hockenheim when – later – he met Senna at the chicane and vanished down the escape road.

(*Above*) The new circuit at Magny-Cours, 1991, and after a spirited but sensible drive Prost accepted second place behind Mansell.

two drivers like this in Formula One then you have an accident in every race. I'm very sorry to see it end like this.'

There is something you should know because it captures in the most simple yet graphic way the full extent of Marlboro McLaren Honda's predicament. After every qualifying session and race in a season Honda, in conjunction with McLaren and Marlboro, produce a special information sheet for journalists. It is extremely detailed, with times, positions, a break-down of any technical specifications and on-the-record quotes from both drivers plus perhaps words from Honda's Project Leader, Osamu Goto, and Ron Dennis giving the overview. It is done professionally, quickly and in several languages and serves two functions: immediate information and when all the sheets are bound at the end of the season (as Honda do) a day by day journal of record to keep. If you thumb through that year you come upon:

'*The team did not produce a press release after the Japanese Grand Prix on Sunday, October 22nd, 1989.*'

The deep waters had spawned a hurricane come in off the Sea of Japan.

Adelaide, where technically Senna could still win the Championship – if appeals against his exclusion at Suzuka were upheld – was a shambles, so wet that Prost did a single lap, pitted and got out of the car. 'I was happy when the race was finished that there had been no serious accident but on the other hand I wonder if that day it was necessary for a driver to be injured – not seriously of course, a wrist or an ankle – uniquely to make officials and drivers understand.' The memory of Pironi remained, Prost exercised an overall concern for driver safety and far from losing his nerve he was demonstrating that he had a bigger nerve than all the rest by doing what he did.

Thierry Boutsen won and Prost saw an interview Boutsen gave in which he said, 'At the end of the race it wasn't dangerous.' This is Prost's riposte: 'It's always easy to say that when you've won, easy to say it when you're sitting in an armchair, easy to say, "No, it wasn't dangerous." '

Prost walked away from the race at Adelaide and from McLaren after 6 years, 92 races, 30 wins, 458 points and now beyond question 3 World Championships. On lap 14 of the Australian Grand Prix Senna, going hard, struck the rear of Martin Brundle's Brabham and that was that, whatever happened to any appeals over Suzuka, whatever lawyers could conjure from the wreckage. Senna hit Brundle because Brundle was masked by a wall of spray, as Prost had been in the untimed session, Hockenheim, 7 August 1982.

Honda did produce a press release and made a stab at humour. Perhaps that was all there was left. They called the release the '*Australian Powerboat Grand Prix*' and it culminated in these words: '*Honda engineers were baffled by the appearance of fish swimming behind the screens of their telmetry monitors.*' Yes, fish in the eye of the hurricane.

Ron Dennis, who had long before taken a corporate decision that whatever Prost said McLaren would not react to it, would subsequently gaze back and say, 'How would I equate Senna and Prost? They are exactly the same with one possible exception, and that is what effect their national tendencies put on their approach. It means, for example, that if you take four nationalities and give them the same problem they might all come to the same solution but they will arrive there using completely different thought processes. When they were driving together I think Ayrton had more to prove than Alain and that reflected a little bit more in the level of commitment Ayrton was prepared to put into things like overtaking – so there was a difference there – but they were very much out of the same mould.'

This is Prost's postscript. 'I had no regrets about leaving McLaren. Everything I did in six years was positive and thus, no regrets. I constantly worked to have good relations with everybody. Or nearly. I left with my conscience at peace thanks to the certainty that I gave the best of myself.' Soon enough he would be saying: 'It is quite true there is a mythology which surrounds Ferrari. It makes a lot of kids and a lot of drivers dream but you must not be blinded by that. The Ferrari myth exists overall outside the team, it exists in people's hearts. The factory is like all other factories. What there is more of is passion.'

Someone wondered irreverently whether, instead of getting himself into the middle of this, he had been tempted to take McLaren's sabbatical money, pack his golf clubs, find a desert island and simply stay there. '*Mais oui*', he liked golf, he said in his own mischievous way, '*Mais oui*', he liked the idea of a desert island but only, you know, '*for 'olidays*'.

Ferrari was always going to be a lot of things. It was never going to be a holiday.

'That first day I went to the factory then drove the car at Fiorano the weather was terrible, rain and fog, but still it was the most emotional day I can remember. I felt a great timidity in myself but the Ferrari people all around me seemed as timid as me. Afterwards what struck me was the space and comfort which was very superior to the McLaren I had been driving. The driving position, so important in Formula One where space is so reduced, is a trump card.' Thus Prost in his mid-thirties, accommodating the emotion and concentrating immediately afterwards on actually driving the car, which is what his sixty-five-page contract demanded that he did. His team-mate, Nigel Mansell, was now into his second year there.

Phoenix, the first race, Prost was troubled by the potential consequences of his relationship with Senna and tried to shake his hand so that at least some sort of *modus vivendi* could be established but Senna refused. You can read whatever you want into that but it was a man of stature making a magnanimous gesture for the well-being of all.

In the race, which Prost would describe as a 'disaster', the engine leaked oil and he retired on lap 21 although he had been as high as fourth; but he won the next, Interlagos, typically from the third row of the grid and approaching mid-season had 23 points, the same as Berger who had replaced him at McLaren. Senna led on 31. During the Canadian Grand Prix, a wet-dry-wet race, Boutsen made a lunge to get through and this is how Prost rationalizes himself and the moment: 'I wasn't driving slower than in 1984 and 1985 but differently. When Boutsen tried to overtake me I knew even before he began his move there was a 90 per cent chance of him going off. I was on my guard. Five years before in an identical case I would perhaps have been taken by surprise. I no longer take superfluous risks. Perhaps they permit glorious feats but over a whole season I come out in front.'

And this is Prost gazing into himself heading towards the French Grand Prix: 'Why do I go on after ten years? It is very difficult to reply to that question. I believe it's a passion. It is a passion which has returned now that constraints have been removed. But there is also the motivation of being in a team like Ferrari, the desire to put them back where they were. If you have been World Champion and done your proving it is enriching to race for the others, the mechanics, the engineers, a team-manager, a mini-society which is counting on you.'

This is the way very mature human beings speak, drawing a much wider pleasure from the winning than a personal exposition of talent; it is – in a very selfish pastime – enjoying something most unexpected: the profound fulfilment of team-play and there is a pertinent example Prost himself (handicap 10, but moving, he insists, towards 8 or even 6, 'I hope!') would appreciate. Europe play the United States in the Ryder Cup every two years and golfers are no less self-centred than racing drivers, perhaps more so. Golfers don't have mechanical failures to blame, only themselves.

The Ryder Cup draws together very different men from England, Scotland, Wales, the Republic of Ireland, Spain, Germany and all have egos in their golfbags as well as clubs, but as if by some magical process they become a team, one for all and all for one, and at crucial moments the fate of all depends on the talent of one. It is so harrowing that strong men who have lived their careers in a monastery of emotional self-denial break down and weep in public, Tony Jacklin, Sam Torrance (crying so much he couldn't speak), Christy O'Connor who having saved all at The Belfry in 1990 crossed himself and sobbed uncontrollably on his wife's shoulder.

We are however speaking of Prost in the traditional Ferrari honeymoon. Rarely does it endure.

He won France, won Britain and after Monza remained within striking distance of Senna, 56 points against Senna's 72. At Monza too a journalist asked pointedly how long the feud was to continue and Prost and Senna publicly made up to great applause. Remember that.

In Portugal, Mansell took pole, Prost alongside him. Poleman was positioned on the left of the track and at the green light Mansell veered wildly across so far that he almost rammed Prost into the pit-lane wall. This was, Mansell, would say, probably the worst start of his life. It was not a judgement Prost would disagree with. Mansell won, Senna second, Prost third.

Prost would complain that he didn't rate Mansell highly in the matter of testing, where teams seek precise information, and didn't rate Mansell highly in setting up a car. Some drivers are better than others at this. Prost did however judge that Mansell is 'hyper-fast, he's someone who is very gifted, who can drive any kind of car, one which is well set-up, badly set-up and so on.' At mid-point in the Championship, however, Mansell had 'practically no chance of becoming champion'.

'You have to understand the interest in Ferrari having a World Champion – for ten years they hadn't had one – and that they spend an enormous amount of money; you have to understand we had done some absolutely incredible testing during the year, we'd done fantastic work, we had truly established – without going into the technical domain – a little trick to get better starts at the races because in comparison with Honda we were getting away badly.'

(Prost had spent two days at Fiorano the week before working on just this; and now had new fuel from Agip to give him extra punch, a short second gear so he could get up through the gears fast, fast, fast and shed Senna.)

That day in Portugal Mansell's car, under the enormous impetus of accelerating off the line, slewed toward Prost, who only had the wall next to him. Prost found it 'absolutely unbelievable. Perhaps I expressed myself badly – again – but I was hopping mad.'

Prost won Spain, Senna at one stage in the lead, out with a punctured radiator. Senna said, 'I thought I had a problem with my tyres which is why I made a pit stop. In fact it was water leaking from the right-hand radiator on to the right-rear tyre. I carried on but when I saw the oil warning light come on as the temperature rose I decided to switch it off and park it. This is the worst possible situation for the Championship.' Senna 78, Prost 69, Berger 40, Mansell 31.

Only Japan and Australia remained and the mathematics were straightforward. Both had eleven finishes but that punished Prost more. If he won Suzuka he had to drop his worst score, two points for being fifth in Canada so a win was worth only seven; if Prost did not win Suzuka the Championship was gone. He might win Australia but it would still only be worth the seven points – two less than he needed.

Senna took pole at Suzuka and controversy was born at that moment. Pole was on the left where the surface of the track was dirtier, affording less grip and the smallest difference would magnify itself when all that power was laid on to the surface. The first corner was a right-hander perhaps 200 metres distant. Senna had asked for pole to be moved to the left and this was refused.

Green.

Under the force of acceleration Senna was dragged slightly towards the centre of the track, Prost less so but they were angled into each other and they kept on coming until they were very close but by then Prost was half a car's length ahead. Within 20 metres he was completely ahead, Senna tucked in behind.

The precise geography: Prost two-thirds of the way over to the left of the width of the track, the nose of the Ferrari angled towards Turn One, Senna positioned half behind but poised to move completely out into all that vacant space on the right. Prost moved towards the centre of the track, the nose still angled behind but, as each metre flicked by, the vacant space was contracting as Prost kept moving across.

For a single instant Prost straightened the Ferrari, the vacant space – the width of two, maybe three cars – no longer contracted and Senna put himself into it. Twenty metres further on Prost began to move across on to the racing line. Senna's front wheels were level with Prost's rear wheels; and they collided, were locked together again, went off together again on to the wide gravel run-off area. It had lasted under 15 seconds.

Prost abandoned any attempt at containing himself. 'What he did is disgusting. I am not ready to fight against irresponsible people who are not afraid to die. Anyone who understands motor racing does not have to ask what happened. He did it on purpose because he saw that I had a good start, that my car was better and that he had no chance to win. So he just pushed me out. What he did is more than unsporting, it is disgusting. I have no problems about losing the World Championship, I have lost many but not this way. From the sporting point of view this is not a good day. Can you imagine what young drivers think when they see things like that in Formula One? They'll think they can get away with anything. I do not like people who do not tell the truth, people who show one thing but are different inside. Everything that has happened here has shown his real face. I hate it, this kind of situation. He has completely destroyed everything. I hope everyone can see he was not honest. I never expected what he did. I thought he was one of the human race. I thought he was hard but fair on the track. Not like this. For him it is much more important to win the Championship than it is for me. It is the only thing that he has in life. He is completely screwed up.'

And: 'In Islam, for someone who is about to die death is a game. The problem here is that we have seen Senna ready to take all the risks to win the Championship. I am not ready to play this game.'

Senna reacted with some savagery of his own. 'I was coming faster than him because I had more acceleration. In the first corner, when you have cold tyres, low pressure, the car heavy [with fuel] you normally brake earlier and if you try hard you can try to overtake. It is difficult, it is risky but in my position I had to try. Prost should have known that. I think he made a big mistake to close the door on me because he took a chance that went wrong.'

And: 'He is always trying to destroy people. He tried to destroy me in the past on different occasions and he hasn't managed. He will not manage because I know who I am and where I want to go.'

Another hurricane off the Sea of Japan and this one stronger. No championship had ever been decided like this: even Suzuka and the chicane the year before had been a race, not just a lunge into a crash within sight of the start line.

Later, when he had the perspective of time, Prost would say: 'On the day I was much quicker than him. He knew that if I was in the lead at the first corner it was finished, he wouldn't see me again. What is firstly not acceptable is his manoeuvre itself but it is also what followed. What happened? No sanctions, nothing at all, practically 50 per cent of people even found ways to say he was right.

'I'll give you a little anecdote. Not a few journalists came to me afterwards and said, "I am completely with you, what he did was disgusting but I am obliged to write against you because I have an editor-in-chief who is asking me to write something hard about you – because it's necessary to go against the current of what the other journalists are doing."

'Friends or not friends, it's not necessary for those people to speak to me any more. I have no wish to speak to them. It is not possible. Me, I don't drive races for audience viewing figures, I drive because I have a passion for it.'

The crash of 1990 was assuming the proportions of a Dreyfus affair and in sporting terms alone was quite unlike anything which had been seen since . . . well, since Joe Louis took the 124 seconds to destroy Max Schmeling. Because of this magnitude, and because it remains an 'incident' of such importance, as I researched this book I asked a final question at interviews: give me your verdict on Suzuka. The answers come from experienced men and prove what anybody who has heard a court case over a car crash could tell you: nothing is simple when witnessed from different standpoints.

'I'm in a minority about this', *John Watson* will say. 'I have, as a driver, tried to be very analytical. In my mind Alain's strategy was wrong. He had a strategy, Senna had a strategy, they both knew the importance of the first corner. On the Monday or Tuesday morning after Suzuka when we landed in Australia I said to Alain, "I'm sorry the thing ended that way but tell me one thing. Why the hell did you not shut the door on him? Why did you give him the chance?" Alain said, "Because I knew if I could take the lead at the start, I could go through the first corner flat in fifth and I knew Senna couldn't." That was fine if Senna wasn't within striking distance but he was coming up alongside.

'So the strategy was from a standing start to go through the first part of the double right-hand corner flat in fifth in a seven-speed gearbox. I know some of the Senna–McLaren strategy and the one thing they had not considered was that if Senna got a nose or whatever inside Alain that Alain would shut the door because that was going to lose him the Championship.

'Alain had a very rigid race plan and once he had committed himself there was no way out of it. Senna committed himself because he did not believe Alain would shut the door. It was a comedy of errors. But the point is that you must not dismiss the mentality of a Senna, a Mansell, a Berger, whoever, you must recognize that mentality. You can't say, "Because I know I can go into that corner flat in fifth I have an advantage, but the other guy is coming down the inside, it looks like he's not going to stop" – you're taking yourself out of the race.

'I do not believe that Senna deliberately and with premeditation drove into Prost, unlike what happened the year before, which I think was wrong. Jackie Stewart, who certainly has the right to make a judgement, also says he would have put himself fully in front of Senna. It's what you do to consolidate your advantage. I would have put myself in a position where Senna had no opportunity to come down the inside. He might have tried to go round the outside but if you have the lead you have control.'

'I think the crash in 1990', *René Arnoux* will say, 'was recompense for the crash in 1989. The difference is that the first happened at slow speed because Alain knew they weren't going quickly at the chicane and the second happened at high speed. The second was repayment for the first. Exactly.'

'I think Senna drove into his back', *Keke Rosberg* will say. 'Are you telling me I'm going to get sued because I say he drove into Alain's back? It's my comment. How can I be sued if I am an expert in motor racing compared to any judge in the world and if my expert opinion is that he drove into somebody's back . . . well, you've got to ask who drove into whom the year before and I'll give you my opinion about that, too. Let me explain that correctly.

'Alain's character is totally unsuited to closing the door, he'd never done it, never blocked another driver on purpose in his life before Suzuka. Now he tried and he did it very badly because it was too late. He didn't know how to do it! I wouldn't like to say he drove into Ayrton, he tried to close the door. Any other driver would have done it twenty metres before and nothing would have happened.

'Suzuka, Part Two, 1990. Everybody is saying Alain left the door open. No, he didn't leave the door open. If he takes a very tight line on to the inside Ayrton is going to overtake him on the outside. All the stuff which the Jackie Stewarts and James Hunts of this world have been saying is crap. If Alain took the tight inside line to close the door Ayrton would have driven a circle around him on the outside.

'It's a very special corner which is very open on the entry and very tight at the exit. Alain took a compromise line which didn't leave enough room on the inside to be overtaken but would give him the speed for entering. The other guy just went for it. If it doesn't work out for the other guy, who cares? [Implication: he's World Champion.]

'These things are done by instinct and instinct does not allow you to think about the consequences. You are fearless and you go for it, it might work, it might not work. Ayrton wasn't considering what colour the car was in front of him, how close they were. There's not time for that. A hundred metres to go, he didn't know how big the gap was or if there was a gap, which side he was going to go.

'The variations you can calculate before the start of a race come in about *171 different versions* so therefore all your calculations are wasted sleep. You might just as well get some sleep the night before and not make the calculations.'

'At the chicane in 1989 I think Senna was wrong,' *Derek Warwick* will say, 'because Prost was in a situation where if he stopped Senna winning he was World Champion – so you do not take chances. And 1990 was the reverse of that. I think Prost was wrong not because he turned in when he shouldn't have done or anything like that but because he knew Senna had nothing to lose and everything to gain.

'He should have given Senna the first corner and hoped that he could beat him on the straight or Senna would break down or whatever, because Senna was not going to back off. Whether Senna was right or wrong is irrelevant. He was not going to.'

'Everything changes around why and how,' *Slim Borgudd* will say, 'because it was the race which counted, but it wasn't Alain's fault. If you're in a race situation in a racing car you can't blame him for being where he was because he was entitled to be there and I think Senna either gambled or calculated in doing what he did. At the time I saw it I thought it was [expletive] of Senna but after five minutes you started to think: well, was it really stupid? He won the Championship.'

'I have raced Suzuka a lot', *Kenny Acheson* will say, 'and I know how difficult it is to overtake on that circuit. I know what position you would have to be in to overtake into that corner whether it be from a standing start or on a lap; there is a certain position and Senna wasn't in it. He would certainly have needed to be at least two-thirds of the way alongside Prost and he wasn't. He wasn't ever near that. In my mind Senna knew he had lost the corner. Senna knew what he was doing, Senna doesn't make mistakes like that. I think Senna did what he had to do to win the World Championship. In his mind I'd say he probably thought that was fair after the year before. People say, "Oh, Prost opened the door." He didn't open the door, he made a clean start, he got away and he moved out to take the right line.

'He and Senna had made up a month or so before. I think he thought he didn't have to think about things like that. If they hadn't made up I don't believe Prost would have opened the door even the little bit he did.'

'I've driven Suzuka a lot of times', *Anders Olofsson* will say, 'and I know that if you're not side by side – or if you're not 100 per cent sure that the guy in front will give you room – there's no way you can pass like Senna tried to do.'

'I can split the fault between them fifty-fifty', *Teo Fabi* will say, 'The first year it was Prost's fault and the second year it was Senna's fault. They did the same thing to each other [chuckle].'

'I say it was fifty-fifty in 1990,' *Jean Sage* will say, 'because Prost opened the door a little bit and Prost knows that Senna is a bit risky and usually Prost is very wise and doesn't do things like that. I apportion the responsibility half and half because one [Senna] is taking too much risk and the other [Prost] moves away and then takes his line again. Prost is the one who can't afford the crash, that's why I don't understand what happened. Did he see Senna or didn't he see him? Many people say Senna could not have taken the corner at the speed he was going, and that's another point . . . '

'You have to look at both races', *Jacky Ickx* will say, 'Suzuka Part Two is the result of Suzuka Part One. In Part One it was obvious Prost knew he was going to be overtaken at the chicane and he completely changed his line compared to the forty-five laps he had done before; and Part Two is the logical answer to Part One even if it was a desperate attempt to overtake.

'I watched the Mexican Grand Prix of 1991 [two drivers on the straight almost coming together] and understood it now seems to be accepted that if a driver is going to be overtaken he changes his line completely to the left or right. I tell you, these things would never have happened twenty years ago. You were on your line and somebody was going to overtake you if he was faster but you never changed your line even *half a metre*. Now you block people to stop them overtaking.

'For any kind of reason it is unacceptable. It is not only not behaving like a gentleman it is also awfully dangerous and if you don't stop the drivers doing these kind of actions it is going to be very . . . difficult. One of these days we are going to have a terrible crash. One of these drivers is very aggressive, a very nice driver but if you do the same thing in football or tennis I guarantee you that you have a "day off" the next weekend.

'I remember a Formula Two race at Montjuich where I tried to overtake Jim Clark in the hairpin. It was obvious I was too fast, I braked too late and I hit him. Afterwards I went straight to him and I said, "*Really I'm sorry about it*," and he said, "*OK, you're sorry and that's OK one time – but not* two *times.*" He was absolutely right, I had no excuse at all and at the time it was a gentleman's sport. Nobody would have done anything like you saw in Mexico or a few times before . . . '

'In my opinion it was 100 per cent Senna's fault', *Stefan Johansson* will say. 'I'm not against Senna at all, I like him and everything but in my view the first man into the corner chooses the line. That's the way I've always been taught to drive, that's one of the unwritten rules between the drivers. You cannot drive through a car if that car is on the line, and there's no [expletive] way you can outbrake anybody into the first corner at Suzuka because you don't brake until you get there. There is absolutely no discussion that there was just no room. If Senna had wanted to get to the finish of that race he would have had to back off and give room to the guy who was in front of him. Prost was totally correct.'

And a cryptic footnote from *The Rat* himself: 'Suzuka? I can't remember who was inside, who was outside . . . ' He was grinning when he said it, grinning his toothy grin.

In the midst of all this *Hughes de Chaunac* provides some basic thinking: 'When you are on the road and a car is following you and it hits you it is always the fault of the car which is behind. That is to say, when there has been an accident and it comes to insurance claims the one behind is culpable, it is he who must be in control of his vehicle.'

That seemed the perfect way to leave it but it wasn't. The twist came all unexpected on the late afternoon of 20 October 1991 when Senna had won his third World Championship and Prost had driven what was almost certainly his last race for Ferrari. Senna's thoughts were still on the Crash of 1990. He spoke vehemently about it and at first sight seemed to have explained everything; but when there was time for hindsight doubts and questions remained.

Senna began by restating his wish that pole position be changed. 'Balestre gave an order not to change. I told myself OK you try and work clean – and then you get [expletive] by stupid people.' Senna recounted his thought process: 'If on Sunday at the start, because I'm in the wrong position, Prost gets the jump and beat me off the line, at the first corner I'll go for it. And he had better not turn in because he's not going to make it. It just happened, I guess. I just wish it hadn't happened. I really wish that I could have had the start because then we could go and go. It's unbelievable that it happened. He got the jump and he was turning in and I hit him. We were both off and it was an [expletive] end to the Championship. It was the result of a bad decision influenced by Balestre. I contributed to it but it was not my responsibility.'

These words almost physically shook Formula One.

Gone was any suggestion that Prost might have been culpable. Instead Balestre, who had been ousted as FISA President, became that.

Perhaps if Prost had known Senna's thought process – I'll take the corner or crash trying to – his natural prudence might have altered his tactics and he would either have ceded turn one or blocked Senna totally out of it. Senna couldn't very well run full in to the back of Prost. Could he?

Prost might have been laughing till tears tumbled and cascaded down his face when he heard Senna's press conference at Suzuka, 20 October 1991, might have been holding his sides. But he wasn't. If turn one had turned out differently, you see, Alain Prost might have had four World Championships, not three.

10

ALL TIME HIGH

Right, that's it, I've done it, I've won and therefore I can win again.

ALAIN PROST, DIJON, 1981

It was only a publicity photograph, static in its composition but no less apt for that. The small neat man wearing sunglasses stood strategically placed behind the right front wheel of a McLaren. One hand steadied a pit board which rested on the ground by his feet. In three tiers the legend on this pit board proclaimed.

PROST
P1
28

Estoril, Portugal, late on the afternoon of 20 September 1987. Jackie Stewart was smiling. 'People might not believe me,' he would say in his clipped, concise Scottish way, 'but I'm glad to see Alain take my record. I am glad that it is he who has done it because he is the one who deserves it. There is no doubt in my mind that he is the best race driver of his generation.'

Some time earlier Prost had brought this McLaren safely round the final right-hander of the Autodromo do Estoril – he'd backed off for the last couple of laps, let his time fall away from the 1:19s to a prudent 1:24 – and then come safely down the straight. As he crossed the line he was 20.493 seconds ahead of Berger. In the end there had been no need to hurry.

He had won his twenty-eighth Grand Prix, beating the total

which Stewart had set and held for fourteen years; Prost was only thirty-two, he was in his prime and a question was born: how many more wins? The answer was always going to be: plenty . . .

Of his generation, to use Stewart's own phrase, only Senna could hope to haul himself up to Prost's total which, at the time of writing stands at forty-four and it may well be that, although by definition these things are dangerous to say, both will establish totals beyond the reach of future generations. After all, Stewart's record was unchallenged between 5 August 1973, his last victory, and that afternoon in Estoril in 1987; only Lauda got close (twenty-five) and Stewart had taken the record from Jim Clark, whose total of twenty-five had lasted since 1968.

Given Prost's stated intentions to remain in Formula One there is a very real possibility that he will double Stewart's total. We are entering places where no human being has been before and, setting Senna aside for a moment, any subsequent driver will need to drive at a consistently elevated level for a decade, free of injury, in a leading car which absolutely dominates several of the seasons of that decade. Otherwise they will never win enough. You won't be able to assault Prost's total by attrition alone, gathering wins here and there and racking them up into a mountain. Time is too short. If you win, say, three races a season it will take you seventeen years to reach fifty.

No man has ever driven seventeen years in Formula One.

Statistics are rightly distrusted although occasionally they are extremely eloquent and incontrovertible. We must return to another of Stewart's phrases: best race driver. Once he had learnt from Lauda, Prost was never obsessed about pole positions and between 1980 and 1990 only managed five in a season once, three in a season twice. In its context: five in a season has also been done by Fangio (twice), Ascari, Phil Hill, Clark, Rindt and Arnoux; six by Clark (three times), Ascari, Stewart and Hunt; seven by Clark, Andretti and Senna, eight by Hunt, Andretti, Senna and Mansell; nine by Lauda (twice), Peterson and Piquet; ten by Senna; thirteen by Senna (twice).

Prost knew exactly what he was about, and that was winning the races. He won more than four World Champions – Ascari, Phil Hill, Hunt and Andretti – together. Their total is only thirty-eight. He won races in turbo cars and non-turbo cars, won them in Renaults and McLarens and Ferraris, won them in whatever they gave him; won them round the streets of Adelaide or the hillside loops of

Austria; won Monaco four years out of five with total precision, won Silverstone two years on the trot and Silverstone is about as far away from Monaco in its demands as you can get; he won 'fuel' races at Imola, beat the heat in Brazil, and so it goes on. No place was safe from him except unlovely, unloved Detroit which he actively disliked anyway. A measure of Prost there, though: fourth in 1984, third in 1986, third in 1987, second in 1988. Never losing sight of the fact that Detroit was a bitch of a circuit – manhole covers, surface breaking up, concrete walls where most races finished resembling a scrapyard – it isn't a bad sequence, is it?

The full multiplying magnificence of Prost's racecraft is revealed by the wins themselves. Here is the full range of his talents and how he – and others – rationalized them. Note, also, how often he was not in the lead at the start.

1. FRANCE (Dijon) 5 July 1981, 80 laps, second row of the grid. Prost was third at the end of the first lap, overtook Watson and tracked Piquet all the way to lap 58 when a downpour halted the race. It was restarted 30 minutes later and now Prost powered past Piquet to beat Watson by 2.29 seconds on the combined time. He set the fastest lap on 64 with 1:9.14. Prost's insight: '*A driver's career begins the day he enters Formula One but his real point of departure is the evening after his first victory. I said to myself,* "Right, that's it, I've done it, I've won and therefore I can win again." *Your mentality changes and from this moment on you go to the start of every race with the object of actually winning.*'

2. HOLLAND (Zandvoort) 30 August 1981, 72 laps, pole. He took the lead immediately but Alan Jones (Williams), a rugged Australian, laid heavy pressure on him and twice attacked at the entry to Tarzan. Prost held his nerve, held his line and would not permit Jones room to go through. On lap 22 they came up to lap Alboreto (Tyrrell) and Prost did hesitate, allowing Jones to elbow past although neither overtook Alboreto. Hammering down the start–finish straight Jones took a 'tow' from Alboreto, moved out and alongside and then discovered Prost out and alongside him. Prost held that all the way to Tarzan and was back in the lead. Jones had tyre troubles, Prost beat Piquet by 8.24 seconds. Jones's insight: '*Oh, he's good all right. He's tough and he drives well. He's learned a lot in a short time.*'

3. ITALY (Monza) 13 September 1981, 52 laps, second row. He made a superb start and took Arnoux for the lead at the mouth

of the first chicane, ran smoothly to the flag beating Jones by 23 seconds. No insight necessary.

4. SOUTH AFRICA (Kyalami) 23 January 1982, 77 laps, third row. He tucked in behind Arnoux until lap 14 when he took the lead. On lap 41 he had a puncture, limped back to the pits but found travelling slowly difficult to accept mentally. The stop for new tyres cast him back to eighth. He flew. He was 2 seconds a lap faster than Alboreto and passed him on lap 45, on lap 49 he set the fastest time of the race, he was gaining on Lauda at just under 2 seconds a lap and took him on 51, he was 3 seconds a lap faster than Watson and took him on 54, scythed past Rosberg on 55, was 2 seconds faster than Reutemann and took him on 61, scythed past Pironi on 62 and was now behind Arnoux, whose tyres were going off. Arnoux had not stopped for fresh ones. The times illustrate it very graphically indeed.

Lap	Arnoux	Prost
63	1:12.714	1:08.704
64	1:13.100	1:09.848
65	1:12.580	1:11.101
66	1:14.108	1:10.078
67	1:14.039	1:09.527

On lap 68 Prost took the lead and finished 14.946 seconds in front of Reutemann, Arnoux third. Prost's insight: '*When I'd come out with new tyres I was eighth a little more than a lap behind Arnoux. I had twenty-five laps left and it was enough.*' Gordon Murray of Brabham came to congratulate him afterwards and wondered aloud about refuelling while you were getting new tyres. Prost's stop had put an idea in his mind: run with tanks half full, build a big lead because the car would be lighter, pit for new tyres and more fuel, win the race. This would happen and change Formula One.

5. BRAZIL (Jacarepagua) 21 March 1982, 63 laps, pole. He was thrust back to third on lap 1 behind Villeneuve and Arnoux, while on lap 6 Piquet and Patrese went by and on lap 11 Rosberg, too. Prost had a misfire. He ran sixth until lap 19 when Lauda took him, re-took Lauda on the next lap and moved up to fifth a lap after that – Arnoux and Reutemann had touched. On lap 30 Villeneuve went off, on lap 33 Patrese spun off (he had blacked out in the heat) and now the order was Piquet, Rosberg, Prost. It remained like that but Piquet and Rosberg were disqualified because their cars weighed less

than 580kg. Their water tanks emptied during the race, making the cars lighter. This, then, was Prost's lucky win. Jean Sage's insight: '*We needed to know if the water tanks were legal. We at Renault could have built light-weight cars, too.*'

6. FRANCE (Paul Ricard) 17 April 1983, 54 laps, pole. He moved firmly into the lead tracked by Patrese (Brabham). A pattern was set, Prost already pulling clear on this first lap. He looked refined, poised, at ease and by the end of lap 2 the gap had grown to 3.23 seconds. He began lapping backmarkers towards the mid-point, feeding in the Renault's turbo power with precise timing, selecting his moments with the same precision, never straying too near the backmarkers. He pitted for new tyres and fuel and it took a long 24.18 seconds – he stalled the car – but Piquet had not pitted yet. When Piquet did (16.07) Prost led by only 10 seconds. Almost immediately he thrust in the fastest lap of the race and, without seeming to go faster, stretched the gap remorselessly. On lap 37 there was a moment of purest irony when he ducked out to lap Arnoux (now Ferrari) on the mile-long Mistral straight and they ran side by side, equidistant, neither man ceding in a great surge towards the corner at the end of the straight. Prost pulled ahead before they reached it and the race was settled in that moment. He beat Piquet by 29.720 seconds. Prost's insight: '*I was so nervous during the last few laps that I started getting pains in my stomach. You know, so many times have I been in this position and something has gone wrong.*'

7. BELGIUM (Spa) 22 May 1983, 40 laps, pole. He was beaten to Eau Rouge, the hill-climb section shortly after the starting line, by De Cesaris (for the second time; there had been a restart). Prost tracked him until lap 22 when De Cesaris's engine went and that left him with a 27-second cushion over Piquet, who subsequently fell back. He beat Tambay by 23.182 seconds. This was the first race at the revised Spa circuit. Prost's insight into its rolling splendour: '*It's a pleasure to come to a place like this, make adjustments to the springs and roll bars and so on and feel the changes working when you go out. That's a nice feeling, very satisfying.*'

8. BRITAIN (Silverstone) 16 July 1983, 67 laps, second row. He settled into third place following Tambay and Arnoux (both in Ferraris). On lap 14 he was directly behind Arnoux, tracked him through the chicane, hounded him along the pit-lane straight and ducked out to take Copse Corner. There was nothing Arnoux could do. Now for Tambay, the team-mate who never was:

Lap	Tambay	Prost
15	1:15.692	1:14.780
16	1:15.709	1:15.688
17	1:15.737	1:14.823
18	1:15.734	1:15.612
19	1:15.666	1:15.343

On lap 20 Prost outbraked Tambay into Copse and

20	1:16.876	1:16.146
21	1:16.108	1:15.189
22	1:15.598	1:14.584

The handling of the Ferrari was giving Tambay trouble and he would eventually be taken by Piquet who led for five laps – from 37 to 41 – while Prost lost time pitting for new tyres. Piquet then pitted himself and Prost moved to victory by 19.161 seconds. Prost's insight: '*A curious feeling suddenly came over me. Apart from a mechanical failure I knew that the race couldn't get away from me. This was an* example *of a race with two faces: from inside the cockpit it was easy, outside it looked very difficult. People thought I was all at sea. I wasn't.*'

9. AUSTRIA (Österreichring) 14 August 1983, 53 laps, third row. He settled into fourth behind Tambay – who at one stage would be disgracefully baulked by Jean-Pierre Jarier (Ligier) – Arnoux and Piquet. Prost had taken Mansell on the first lap. On lap 22 he took Piquet – they banged wheels – but Piquet retook him. Prost now pitted for tyres and fuel which pushed him back to seventh but other pit stops were coming and by lap 31 he was third behind Piquet and Arnoux. On lap 38 Piquet lost boost and now Prost attacked Arnoux. He took him on lap 48 – Arnoux had lost fourth gear – and Prost ran safely enough to the end, crossing the line 6.835 seconds ahead. Nigel Roebuck's insight: '*As I talked to Prost afterwards it was difficult to believe that he had recently completed a winning Grand Prix drive. Not a bead of sweat, let alone matted hair. His voice was calm and low – until the Jarier incident was mentioned.* "It was really very bad. Jarier was fighting for fifteenth place or whatever it was, and I understand that. You have to fight wherever you are but you must respect the people who are lapping you – who are also racing." '

10. BRAZIL (Jacarepagua) 25 March 1984, 61 laps, second row. This was his first drive for McLaren, the new car hadn't run

much and it was the first race with a limit of 220 litres of fuel. In other words, keep one eye on the gauge. From the second row he was quite content to be tenth completing the opening lap. His own word is . . . cautious. He was pacing himself, took Arnoux on lap 9 to get himself into the points. On lap 13 he took Tambay, Alboreto spun and that was fourth. On lap 16 he took Mansell and now Warwick lay ahead of him, Lauda clearly in the lead.

Lap	Warwick	Prost
16	1:40.925	1:39.620
17	1:39.854	1:39.666
18	1:40.327	1:40.112
19	1:39.999	1:39.769
20	1:39.902	1:38.624
21	1:40.120	1:38.347
22	1:41.106	1:39.248
23	1:40.118	1:39.845

You see how Prost does it, every lap quicker except one and yet none dramatically so. He now took Warwick and when Lauda's electrics went on lap 38 he found himself in the lead. He pitted immediately for tyres, ceding second place to Warwick who constructed a 30-second lead until, with ten laps to go, Warwick's suspension broke. Prost won from Rosberg, 40.514 seconds behind. Prost's insight: '*This was an important victory because it was the first for McLaren and it* cleansed my spirit *from all the accumulated problems of the winter after I'd left Renault.*'

11. SAN MARINO (Imola) 6 May 1984, 60 laps, front row. He beat Piquet from the line and built a cushion which reached 13 seconds by lap 10 – but on lap 20 he spun. It was an amazing moment, a moment when he suddenly looked prey to human error. He gathered the spin deftly and as he passed the pits he tapped his helmet as if to say sorry. He had been running smoothly in the 1:35s but that errant lap went out to 1:41. He pitted for tyres on lap 30 and moved comfortably to the end beating Arnoux by 13.416 seconds. Prost's insight: '*The spin was not my fault, maybe, but what* caused *it was my fault. I was using the carbon fibre brakes on the car and I probably overheated them in the first part of the race when I was trying to build a lead. After that they didn't work evenly, which is why I spun. I was lucky, no?*'

12. MONACO (Monte Carlo) 3 June 1984, 77 laps, pole. The

race in the thunderstorm. Prost reached Ste Devote first, a crucial moment. Mansell settled behind.

Lap	Prost	Mansell
1	2:05.735	2:06.678
2	1:58.764	2:00.136
3	1:57.403	1:58.104
4	1:58.926	1:58.378
But . . .		
8	1:56.412	1:55.682
9	1:56.391	1:56.235
10	1:57.471	1:56.471

On lap 11 Prost was moving towards the tunnel when he came upon Corrado Fabi's Brabham. It rested across the track after a spin. Prost threaded past it, inadvertently brushing against a marshal. In the confusion Mansell took him and led a Grand Prix for the first time in his life. Five laps later he too spun and Prost was back in the lead. He held that to lap 31, Senna, young, eager, fearless, catching him fast.

Lap	Prost	Senna
28	2:00.193	1:56.628
29	1:59.436	1:56.666
30	2.02.598	1:59.008
31	2:03.766	1:59.433

At this point Ickx stopped it, Prost 7.446 seconds ahead of Senna. Prost's insight: '*This was strictly the reverse of Great Britain in 1983. It looked easy from the outside but it was hell in the cockpit – the rain, a problem with my brakes and Senna on my heels. I was on the limit throughout and all that for half points because the race was stopped when it was. The other half of those points was going to cost me cruel at the end of the season.*'

13. GERMANY (Hockenheim) 5 August 1984, 44 laps, pole. He was in the spare because the race car had developed fuel pump problems – and he was beaten to the first corner by De Angelis. Now watch Prost as he becomes more comfortable in the car.

LAP	DE ANGELIS	PROST
1	2:01.238	2:01.570
2	1:55.202	1:55.483
3	1:54.934	1:55.230
4	1:55.029	1:54.996
5	1:55.097	1:54.709
6	1:54.954	1:54.967
7	1:54.776	1:54.837

On lap 8 De Angelis blew up and Prost had to lift off to miss him. That gave Piquet the impetus to catch him and take him at the chicane. Meanwhile Lauda was coming hard. Piquet's gearbox went on lap 22 and it became a straightforward heavyweight contest, Prost *v.* Lauda, over the remaining twenty-two laps. The fulcrum of the race lay between laps 27 and 31.

LAP	PROST	LAUDA
27	1:55.153	1:54.855
28	1:53.933	1:54.105
29	1:53.843	1:53.778
30	1:54.519	1:56.061
31	1:53.538	1:54.273

At this point Lauda, mindful of the state of his rear tyres, accepted second place and they ran like that to the end, Prost winning it by 3.149 seconds. Prost's insight: '*The spare car was good, really good but of course I was worried because it was the spare car. I was so worried that I actually felt sick in my stomach during the race waiting for something to go wrong. This was a race that I absolutely had to win and if it looked easy to people watching it wasn't like that in my* mind. *Psychologically it was tough. I had this* monument *called Lauda who I felt I could beat but who had made such an impression on me. I couldn't ignore the almost* sentimental *aspect of that* feeling *but I needed the win to impose myself on the Championship*.'

14. HOLLAND (Zandvoort) 26 August 1984, 71 laps, pole. He was beaten to Tarzan by Piquet who began to draw away but on lap 11 when Piquet's lead had grown to 6 seconds his engine went. The McLaren heavyweights started slugging again over the remaining sixty-one laps. Prost had chosen a harder compound tyre than Lauda because it would last longer. It worked. Prost backed off towards the end so that the winning margin, 10.283 seconds,

had no particular meaning. Prost's insight: '*I knew that I would have a problem in the first half of the race because Nelson and Niki would be in better shape with their softer tyres but I also knew that if the race was hard my tyres would let me fight for longer. I think I made the right choice.*'

15. EUROPE (Nürburgring) 7 October 1984, 67 laps, front row. A pressure race as the Championship moved towards its climax (Lauda going into it with 63 points, Prost 52½ and only Portugal to come). Prost had had a bizarre moment during the morning warm-up, spinning off and striking an official safety car. The whole of the McLaren's rear had to be replaced. From the green he took the lead and simply stayed there. This was total, complete, all-enveloping control, smooth, precise and when it was done and the Championship was still alive he thrust both hands out of the cockpit and waved and waved for all the world to see. He had beaten Alboreto by 23.911 seconds but nobody cared about that. The important finisher was Lauda, only fourth. Prost's insight: '*My car was the most perfect I had known in a race.*'

16. PORTUGAL (Estoril) 21 October 1984, 70 laps, front row. The Championship decider which is fully discussed in Chapter 8.

17. BRAZIL (Jacarepagua) 7 April 1985, 61 laps, third row. He settled in behind Rosberg and Alboreto. Rosberg's turbo went on lap 10, Prost stalked Alboreto and on lap 19 Alboreto missed a gear in front of the pits. Prost was through. He backed off towards the end and beat Alboreto by 3.259 seconds. Lauda had gone out on lap 27 when the engine's electronics failed. Prost's insight: '*There was a little green light which told you if there was a malfunction in the engine management system and I was beginning to wonder if I'd share the same fate as Niki.*' That's why he backed off. He had now moved ahead of Stirling Moss's total of sixteen wins. Moss drove sixty-six races between 1951 and 1961. This was the beginning of Prost's sixth season and he had driven seventy-three times.

THE ONE that got away and would have been number 18 was SAN MARINO (Imola) 5 May 1985, 60 laps, third row. He was fourth after the first lap but moved up and when Johansson (Ferrari) ran out of fuel with three laps to go, won it. He was then disqualified because the McLaren weighed less than the regulation 540kg. Prost's insight: '*A complete victory, one of my best in terms of attack, tactics, sweet mechanically. I'd have accepted being thrown out after a crappy victory but not after one like that and all for 1,700 grammes under the limit.*'

18. MONACO (Monte Carlo) 19 May 1985, 78 laps, third row. This one seemed improbable because (in theory) you can't really win from that third row round the streets. He accepted that Alboreto's Ferrari would be the fastest car in the race and decided to be patient. Senna seized the lead, Mansell behind then Alboreto and Prost. He took Mansell on lap 2 and later moved into second place behind Alboreto when Senna's engine gave way. Patrese and Piquet crashed and on lap 18 Alboreto spun on oil which had been dropped, letting Prost through. Prost knew Alboreto would come back at him. Alboreto was quicker, you see. At Ste Devote, Alboreto jinked through and Prost did not close the door. He was mildly surprised to note that Alboreto wasn't pulling away as he had anticipated. Debris from the Patrese–Piquet crash had punctured Alboreto's left rear tyre and he needed to pit. Prost was back in the lead. Deep into the race Alboreto struck back yet again – Prost had the boost turned firmly down to conserve the car – and it rained. Both drivers decided to settle for what they had, Prost crossing the line 7.541 seconds ahead. Prost's insight: '*I had to be patient, which was difficult because it is not one of my natural characteristics. I knew I had to bide my time, I knew I had to wait and I did wait.*'

19. BRITAIN (Silverstone) 21 July 1985, 65 laps, second row. He was fourth after lap 1 behind Senna, Rosberg and Mansell, dropped another place when De Cesaris came through. Senna and Rosberg set off into the distance across Silverstone's broad acres. Prost knew they would all be marginal on fuel. He went past Mansell on lap 7 and De Cesaris on lap 9. That was done at Woodcote, the fast-fast-fast right-hander, and it was done clinically: by simply outbraking him. Rosberg lay ahead.

Lap	Rosberg	Prost
9	1:14.158	1:13.527
10	1:14.463	1:12.630
11	1:14.083	1:12.361
12	1:13.217	1:12.792
13	1:12.914	1:12.140
14	1:13.303	1:11.966
15	1:13.714	1:11.646

The decisive lap was 13, Rosberg's fastest of the race but Prost was quicker still. At the end of lap 16 Prost went through – at Woodcote again. Senna was 9 seconds ahead. By lap 30 Prost had caught him and attacked, Senna edged away in the traffic but Prost caught him again with a stunning lap of 1:09.886 on 43. Senna now accelerated away again – this was racing. Then Senna's Lotus developed a misfire. On lap 58 it seemed to have cleared itself, hadn't, and at Copse Corner Prost was with him, at Becketts – a left-right twist – he was through; but the misfire did clear and Senna retook Prost at Stowe, the misfire returned and Prost retook him at Copse. Senna ran out of fuel and Prost won it by a lap from Alboreto. Prost's insight: '*If I had stayed with Senna before he had the misfire I don't think I would have had enough fuel to finish the race. All I knew was that I couldn't put my boost up because I would have run out.*' In the matter of economy Prost was a master, too.

20. AUSTRIA (Österreichring) 18 August 1985, 52 laps, pole. A lot of crashing at the start and at the restart. There had been worries about a CV joint on the McLaren as it sat on the grid and briefly Prost even contemplated changing to the spare car, although that would have meant starting from the pit lane. As it was the race was declared to be an entirely new one allowing Prost to change to the spare. Lauda took the lead, Prost took it from him at the Hella Licht curve and these two pulled clearly away. But Prost had made a tactical error, choosing B compound tyres on the left of the car (everybody else was on Cs) and on lap 26 he pitted for fresh tyres (Cs incidentally). Lauda now had a lead of 30 seconds but Prost carved into it.

LAP	LAUDA	PROST
29	1:31.856	1:29.553
30	1:30.406	1:31.172
31	1:31.164	1:29.953
32	1:32.238	1:29.494
33	1:32.076	1:29.451

Lauda responded and on lap 38 set his fastest time, 1:30.052, but Prost was flying and thrust in 1:29.241 – the quickest of the race. A lap later Lauda's turbo went and Prost finished 30.002 seconds ahead of Senna. Prost's insight: '*Well, the car was superb.*'

21. ITALY (Monza) 8 September 1985, 51 laps, third row. He was third after lap 1 behind Rosberg and Mansell, fourth after lap 2 (Senna overtaking him), second after lap 4 (retaking Senna, Mansell misfire) but 7 seconds behind Rosberg. Prost had chosen only B compound tyres and calculated that although the Honda in

Rosberg's Williams was clearly faster than his TAG, Rosberg – who had a C compound on his right front – would have to make a stop. He did on lap 28 and mounted a typical charge.

Lap	Prost	Rosberg
34	1:30.643	1:29.239
35	1:31.155	1:28.989
36	1:31.597	1:28.892
37	1:30.416	1:29.831
38	1:29.917	1:28.795
39	1:30.776	1:28.421

Mentally Prost had accepted that he would finish second and was already nursing the notion of six points towards the Championship; Rosberg's Honda engine was quicker and Prost's tyres were worn now. Down the short, sharp surge to the parabolica on lap 40 Rosberg went by on a power play but four laps later the engine let go. Prost won it from Piquet by 51.635 seconds. Prost's insight: '*There was absolutely nothing I could do. The power of the Honda was fantastic and I was slow anyway because of hard, worn tyres. Second place, I had thought, was not too bad. The win was a bonus. I arrived at Monza with a three-point advantage over Alboreto and left with twelve points. My situation was completely altered because I now had a one-win cushion and you start to reason differently: the person behind has no alternative. He has to attack.*'

22. SAN MARINO (Imola) 27 April 1986, 60 laps, second row. He was behind Piquet and Senna at the end of lap 1 but took Senna on lap 4 – a muscular move at the corner called Tosa. Piquet (now Williams) pulled away and Rosberg (now McLaren) took Prost on lap 5. They ran together. Piquet pitted for new tyres on lap 29, Prost a lap later and McLaren did it fast enough to have Prost back out in front of him. Rosberg hadn't stopped yet and was in the lead. When he did Prost went cleanly through and won it from Piquet by 7.645 seconds. Prost's insight: '*All the time I thought about minimum boost, saving fuel. No, this was not racing (with the fuel restriction) but you still have to find a way to win, a way to do it better than the others.*'

23. MONACO (Monte Carlo) 11 May 1986, 78 laps, pole. He took the lead immediately from Senna, made his tyre stop on lap 35, caught Senna who had not yet pitted and actually toyed with the notion of overtaking him. Rosberg tried to mount an assault but

every time he did Prost responded. Senna did pit on lap 42 and Prost now commanded the race by making a long, sweeping gesture.

Lap	Prost	Rosberg
47	1:27.227	1:27.457
48	1:27.255	1:27.342
49	1:28.094	1:29.391
50	1:26.694	1:27.535
51	1:26.607	1:27.759

In its scope this was magnificent and lap 51 remained the fastest of the race. He beat Rosberg by 25.022 seconds. Rosberg's insight: '*Alain was simply too strong for any of us.*' Prost's insight: '*One of the most complete races of my career. When the car is perfect and the feeling of domination gets hold of you you feel unassailable. An adversary approaches? All you have to do is increase your rhythm a little and the gap opens again. This is real delight, the* dream. *I don't however class it as among my most* beautiful *wins but among the easiest because, as is well known, some sixth places are harder to get than some victories.*'

24. AUSTRIA (Österreichring) 17 August 1986, 52 laps, third row. He followed Berger and Teo Fabi (both Benettons) until lap 17 when Fabi's engine blew. Prost's insight: '*I could do nothing against them, especially as we knew they would probably not need a tyre stop. I only hoped they would "take care" of themselves. If they did I felt pretty confident. Because I'd changed the set-up of my car so much I wasn't sure how my front tyre wear would be. Therefore during the first half of the race I ran minimum boost and I didn't push too hard.*' Berger's engine developed a misfire, Mansell went with a broken drive shaft and Prost finished a lap ahead of Alboreto.

25. AUSTRALIA (Adelaide) 26 October 1986, 82 laps, second row. This race is fully described in Chapter 8. Because Prost retained the Championship the fact that he had now passed Juan Manuel Fangio's total was largely obscured. Fangio drove only fifty-one races between 1950 and 1958. Prost was now in his seventh season and had driven 105.

26. BRAZIL (Jacarepagua) 12 April 1987, 61 laps, third row. The new McLaren had not been tested much and in qualifying Prost was careful not to go near the 4.0 bar maximum. The road holding wasn't right and for race day warm-up Gordon Murray favoured

moving the wing settings, Prost didn't and wanted them reduced. It worked. At the end of lap 1 he was seventh, took Boutsen on lap 3, Fabi on lap 8, was into second place on lap 11 when Mansell pitted for tyres, led on lap 13 when Senna pitted for tyres, only sacrificed the lead to Piquet when he pitted for tyres himself, retook it during Piquet's stop and ran smoothly to the end 40.547 seconds in front. At no stage had he stretched the car! Prost's insight: '*An amazing race for me, different car, different engine, a different race engineer, Neil Oatley, and . . . everything perfect.*'

This win took him past Lauda and Jim Clark. Lauda had retired in 1985, of course. His career had begun in 1971 and he had driven 171 races. Clark, killed in 1968, had begun in 1960 and had taken only seventy-two races to reach his total. Prost had now driven 106 and only Stewart and the absolute record lay ahead.

27. BELGIUM (Spa) 17 May 1987, 43 laps, third row. He was third until lap 10 of a restarted race. On the opening lap Mansell and Senna crashed and on lap 10 Piquet was halted by a turbo problem and Alboreto by a wheel bearing. Prost made no mistake and crossed the line 24.764 seconds ahead of Johansson. Prost's insight: '*Mansell and Senna I knew about and then on the second lap Berger went [engine]. I only had Piquet and Alboreto to worry me. Alboreto was weaving a bit when I tried to pass him once or twice and Piquet began to get away but I wasn't going to risk anything so early in a race. There was plenty of time. When I was in the lead there was nothing to do except hope that the rain kept away.*' Stewart's record total was now equalled.

28. PORTUGAL (Estoril) 20 September 1987, 70 laps, second row. He was fifth after lap 2, was taken by Alboreto and ran sixth until lap 12 when Senna had mechanical problems. That was fifth. Mansell's electrics went on lap 13 and that was fourth. After the pit stops he was second behind Berger and applied the pressure.

Lap	Berger	Prost
53	1:22.908	1:20.230
54	1:22.216	1:20.466
55	1:21.640	1:20.435

Prost was using full boost, Berger resisting the pressure; he was however concerned about the condition of his tyres. Berger did respond.

63	1:19.957	1:20.761
64	1:19.868	1:19.591
65	1:20.795	1:19.509

And that was Prost's fastest of the race. On lap 68 Berger made a brave decision. If he could screw everything out of the car he might gain a 3-second cushion and it would be enough to keep Prost at bay – but his tyres wouldn't stand it and he spun. And that was Stewart's record gone. Stewart's insight, which bears repeating: '*There is no doubt in my mind that he is the best race driver of the generation.*'

29. BRAZIL (Jacarepagua) 3 April 1988, 60 laps, second row. Honda power now and Prost had a clear road because Senna, on pole, suffered gear section problems and began from the pit lane. Mansell angled his Williams across the track feeling for the racing line for turn one, a right hander, but Prost hugging the rim of the track got there first and was not seen again. He held his lead throughout, even during his pit stop, although Berger made a determined late rush at him. Berger's insight: '*I thought his tyres might be finished but of course they were not. He was just being careful with the fuel. I should have known better.*' Prost won it by 9.873 seconds. Prost's insight: '*The car felt very comfortable and I was not even worried when Gerhard started to attack after his second tyre stop because I still had something in hand to respond if necessary.*'

30. MONACO (Monte Carlo) 15 May 1988, 78 laps, front row. At the green Berger stole between Senna, on pole, and Prost and the order settled into Senna, Berger, Prost who couldn't find a way through until lap 54 when he outbraked Berger at Ste Devote. Senna was now 46 seconds ahead and essentially uncatchable but he crashed on lap 67, a straightforward lapse of concentration. Prost's insight: '*My big problem was not getting second gear at the start which meant sitting behind Berger for so long. The car itself ran perfectly.*'

31. MEXICO (Mexico City) 29 May 1988, 67 laps, front row. Prost, alongside Senna, made the better start and stayed there although in traffic Senna was more incisive. At one stage Prost was content to stay behind a backmarker awaiting his moment rather than forcing it, was prepared to sacrifice the second and a half he lost. He finished 7.104 seconds ahead of Senna. Prost's insight: '*In the first half I was a bit worried about tyre wear because the surface was not good, but as the race progressed more rubber went down*

on the track surface and the problem disappeared. It was the same with the fuel. I seemed to be using too much although we hadn't expected consumption to be a problem. Later on it was OK even though I was pushing really hard to keep clear of Ayrton.'

32. FRANCE (Paul Ricard) 3 July 1988, 80 laps, pole. He took the lead immediately, lost it during his tyre stop on lap 36, regained it on lap 61 after a magnificent struggle.

LAP	SENNA	PROST
55	1:12.398	1:12.456
56	1:12.046	1:12.067
57	1:12.640	1:12.680
58	1:12.220	1:12.239
59	1:12.384	1:12.277
60	1:12.406	1:12.403

Senna had a problem with the gearlever ('it felt spongy') and finished 31.752 seconds behind. Prost's insight: '*I think Ayrton lost downforce when he was following another car through the fast corner at le Beausset because he ran wide in the dirt. I took him with a supreme effort in a way I didn't think possible and then I braked very late at the next corner. Both us had been at the absolute limit. It was superb.*'

33. PORTUGAL (Estoril) 25 September 1988, 70 laps, pole. Senna got away first. As they crossed the line to complete lap 1 Prost tried to go through, Senna moved over on him and they almost crashed. Prost elbowed through and vanished, winning it from Capelli by 9.553 seconds. Prost's insight: '*I did a very good race by controlling everything. By that I mean fuel consumption, tyres and also the physical aspect because this was a hard race. Capelli was very quick, very competitive so it was never easy. I knew Ivan and the leading normally aspirated cars would be difficult to beat because we had fuel consumption problems. In the first laps I used minimum power but I had to push when Ivan was close.*'

34. SPAIN (Jerez) 2 October 1988, 72 laps, front row. He got cleanly away but came under attack from Mansell.

LAP	PROST	MANSELL
10	1:30.603	1:30.396
11	1:30.442	1:30.858
12	1:30.268	1:31.186
13	1:30.924	1:30.992
14	1:30.624	1:29.885
15	1:29.975	1:30.058

Nigel Roebuck's insight: '*The Prost–Mansell duel was fascinating. On the one hand you marvelled at Nigel's relentlessness and fight, his occasional blistering laps which brought him close to the McLaren; on the other you were lost in admiration for Alain's utter calm, absolute refusal to be flustered into braking a yard too late. Even with the Williams large in his mirrors he continued to change up at precisely the same points every lap; his line through the first turn never wavered a trace. They were at their closest – virtually nose to tail – from laps 23 to 25 . . .*'

LAP	PROST	MANSELL
23	1:30.038	1:29.567
24	1:30.252	1:30.279
25	1:30.960	1:30.816

Mansell had problems with a rear wheel on lap 47 and that settled it, Prost winning by 26.232 seconds. Prost's insight: '*My two main problems were fuel consumption and tyre wear. I had decided not to stop for tyres because my radio wasn't working and I didn't have the information I needed but my crew showed me a signal and I came in for a very quick stop. I was right on the limit of the consumption but within the permitted tolerance of the system.*'

35. AUSTRALIA (Adelaide) 13 November 1988, 82 laps, front row. He got cleanly away but Berger had told him his Ferrari wouldn't have enough fuel to finish if he drove it hard – so he intended to enjoy himself. Berger took the lead on lap 14 at the end of the straight but crashed into Arnoux on lap 26. On lap 46 several cars were involved in another crash. Prost had no choice but to run through the debris and a front-wing endplate perished, making the car understeer. Prost's insight: '*From then on it was a matter of playing with the front roll-bar and damper settings to try and minimize the problem. For the rest of the race the car was*

very difficult to drive.' You'd barely have known. This is Prost's sequence before, during and after:

Lap 45	1:22.555
Lap 46	1:21.650
Lap 47	1:21.559
Lap 48	1:22.548
Lap 49	1:22.375
Lap 50	1:21.594

And on lap 59 he set his fastest time – and that of the whole race – with 1:21.216. He beat Senna by 36.787 seconds. Prost's insight: '*Quite a race!*'

36. USA (Phoenix) 4 June 1989, 75 laps, front row. He had had a fraught final qualifying session. 'I crashed my race car in the morning – my own fault – and badly damaged a monocoque, for the first time since I joined McLaren. Then I had a slight engine problem with the spare car. During the afternoon my rear brake calipers were getting hot and I also got caught up in traffic.' After all that he judged the front row a good place to be. He might have reached turn one in the lead but on his side of the track there was a bump, he was changing gear as he reached it and he had wheelspin, the rev counter went wild and briefly the engine cut. Senna pulled away. As the race unfolded Prost started to watch the water and oil temperatures with mounting concern and when he was directly behind Senna 'they began to frighten me'. He backed off, let them settle and then started to move. Senna had a misfire. Prost could win it at a canter and did, by 39.696 seconds from Patrese. Prost's insight: '*The track was breaking up a little towards the end but I had chosen the harder B compound tyres which helped the handling as the surface grip improved in the second half of the race.*'

37. FRANCE (Paul Ricard) 9 July 1989, 80 laps, pole. He took the lead and never lost it. Prost's insight: '*I tried to conserve my tyres throughout because this track has an extremely abrasive surface and I think my tactics paid off. They were in good condition at the end. I didn't have any real pressure from anyone but Berger, Nannini, Capelli and others were not too far behind in the early part so I had to concentrate on keeping my rhythm.*' He won it from Mansell by 44.017 seconds.

38. BRITAIN (Silverstone) 16 July 1989, 64 laps, front row. He made a better start but Senna took him towards Copse, powering

down the inside – Prost wasn't pleased about how close Senna came – and it stayed like that until lap 12 when Senna, with a lead of 0.787 seconds, spun off ('I had difficulty selecting third gear on the downchange almost from the start. Four or five laps before I spun I almost went off at the same place. Eventually I couldn't get the gear and that was that. I couldn't take the corner in neutral!'). Prost's insight: '*We were using the new transverse gearbox for the first time and we were not fully certain about its reliability. You can't really attack the corners because you never know if the gear is going in or not. You have to leave some margin. I was quite happy to run second behind Ayrton in the opening stages. I felt I was having an easier time but you cannot get too close to another car on such a fast circuit because of the aerodynamic turbulence. I saw him have two or three moments before he eventually went off.*' Prost now had to hold Mansell at bay.

Lap	Prost	Mansell
20	1:13.367	1:14.049
21	1:14.608	1:14.023
22	1:14.698	1:15.110
23	1:15.057	1:14.549
24	1:13.337	1:15.766

On lap 43 Mansell had a puncture and that left Prost with a lead of 54 seconds. He eased off towards the end, beating Mansell by 19.369 seconds.

39. ITALY (Monza) 11 September 1989, 53 laps, second row. Prost was publicly unhappy about getting equal treatment with Senna and was not mollified when Senna broke clear, Prost running fourth. He took Mansell on lap 21, Berger on 41 and Senna broke down on lap 45. Prost's insight: '*It was luck, my good luck and Ayrton's bad. The way my engines were during the meeting I couldn't get near him.*'

40. BRAZIL (Interlagos) 25 March 1990, 71 laps, third row. Senna and Berger broke clear followed by Boutsen and Prost, now with Ferrari. On lap 8 Boutsen took Berger and on lap 17 Prost did, too. At the pit stops Boutsen's brakes failed – he almost ran into a mechanic – and although he re-emerged he was no longer in contention. Senna had a long stop – a problem with the left rear wheel – but still held a lead of more than 10 seconds. Past the halfway mark Senna tried to lap Nakajima. 'I followed him

through three corners and then he seemed to open the door as if to let me through. As I went inside him he came across me and my nose was lost against his rear wheel.' Nakajima had moved aside but that put him on a dusty part of the track and there was nothing he could do except apologize. Prost ran smoothly to the end, 13.564 seconds in front of Berger. Prost's insight: '*Second race for Ferrari, first victory, fantastic. We proved the car had a good performance and was reliable, particularly after the problems we had had in the first race, Phoenix.*'

41. MEXICO (Mexico City) 24 June 1990, 69 laps, seventh row. Qualifying was a disaster, lack of grip, a spin, engine down on power and he was thirteenth on the grid. He hadn't been that low since 1980. Very quietly he said that the race would be different. The car was well set-up. He was still thirteenth after lap 1 but realized that the Ferrari was actually quicker than all the others – an interesting realization with 68 laps left. He moved past Nannini on lap 2, De Cesaris on lap 3, Martini on lap 4, Warwick on lap 7 . . . by lap 13 he was sixth, by lap 55 second and on lap 61 he took Senna for the lead. He swarmed him and eventually swamped him on the straight on a power play, got a tow, flicked the Ferrari out and was gone. Senna had a puncture and Prost beat Mansell by 25.351 seconds. Prost's insight: '*It may be my best victory, and not because I started thirteenth but for the way it was constructed. When you're behind the wheel you are aware of what people outside aren't, flashes, little tricks, you can almost sniff these things which subconsciously guide you. Sometimes you have to sacrifice your second qualifying session to prepare better for the race itself or try something which you hadn't thought about before but now seems the right thing to do. From that moment, whether you're on pole or the seventh row, nothing can stop you.*'

42. FRANCE (Paul Ricard) 8 July 1990, 80 laps, second row. He ran sixth early on, the engine cutting out every time he changed into top. He pitted for tyres on lap 28 when he was eighth and flew. Within seven laps he was third behind Capelli and Mauricio Gugelmin. He took the latter on lap 54, outbraking him into the first corner clean and swift, holding the car's balance perfectly as he hugged the inside.

LAP	CAPELLI	PROST
54	1:10.031	1:09.170
55	1:09.764	1:08.508
56	1:08.737	1:09.615
57	1:09.244	1:08.770
58	1:10.567	1:08.579

After lap 60 the gap was 0.432 but while Prost could close up he couldn't get past and that became a dilemma: he wanted the win, of course, but six points would have been useful towards the Championship. Moreover he had a blister on a tyre and it made the car vibrate. On lap 78 he thrust the Ferrari ahead at le Beausset: a right-hander looming and Prost pressed the Ferrari right up to Capelli, jinked right and held the inside line. In total safety. Fast as you can blink your eye. Soon after Capelli had engine trouble and Prost beat him by 8.626 seconds. Prost's insight: '*It was the old story. When I was some way behind Ivan I was much quicker but when I caught him up the balance of my car was upset by the turbulence from his.*'

43. BRITAIN (Silverstone) 15 July 1990, 64 laps, third row. He ran fifth early on to save his tyres, was fourth after Senna spun, third when he took Boutsen, second when he took Berger ('right from the start the car was very difficult to drive. I thought I would lose control on the faster corners,' Berger said) and grasped the lead when Mansell's gearbox began to misbehave. It was done on the exit to Becketts, the left-hander: Alex Caffi (Arrows) – a backmarker – with Mansell tight on him and Prost tight on Mansell, watching, watching, watching. They flowed out of Becketts, Caffi far to the right. The timing and anticipation was almost unreal. Before Mansell had ducked out to take Caffi, Prost had already ducked out to take him, going far to the left to use the full width of the track. For a fleeting instant they ran three-abreast but Prost screwed just a little more power out of his car than Mansell could down Hangar Straight and reached Stowe Corner first. Later Mansell dropped out, gearbox, and Prost beat Boutsen by 39.092 seconds. Prost's insight: '*No real problems . . .*'

44. SPAIN (Jerez) 30 September 1990, 73 laps, front row. He tracked Senna but lacked the power to overtake him. Jerez isn't an easy place to do that. This is how he worked it out: 1) My Ferrari is better than Senna's McLaren through the fast corners. 2) The only sensible place to overtake is at the end of the straight but Senna is

out-accelerating me on that straight so that I can't out brake him for the corner at the end of it. 3) If I can get in front I will win easily. 4) The best chance is to have a faster pit stop and get out of the pits before he does. Therefore I will cling to him all the way to the pit stops. Lap 25: Prost stops, 6.17 seconds. He knows he must fly now. Lap 26: Senna stops, 5.71 seconds but Prost has been flying and as Senna slips from the pit lane exit Prost is upon him – and with all the ferocity, all the momentum of travelling at high speed. Turn One is a right-hander and Prost goes outside Senna, takes him – they weren't far apart. But the race is settled. He beat Mansell by 22.064 seconds. '*You can say your car is two seconds quicker that someone else's but proving it is something else. Here I had the opportunity.*'

11

A STING IN THE TALE

> From time to time he was braking prematurely, which was really underhand . . . next time I'll try to take him on the inside and I'll run him off.
>
> ALAIN PROST

Gerard Ducarouge made a noise rendered incoherent by anger, cocked his fist and punched the canvas wall. Whether he hit anyone is hard to say. There were too many fast-moving targets, too much of a chaotic mêlée, too many people gripped by self-interest. From where I was standing I don't think they were even aware of the punch.

Friday, 9 August 1991. The sun was hanging low beyond the gently rolling hills of the Hungaroring that late afternoon but it was still hot enough to burnish and that somehow fuelled it. The irritant of heavy sweat was on every forehead.

The Elf motorhome is normally a sanctuary for journalists. Outside it under a white awning half a dozen tables are arranged so that they can shade themselves and take a coffee, a fruit juice or perhaps a glass of wine. Elf is there among the team's motorhomes, all arranged in a row in the paddock down the concrete steps from the pits, and by its nature the sort of place where great events are endlessly discussed but not made.

By a quirk which can only be regarded as bizarre, Elf had something invaluable: a video player which could play French cassettes. France works to a system called Secam and it is not compatible with the VHS used virtually everywhere else in Europe. To Elf this Friday afternoon by pressing invitation came Prost and Senna and several FISA officials to watch a tape of the race before, the German Grand Prix at Hockenheim, and an interview which Prost gave immediately after it.

In a communiqué, FISA laid out the background from the Hockenheim TV interview thus: 'Alain Prost, in a new fit of rage, points a vengeful finger at Ayrton Senna: "I went on to the grass once or twice at 320kph. From time to time he was braking prematurely, which was really underhand. I therefore tried everything I could but next time I'll try to take him on the inside and I'll run him off, that's for sure. I'll play Mansell's and Renault's game right to the end of the Championship if that's the way it is because he [Senna] is completely out of order and the Federation is incapable of taking decisions; they fined [Mauricio] Gugelmin and [Aguri] Suzuki 10,000 dollars at Magny-Cours and Silverstone, but nobody does anything with regard to the top drivers. If regulations exist they must be the same for everybody.'

This background, stemming from a race which had been cleanly and clearly dominated by Mansell and Patrese while Prost struggled to overtake Senna and eventually went off at the chicane in what proved to be a last, final, nearly desperate attempt to achieve that, chilled Formula One. The fact that Prost didn't like Senna and Senna didn't like Prost had been open knowledge for two years, the fact that they had twice crashed at Suzuka had been chilling enough but now here was Prost gripped by the anger we know so well threatening to 'run' Senna off.

Racing is inherently dangerous even without this. Consider it: the Williams which Mansell was driving would do 0 to 200 mph and stop in 14 seconds. It would brake from 180 mph to 55 in 1.75 seconds. In a tight sequence of corners it generated G forces so extreme that Mansell had difficulty 'physically dragging' his eyeballs round to focus on the next corner coming up.

These are machines which, when they are moving in clusters, demand the utmost prudence from every man handling them. FISA, under the umbrella of the world body the FIA (Fédération Internationale Automobile) could no longer claim to run Formula One if they allowed Prost's words to stand unchallenged or, more pertinently, unpunished.

Their communiqué also gave their decree:

Attention Mr John Corsmit,
Stewards' Office, Hungaroring.
Urgent and important.

According to Articles 170 and 177 of the Sporting Regulations of the 1991 FIA Formula One World Championship, and after seeing the video tape of the German Grand Prix as well as an interview given by driver Alain Prost to French television, the Special Commission of Inquiry for Safety has decided

1) In pursuance of Article 58 of the International Sporting Code and 29 of the FIA Statutes, to give a warning to the drivers Ayrton Senna and Alain Prost for their conduct during the German Grand Prix, and to inflict upon Alain Prost a suspension for one Grand Prix, with suspended effect, by reason of the declaration he made in a televised interview concerning the FISA. You are therefore requested to convoke these two drivers to your office today at 3.30pm in order to inform them of these decisions.

(Signed) YVON LEON,
The Secretary General of the FISA.

And then of course they needed to play the video, which took them along the paddock to the normally becalmed waters of the Elf motorhome. They were closeted securely within and like a sharp, sharp whisper the news spread. Within a little while the photographers had begun to gather among those half-dozen tables and more photographers came and then more until they were shoulder to shoulder cheek to jowl round the door, were standing on the chairs and tables; and they merged into a solid mass, each weighted by the equipment they carry, each needing a vantage point to catch the moment, whatever that would be. And as I say, the heat didn't help. Nor did the wait. They were there two hours while inside Prost and Senna made another attempt at reconciliation.

The Ligier motorhome, with its own awning, was directly next to Elf, divided by the canvas wall. Thierry Boutsen was preparing to give an interview to a lone journalist who fiddled with his tape-recorder, setting it up. Boutsen wondered quite what was happening at Elf. All he could see through the canvas wall was the backs of the photographers facing away from him.

Without warning Prost and Senna emerged down the tight little stairwell from the motorhome and were hemmed. A ripple passed through the photographers, they lurched forward instinctively, under the impetus of the lurch they began to spill and elbow and topple and one of them tumbled back into the canvas wall and might have come clean through, dragging it down. Ducarouge, Ligier's designer, cocked the fist and punched. It was a useful right hook. Boutsen rose, bemused, and a brief smile of irony spreading all across his face, rose to have a look, was shaking his head. I was standing next to him and I didn't see much either except the jostling and tumbling going on and on.

Evidently both men – they were smiling, too – made restrained little speeches about peace, or at least about giving peace another chance. Then they were gone, each their separate ways. It was a cameo of a season, maybe even a cameo of a life.

No man had ever endured, experienced or simply lived through such a season. Just as the cars themselves are inherently dangerous so Grand Prix racing is inherently tumultuous; it is, as we have seen, played out on the stage of extremes and excuse me for restating that. But 1991 was something else again: charged with venom, with bitter turmoil within Ferrari and without, with sinister politics, with hirings and firings, with Prost using obscenities about the Italian Press – they demanded an apology, considered legal action and he did say he was unwise to use the obscenities but he did not moderate his position; and then there was the strange interlude of Umberto Agnelli, brother of Gianni (who owns Fiat who own Ferrari) stirring it all, the strange interlude of Prost speaking of his team-mate Jean Alesi in ominous words at Silverstone; and always in the foreground or the background Ayrton himself; and then there was . . .

But, observing chronological order, we come back to *J'ACCUSE*, to Imola in the spring and that test session where, all else aside, it snowed. Senna had won the opener round the streets of Phoenix from Prost, who had clutch problems and worse made a pit stop for tyres which went wrong. The flickering figures on the world's television screens froze at 15.87 seconds, double the normal time it takes, before he moved away. The mechanics had had to struggle with the right rear. 'These things happen,' Prost would say. 'We should remember that often mechanics help you to win a race with a quick stop.'

It left him in seventh place and now he demonstrated all his touch. He worked his way up to fourth, Senna a long way down the road followed by Alesi and Piquet (Benetton). They rounded a left-hander and Alesi hugged the right of the track, Piquet moving out to overtake him, Prost tracking Piquet. As Piquet drew level with Alesi, Prost had a brief look outside Piquet; as Piquet drew clear of Alesi, Prost had a brief look inside and with exquisite timing went into the gap between Alesi and Piquet; and that was second place.

He fought bad handling to be fourth in Brazil and now the bill-boards of France were being prepared for *J'ACCUSE*. In a long interview Prost began by saying: 'When something doesn't work it's always necessary to find people who are guilty. Or excuses. That's virtually the same thing. One day someone is guilty, another day someone else is guilty. Today there's talk of Steve Nichols [a designer] because the chassis is involved. For me that's a scandal, truly a scandal because it's not at all his fault. It's too easy to incriminate someone in particular. We're all guilty or no one is guilty. What is certain is that the choice of attacking the season with the 642 car was not made by Steve Nichols or me but by the management.'

Question: Since Brazil is the team in crisis?

'Crisis is almost the normal state at Ferrari. When you win there is a crisis of optimism. The problem is that there are one or two people in the team who have slight experience of Formula One. It's possible for them to think that if a car is competitive at the end of a season you must keep it for the start of the next season. That was true ten years ago. Now things change from race to race.' (Ferrari's car, designated the 642, had finished 1990 well, of course.)

Prost confirmed that he could speak to Gianni Agnelli whenever he wished. All he had to do was pick up the receiver and dial the number or go round. And there was a sting in the final paragraph of the interview. 'The structure put in place by Ron Dennis [at McLaren] is much more effective than ours. He was a mechanic, he knows Formula One well, he's been in motorsport for a long time and he doesn't hesitate to lend a hand when it's necessary. Ron Dennis is a leader of men, a catalyst of energies, he is completely respected and that's what's missing here.'

This was not exactly good news for Ferrari's sporting director Cesare Fiorio, although he and Prost agreed at the San Marino Grand Prix a few weeks after the test to leave the politics alone for the weekend. Now shallow water claimed Prost who, on the parade lap taking him to the starting grid, ran into a puddle and spun away never to return. Alesi was gone, too, by lap 3 when he went off trying to overtake Stefano Modena (Tyrrell). That word crisis was howling and baying from every Italian headline.

Prost ran second at Monaco before Mansell took him and was fifth after a late pit stop because he had suspension problems. A week later Fiorio was gone and Prost had won what someone described as 'a battle of wills'. Piero Ferrari, Enzo's son, took over as part of a triumvirate. There was blood on the floor, not water. Fiorio departed proclaiming no bitterness and would not remain silent for long.

The season was slipping away. In Canada, Prost's gearbox failed and he got only as far as lap 16 in Mexico when a misfire halted him. The new Ferrari, the 643, was ready for France – at Magny-Cours, a circuit new to Formula One – and Prost put it on the front row of the grid. Twice in the race he was overtaken by a very aggressive Mansell and accepted a safe second place 'for the team as much as for myself.' Afterwards, speaking in the soft, mellow way he does into microphones, he said: 'Yes, the best is yet to come.'

It was without question the correct decision to settle for second and a mature one, too. Mansell, eternally combative, felt the season slipping away from himself; had announced his retirement the season before, departing Prost, Ferrari and the whole thing for the sake of his family, had been lured to join Williams by Frank himself with a golden contract and the only possible justification for changing his mind: to win the World Championship. At Magny-Cours, the Williams flying, Mansell went for the win and the ten points he needed to haul himself nearer to Senna at the head of the table and justify the decision.

Prost knew that if you take a new car to second place you're moving in the right direction and what would they all have said if he'd tangled with Mansell and they had crashed instead?

Umberto Agnelli had a different view, said aloud how much he admired Senna and questioned Prost's motivation. To appreciate what this means you have to consider several factors. Umberto was not directly involved in Ferrari although he was vice-president of Fiat and therefore a man of some consequence. By citing Senna's name he was either being naïve or extremely provocative. By citing Prost's motivation he was being plain silly. Didn't Umberto Agnelli know after all these years that Alain Prost always extracts the maximum by using the minimum? Didn't he know that Alain Prost always extracts whatever a car has to offer and has always done? Didn't he know what failure at Ferrari meant to Prost?

Umberto Agnelli must have been aware that the headlines would be howling and baying again and they did, and they did. Prost gave a television interview and compared the journalists to something I won't mention here, which enraged them – itself an amazing thing, given the latitude they daily grant themselves.

Prost also delivered ripostes in two interviews to the written media. To *Gazetta dello Sport* he said: 'With the help of Cesare Fiorio the Press began to criticize me. Today if there is a person who should shut his mouth it is Fiorio, and I mean it. If he continues to make comments it will be very dangerous to him. Fiorio has led everyone to believe that the Ferrari wins were his wins. The opposite is true. The wins were due to the whole team.'

To *Auto Hebdo* he said: 'The words of Umberto Agnelli, a very important and influential person, have hurt me. Before coming to Ferrari I underestimated the enormous pressure on Ferrari drivers, engineers and mechanics. It's all the more difficult because of that. It's impossible to read an article about me without criticism and that hurts me as a driver and a human being.'

His conclusion: If Ferrari want Senna, go hire Senna.

Gianni Agnelli would be on the phone to Prost, saying sorry . . .

Alesi was aggressive at Silverstone and overtook Prost on muscle, power-play or exuberance, depending on your viewpoint. 'It was pass or crash', Prost said. 'I was surprised, I must say.' Was this another undercurrent of tension surfacing? We didn't know, we didn't know. Mansell won Silverstone by driving a beautifully controlled race, Prost third, Senna out of fuel at the end but classified fourth; and the Championship was tightening, Senna 51, Mansell 33, Patrese 22, Prost 21.

At Hockenheim the Italian Press demanded an apology from Prost who had confessed that although he normally doesn't read their coverage the 'people at the factory do' and frankly it was getting on his nerves. Prost withdrew the obscenities – but no more.

The German Grand Prix was conducted on two levels. Mansell, at this moment in his career become masterful, took the lead and headed off into the distance but Patrese, who potentially ought to have been doing the same thing, had made a bad start and was working his way up through the field. For the initial part of the race it was Mansell, Berger, then in tandem Senna, Prost, Patrese in that order. Patrese took Prost and Senna – seemingly without difficulty – and that made people wonder. Prost tracked Senna lap on lap but could not take him. This went on . . . and on, Prost looking, attacking, probing, Senna defending or – this is a fine point – baulking. It went on until lap 38 of forty-five when, at the chicane, Prost went for it, Senna's McLaren seemed to twitch towards him and Prost kept straight on down the escape road.

Prost then gave The Interview, said he would 'run' Senna off and all at once we are on tables and chairs outside the Elf motorhome, the Hungaroring, Friday, 9 August 1991, and Gerard Ducarouge is cocking his fist.

It is necessary to listen to both drivers.

Senna: 'What happened in the past is past, when we were teammates and when we were not. It was not pleasant for anyone, not only us. It was a frustrating and stressful time. The situation would be good for me but not for the other and then the other way round. I don't think we were ready to try it last year [peace, declared at Monza] but now one year later I have to believe it will work. Maybe it won't. Only time will tell. I cannot say.

'It would not have happened if we had not been brought to the same room to discuss something regarding him and me [the Hockenheim race]. Once we were in the room it was a natural thing which developed by itself. I honestly believe that as much as I have had enough of this he has had more than enough. Different timing can sometimes change a situation.'

Prost: 'I am not upset by the threatened ban. If this is an attempt to gag me it won't. If I have something to say, particularly if it concerns safety, I will say it.

'Ayrton and I talked for nearly two hours and cleared up a lot of things. OK, once or twice it got a bit heated but generally it was friendly. I'm not going to say anything about what was actually said because we both promised not to do that. The discussion was private.'

The consequences were always going to be public, although not at the Hungaroring where Senna led from flag to flag and Prost, at one point fourth but never within (if I can put it in such a way) striking distance, retired when the engine went. At Spa, Senna took pole, Patrese alongside, Prost behind, but three hours after the final qualifying session scrutineers decided that Patrese's Williams violated the rules (reverse gear didn't work and you have to have reverse). They relegated him to his Saturday position, seventeenth, and his place on the grid – directly in front of Prost – was left vacant. It might have been important because it gave Prost a clear run to Eau Rouge, the hairpin a mere hundred metres from the start line and so tight that whoever gets there first has an instant advantage: you can start to build a race-long lead from exactly there. Senna got away fast, holding the inside line and Prost got away fast too, flirted with trying to take Eau Rouge from Senna – the Ferrari twitched under braking – but couldn't, settled into second place and held that under attack from Mansell until the second lap when Mansell went through on stark power. A lap later tongues of fire were licking the back of the Ferrari, smoke enveloped the engine and Prost simply pulled off. Some you win, some you lose like this.

Monza was more promising and just to demonstrate the almost unimaginable demarcation line between that and fulfilment here are the times from the final qualifying session. Please remember they are to hundredths of a second.

Senna	1:21.245
Mansell	1:21.247
Berger	1:21.346
Patrese	1:21.372
Prost	1:21.285
Alesi	1:21.890

They were set on a circuit 3.604 miles long, including two chicanes. In the race Senna took the lead tracked inevitably by Mansell and Patrese, Prost holding station fourth although young Michael Schumacher – the German who had been plucked into Formula One by the Eddie Jordan team when their driver, Bertrand Gachot, went to prison for assaulting a London taxi driver and who now, amid much acrimony, had departed Jordan for Benetton – mounted an assault on him. Prost resisted that firmly enough and after Patrese dropped out and Senna pitted for tyres found himself in second place behind Mansell.

Senna of course was charging with those new tyres and towards the end of the race came upon Prost. It might have been a sharp encounter bearing in mind its antecedents but Prost kept the Ferrari pointed straight ahead so that Senna could duck out and overtake. Peace, brother. Prost finished a solid third.

There was even levity during the post-race press conference when Mansell, 18 points behind Senna, said he intended to battle him all the way and Senna, in that quiet way he has, said naturally he would prefer to win races and settle it before Japan. Bearing in mind the antecedents, we could all summon a smile. So could Prost, who, in that quiet way he has, said that if it did go as far as Japan he was looking forward to watching developments 'from behind'. He added mischievously that maybe it was the only way he could win a race in 1991, Mansell and Senna taking each other out. After all, the last season when he hadn't won was . . . 1980.

Portugal was, well, a race like so many before across the season, third row of the grid and a retirement on lap 40 – engine – but he hadn't been within sight of the leaders before that. The rumour mill was much more interesting and began to grind out all sorts of theories, the most notable of which was that Prost was thoroughly fed up with the politics and hysteria surrounding Ferrari and although he had re-signed for 1992 he might decide to sit out the season – his Ferrari contract precluded him from driving for another team – and concentrate his energies on helping to found a much-vaunted French super-team by expanding Ligier, Renault engines, and with himself back in the cockpit in 1993 for a major assault on the Championship. As the nights began to shorten into autumn that had to be more appealing than more punishment at Ferrari. Or did it? Rumour mills always leave you asking that kind of question. The other point of interest was that Prost had been due to make a statement at Portugal and hadn't. He was going to Spain in a week but, well, that was maybe a rumour too . . .

In Spain he said, 'I don't want to talk about my decision but I will give you my opinion. Ferrari's performance this season has not been a good one. I would like to have a Ferrari with which I can win races and fight for the World Championship. My challenge was and is to see a winning Ferrari but if we want to see that for sure there is a lot that must be changed.'

Interestingly enough he ran a strong second in the race and finished there, and this a wet-dry Grand Prix. 'If I had not been racing for Ferrari today but for myself I would have started on slick tyres and I would have won because of that. I only began on wet-weather tyres because there wasn't enough time to change to slicks before the start, because I wasn't allowed to, because of the awfully stupid pressure on us today at Ferrari.' The words were enigmatic and ambivalent and of course we might get the statement in Japan, which was next . . . or confirmation of a couple of other rumours. The first: Ligier had offered him thirty million dollars to help organize the super-team, testing then driving for it. The second: that he would rejoin McLaren in 1993, perhaps partnering Senna. It was a staggering thought but very, very intriguing, too. Wasn't it?

In Japan he was a distant fourth which brought him within

touching distance of another landmark, 700 points in his career. He now had 699½, hugely more than anybody else. On the evening of 20 October 1991 the all-time leader board read:

Prost 699½
Senna 486
Piquet 484
Lauda 420½
Stewart 360
Mansell 358
Reutemann 310
Graham Hill 289
Fittipaldi 281
Fangio 277½

After Japan, Ferrari fired Prost, who had said, 'Basically the difference between an English and Italian team is in the way they listen to their drivers. I've pointed out and underlined the defects of Ferrari throughout the season but no one really listened to a word I said. When I was at McLaren every remark was taken into account from Ron Dennis down to the lowest mechanic.' Later in a statement he also said, 'While I regret that I should be in a contentious situation with Ferrari I am relieved that what for me has been a very unsatisfactory season has been brought to an end.'

Could Ferrari truly stop him driving for another team in 1992? Prost really ought to have given Teddy Mayer a phone call about that so they could discuss a man's right to work; which is almost where we came in.

Oh, there was talk of a swop, Patrese to Ferrari – but Ferrari signed Ivan Capelli; talk of Mansell going to Ferrari for 17 million dollars – but Ferrari signed Ivan Capelli; talk of Prost joining the Eddie Jordan team, which would have been the ultimate Christmas present. Meanwhile Prost was talking to Ligier who had – nudge, nudge, wink, wink – Renault engines and that would have given a very Gallic equation: French team + French leading driver + Elf + Renault.

The real sting in the tale was that as Christmas approached the most successful driver of all time had no drive at all.

12
STATISTICS

P = pole position, FL = fastest lap, R = retired, DNS = did not start, DSQ = disqualified.

KARTING

1973, French and World Junior champion, 2nd in French seniors, 14th World Championships. 1974, French Senior champion, not in top ten in Worlds. 1975, French Senior champion, not in top ten in Worlds.

1976

FORMULA RENAULT FRANCE

4 Apr	Le Mans	Martini MK17-Renault	1
18 Apr	Nogaro	Martini MK17-Renault	1 P/FL
1 May	Magny-Cours	Martini MK17-Renault	1 P/FL

FORMULA RENAULT EUROPE

9 May	Dijon	Lola T410-Renault	R P
16 May	Zolder	Lola T410-Renault	R

FORMULA RENAULT FRANCE

23 May	Clermont Ferrand	Martini MK17-Renault	1 P/FL
20 Jun	Folembray	Martini MK17-Renault	1 P
27 Jun	Rouen	Martini MK17-Renault	1 FL
4 Jul	Paul Ricard	Martini MK17-Renault	1 FL
11 Jul	Magny-Cours	Martini MK17-Renault	1 P/FL

5 Aug	Dijon	Martini MK17-Renault	1 P/FL
19 Aug	Nogaro	Martini MK17-Renault	1 FL
30 Sep	Albi	Martini MK17-Renault	1 FL
17 Oct	Paul Ricard	Martini MK17-Renault	1 FL
24 Oct	Imola	Martini MK17-Renault	R FL

1977

FORMULA RENAULT EUROPE

27 Mar	Le Mans	Martini MK20 Renault	3
11 Apr	Nogaro	Martini MK20 Renault	1 FL
17 Apr	Hockenheim	Martini MK20 Renault	5
1 May	Magny-Cours	Martini MK20 Renault	1
22 May	Monte Carlo	Martini MK20 Renault	2 FL
29 May	Pau	Martini MK20 Renault	2 FL
5 Jun	Zolder	Martini MK20 Renault	R P
19 Jun	Clermont Ferrand	Martini MK20 Renault	3
26 Jun	Rouen	Martini MK20 Renault	1 P/FL
3 Jul	Dijon	Martini MK20 Renault	13

GRAND PRIX DE NOGARO (F2)

10 Jul	Nogaro	Elf 2J-Renault	10

FORMULA RENAULT EUROPE

10 Jul	Nogaro	Martini MK20 Renault	1 P
17 Jul	Magny-Cours	Martini MK20 Renault	R P
24 Jul	Paul Ricard	Martini MK20 Renault	5
11 Sep	Monza	Martini MK20 Renault	1 FL
25 Sep	Albi	Martini MK20 Renault	1 FL

GRANDE PREMIO DO ESTORIL (F2)

2 Oct	Estoril	Elf 2J-Renault	R

FORMULA RENAULT EUROPE

15 Oct	Paul Ricard	Martini MK20 Renault	7 FL

1978

EUROPEAN FORMULA THREE

23 Apr	Zolder	Martini MK21B Renault	10

MONACO FORMULA THREE

7 May	Monte Carlo	Martini MK21B Renault	4

EUROPEAN FORMULA TWO

15 May	Pau	Chevron B40-Hart	R

EUROPEAN FORMULA THREE

28 May	Nürburgring	Martini MK21B Renault	R
4 Jun	Dijon	Martini MK21B Renault	10
25 June	Monza	Martini MK21B Renault	14

BP FORMULA THREE

2 Jul	Paul Ricard	Martini MK21B Renault	3

EUROPEAN FORMULA THREE

16 Jul	Magny-Cours	Martini MK21B Renault	R
26 Aug	Donington Park	Martini MK21B Renault	6

VANDERVELL FORMULA THREE

28 Aug	Silverstone	Martini MK21B Renault	3

EUROPEAN FORMULA THREE

17 Sep	Jarama	Martini MK21B Renault	1 P/FL
8 Oct	Vallelunga	Martini MK21B Renault	R

1979

EUROPEAN FORMULA THREE

18 Mar	Vallelunga	Martini MK27 Renault	2 FL
16 Apr	Österreichring	Martini MK27 Renault	1
23 Apr	Zolder	Martini MK27 Renault	1
1 May	Magny-Cours	Martini MK27 Renault	1 FL
20 May	Donington Park	Martini MK27 Renault	3

MONACO FORMULA THREE

26 May	Monte Carlo	Martini MK27 Renault	1 P/FL

EUROPEAN FORMULA THREE

4 Jun	Zandvoort	Martini MK27 Renault	1 P/FL
24 Jun	Monza	Martini MK27 Renault	R

VANDERVELL FORMULA THREE

14 Jul	Silverstone	Martini MK27 Renault	14

EUROPEAN FORMULA THREE

5 Aug	Knutstorp	Martini MK27 Renault	1 P/FL
12 Aug	Kinnekulle	Martini MK27 Renault	R P
9 Sep	Jarama	Martini MK27 Renault	1 P/FL

FRENCH FORMULA THREE

15 Sep	La Châtre	Martini MK27 Renault	1 FL
22 Sep	Albi	Martini MK27 Renault	1 FL

1980

FORMULA ONE

13 Jan	Argentina	McLaren M29B Cosworth DFV	6
27 Jan	Brazil	McLaren M29B Cosworth DFV	5
1 Mar	S. Africa	McLaren M29B Cosworth DFV	DNS
4 May	Belgium	McLaren M29B Cosworth DFV	R
18 May	Monaco	McLaren M29B Cosworth DFV	R

NON-CHAMPIONSHIP

1 Jun	Spain	McLaren M29B Cosworth DFV	R

FORMULA ONE

29 June	France	McLaren M29B Cosworth DFV	R
13 Jul	Britain	McLaren M29B Cosworth DFV	6
10 Aug	Germany	McLaren M29B Cosworth DFV	11
17 Aug	Austria	McLaren M29B Cosworth DFV	7
31 Aug	Holland	McLaren M30B Cosworth DFV	6

14 Sep	Italy	McLaren M30B Cosworth DFV	7
28 Sep	Canada	McLaren M30B Cosworth DFV	R
5 Oct	USA East	McLaren M30B Cosworth DFV	DNS

1981

15 Mar	USA West	Renault RE228EFI	R
29 Mar	Brazil	Renault RE228EFI	R
12 Apr	Argentina	Renault RE228EFI	3
3 May	San Marino	Renault RE228EFI	R
17 May	Belgium	Renault RE30EFI	R
31 May	Monaco	Renault RE30EFI	R
21 Jun	Spain	Renault RE30EFI	R
5 Jul	France	Renault RE30EFI	1 FL
18 Jul	Britain	Renault RE30EFI	R
2 Aug	Germany	Renault RE30EFI	2 P
16 Aug	Austria	Renault RE30EFI	R
30 Aug	Holland	Renault RE30EFI	1 P
13 Sep	Italy	Renault RE30EFI	1
27 Sep	Canada	Renault RE30EFI	R
17 Oct	USA	Renault RE30EFI	2

1982

23 Jan	S. Africa	Renault RE30BEFI	1 FL
21 Mar	Brazil	Renault RE30BEFI	1 P
4 Apr	USA West	Renault RE30BEFI	R
25 Apr	San Marino	Renault RE30BEFI	R
9 May	Belgium	Renault RE30BEFI	R P
23 May	Monaco	Renault RE30BEFI	R
6 Jun	USA East	Renault RE30BEFI	P/FL
13 Jun	Canada	Renault RE30BEFI	R
3 Jul	Holland	Renault RE30BEFI	R
18 Jul	Britain	Renault RE30BEFI	6
25 Jul	France	Renault RE30BEFI	2
8 Aug	Germany	Renault RE30BEFI	R
15 Aug	Austria	Renault RE30BEFI	R
29 Aug	Switzerland	Renault RE30BEFI	2 P/FL
12 Sep	Italy	Renault RE30BEFI	R
25 Sep	USA	Renault RE30BEFI	4 P

NON-CHAMPIONSHIP

7 Nov	Australia	Ralt RT4-Ford BDA	1 P

1983

13 Mar	Brazil	Renault RE30CEFI	7
27 Mar	USA West	Renault RE4OEFI	11
17 Apr	France	Renault RE4OEFI	1 P/FL
1 May	San Marino	Renault RE4OEFI	2
15 May	Monaco	Renault RE4OEFI	3
22 May	Belgium	Renault RE4OEFI	1 P
5 Jun	USA East	Renault RE4OEFI	8
12 Jun	Canada	Renault RE4OEFI	5
16 Jul	Britain	Renault RE4OEFI	1 FL
7 Aug	Germany	Renault RE4OEFI	4
14 Aug	Austria	Renault RE4OEFI	1 FL
28 Aug	Holland	Renault RE4OEFI	R
11 Sep	Italy	Renault RE4OEFI	R
25 Sep	Europe	Renault RE4OEFI	2
15 Oct	S. Africa	Renault RE4OEFI	R

1984

25 Mar	Brazil	McLaren MP4/2TAG	1 FL
7 Apr	S. Africa	McLaren MP4/2TAG	2
29 Apr	Belgium	McLaren MP4/2TAG	R
6 May	San Marino	McLaren MP4/2TAG	1

SALOON CAR RACE

12 May	Nürburgring	Mercedes Benz 190E	15

FORMULA ONE

20 May	France	McLaren MP4/2TAG	7 FL
3 Jun	Monaco	McLaren MP4/2TAG	1 P
17 Jun	Canada	McLaren MP4/2TAG	3
24 Jun	USA East	McLaren MP4/2TAG	5
8 Jul	USA	McLaren MP4/2TAG	R
22 Jul	Britain	McLaren MP4/2TAG	R
5 Aug	Germany	McLaren MP4/2TAG	1 P/FL
19 Aug	Austria	McLaren MP4/2TAG	R
26 Aug	Holland	McLaren MP4/2TAG	1 P
9 Sep	Italy	McLaren MP4/2TAG	R

7 Oct	Europe	McLaren MP4/2TAG	1
21 Oct	Portugal	McLaren MP4/2TAG	1

1985

7 Apr	Brazil	McLaren MP4/2BTAG	1 FL
21 Apr	Portugal	McLaren MP4/2BTAG	R
5 May	San Marino	McLaren MP4/2BTAG	DSQ
19 May	Monaco	McLaren MP4/2BTAG	1
16 Jun	Canada	McLaren MP4/2BTAG	3
23 Jun	USA East	McLaren MP4/2BTAG	R
7 Jul	France	McLaren MP4/2BTAG	3
21 Jul	Britain	McLaren MP4/2BTAG	1 FL
4 Aug	Germany	McLaren MP4/2BTAG	2
18 Aug	Austria	McLaren MP4/2BTAG	1 P/FL
25 Aug	Holland	McLaren MP4/2BTAG	2 FL
8 Sep	Italy	McLaren MP4/2BTAG	1
15 Sep	Belgium	McLaren MP4/2BTAG	3 P/FL
6 Oct	Europe	McLaren MP4/2BTAG	4
19 Oct	S. Africa	McLaren MP4/2BTAG	3
3 Nov	Australia	McLaren MP4/2BTAG	R

1986

23 Mar	Brazil	McLaren MP4/2CTAG	R
13 Apr	Spain	McLaren MP4/2CTAG	3
27 Apr	San Marino	McLaren MP4/2CTAG	1
11 May	Monaco	McLaren MP4/2CTAG	1 P/FL
25 May	Belgium	McLaren MP4/2CTAG	6 FL
15 Jun	Canada	McLaren MP4/2CTAG	2
22 Jun	USA East	McLaren MP4/2CTAG	3
6 Jul	France	McLaren MP4/2CTAG	2
13 Jul	Britain	McLaren MP4/2CTAG	3
27 Jul	Germany	McLaren MP4/2CTAG	6
10 Aug	Hungary	McLaren MP4/2CTAG	R
17 Aug	Austria	McLaren MP4/2CTAG	1
7 Sep	Italy	McLaren MP4/2CTAG	DSQ
21 Sep	Portugal	McLaren MP4/2CTAG	2
12 Oct	Mexico	McLaren MP4/2CTAG	2
26 Oct	Australia	McLaren MP4/2CTAG	1

1987			
12 Apr	Brazil	McLaren MP4/3TAG	1
3 May	San Marino	McLaren MP4/3TAG	R
17 May	Belgium	McLaren MP4/3TAG	1 FL
31 May	Monaco	McLaren MP4/3TAG	R 9
21 Jun	USA East	McLaren MP4/3TAG	3
5 Jul	France	McLaren MP4/3TAG	3
12 Jul	Britain	McLaren MP4/3TAG	R
26 Jul	Germany	McLaren MP4/3TAG	R 7
9 Aug	Hungary	McLaren MP4/3TAG	3
16 Aug	Austria	McLaren MP4/3TAG	6
6 Sep	Italy	McLaren MP4/3TAG	15
20 Sep	Portugal	McLaren MP4/3TAG	1
27 Sep	Spain	McLaren MP4/3TAG	2
18 Oct	Mexico	McLaren MP4/3TAG	R
1 Nov	Japan	McLaren MP4/3TAG	7 FL
15 Nov	Australia	McLaren MP4/3TAG	R
1988			
3 Apr	Brazil	McLaren MP4/4 Honda RA168E	1
1 May	San Marino	McLaren MP4/4 Honda RA168E	2 FL
15 May	Monaco	McLaren MP4/4 Honda RA168E	1
29 May	Mexico	McLaren MP4/4 Honda RA168E	1 FL
12 Jun	Canada	McLaren MP4/4 Honda RA168E	2
19 Jun	USA East	McLaren MP4/4 Honda RA168E	2 FL
3 Jul	France	McLaren MP4/4 Honda RA168E	1 P/FL
10 Jul	Britain	McLaren MP4/4 Honda RA168E	R
24 Jul	Germany	McLaren MP4/4 Honda RA168E	2
7 Aug	Hungary	McLaren MP4/4 Honda RA168E	2 FL
28 Aug	Belgium	McLaren MP4/4 Honda RA168E	2

11 Sep	Italy	McLaren MP4/4 Honda RA168E	R
25 Sep	Portugal	McLaren MP4/4 Honda RA168E	1 P
2 Oct	Spain	McLaren MP4/4 Honda RA168E	1 FL
30 Oct	Japan	McLaren MP4/4 Honda RA168E	2
13 Nov	Australia	McLaren MP4/4 Honda RA168E	1 FL

1989

26 Mar	Brazil	McLaren MP4/5 Honda RA109E	2
23 Apr	San Marino	McLaren MP4/5 Honda RA109E	2 FL
7 May	Monaco	McLaren MP4/5 Honda RA109E	2 FL
28 May	Mexico	McLaren MP4/5 Honda RA109E	5
4 Jun	USA	McLaren MP4/5 Honda RA109E	1
18 Jun	Canada	McLaren MP4/5 Honda RA109E	R P
9 Jul	France	McLaren MP4/5 Honda RA109E	1 P
16 Jul	Britain	McLaren MP4/5 Honda RA109E	1
30 Jul	Germany	McLaren MP4/5 Honda RA109E	2
13 Aug	Hungary	McLaren MP4/5 Honda RA109E	4
27 Aug	Belgium	McLaren MP4/5 Honda RA109E	2 FL
10 Sep	Italy	McLaren MP4/5 Honda RA109E	1 FL
24 Sep	Portugal	McLaren MP4/5 Honda RA109E	2
1 Oct	Spain	McLaren MP4/5 Honda RA109E	3

22 Oct	Japan	McLaren MP4/5 Honda RA109E	R FL
5 Nov	Australia	McLaren MP4/5 Honda RA109E	DNS

1990

11 Mar	USA	Ferrari 641/034	R
25 Mar	Brazil	Ferrari 641/034	1
13 May	San Marino	Ferrari 641/034	4
27 May	Monaco	Ferrari 641/034	R
10 Jun	Canada	Ferrari 641/034	5
24 Jun	Mexico	Ferrari 641/034	1 FL
8 Jul	France	Ferrari 641/034	1
15 Jul	Britain	Ferrari 641/034	1
29 Jul	Germany	Ferrari 641/034	4
12 Aug	Hungary	Ferrari 641/037	R
25 Aug	Belgium	Ferrari 641/037	2 FL
9 Sep	Italy	Ferrari 641/037	2
23 Sep	Portugal	Ferrari 641/037	3
30 Sep	Spain	Ferrari 641/037	1
21 Oct	Japan	Ferrari 641/037	R
4 Nov	Australia	Ferrari 641/037	3

1991

10 Mar	USA	Ferrari 642/123	2
24 Mar	Brazil	Ferrari 642/123	4
28 Apr	San Marino	Ferrari 642/124	DNS
12 May	Monaco	Ferrari 642/123	5
2 Jun	Canada	Ferrari 642/123	R
16 Jun	Mexico	Ferrari 642/123	R
7 Jul	France	Ferrari 643/128	2
14 Jul	Britain	Ferrari 643/128	3
28 Jul	Germany	Ferrari 643/129	R
11 Aug	Hungary	Ferrari 643/129	R
25 Aug	Belgium	Ferrari 643/129	R
8 Sep	Italy	Ferrari 643/130	3
22 Sep	Portugal	Ferrari 643/130	R
29 Sep	Spain	Ferrari 643/130	2
20 Oct	Japan	Ferrari 643/130	4

INDEX